CW01647744

*Abo*ı

Robert Fraser's biography of the poet George Barker was a *Spectator* book of the year; his life of the poet David Gascoyne topped the *Independent*'s list of new biographies. He has also published books about Marcel Proust, the anthropologist Sir James Frazer, and the print history of Africa and India. In Africa he adapted *Charley's Aunt* for the local stage; whilst teaching in Cambridge he inherited a fellow's set once occupied by A. E. Housman; at the Open University, where he is Professor Emeritus, his office was in a building named after Harold Wilson. He is a Fellow of the Royal Society of Literature, the English Association and the Royal Asiatic Society. He lives mainly in London.

by the same author

LITERATURE, MUSIC AND COSMOPOLITANISM: CULTURE AS MIGRATION

BOOK HISTORY THROUGH POSTCOLONIAL EYES: RE-WRITING THE SCRIPT

BOOKS WITHOUT BORDERS edited with Mary Hammond

1: THE CROSS-NATIONAL ELEMENT IN PRINT CULTURE

2: PERSPECTIVES FROM SOUTH ASIA

THE FOUNDERS' GIFT: IMPRESSIONS FROM A COLLECTION

FOX HILL IN THE SNOW AND OTHER POEMS

THE MAKING OF *THE GOLDEN BOUGH*: THE ORIGINS AND GROWTH OF AN ARGUMENT

THE GOLDEN BOUGH: A NEW ABRIDGEMENT

SIR JAMES FRAZER AND THE LITERARY IMAGINATION: ESSAYS IN AFFINITY AND INFLUENCE (editor)

PROUST AND THE VICTORIANS: THE LAMP OF MEMORY

VICTORIAN QUEST ROMANCE: STEVENSON, HAGGARD, KIPLING AND CONAN DOYLE

THE CHAMELEON POET: A LIFE OF GEORGE BARKER

THE COLLECTED POEMS OF GEORGE BARKER (editor)

THE SELECTED POEMS OF GEORGE BARKER (editor)

NIGHT THOUGHTS: THE SURREAL LIFE OF THE POET DAVID GASCOYNE

THE HORNED APE

LIFTING THE SENTENCE: A POETICS OF POSTCOLONIAL FICTION

A COMMENTARY ON EDWARD BRATHWAITE'S *MASKS*

THE NOVELS OF AYI KWEI ARMAH: A STUDY IN POLEMICAL FICTION

BEN OKRI: TOWARDS THE INVISIBLE CITY

WEST AFRICAN POETRY: A CRITICAL HISTORY

READING AFRICAN POETRY

THIS ISLAND PLACE

ACKNOWLEDGEMENTS

Several people have helped nurture this small book. Jenny Uglow, Blake Morrison, William St Clair, Sarah Bakewell and Iain Sinclair cast their eyes over various drafts and generously lent their advice, as did Benjo Fraser, Maria Thanasi, David and Margaret Hancock, and my affectionate companion, Dr Brigid Allen. Croydon University Hospital (formerly the Mayday) allowed me access to Catherine's medical records, which fill two hefty drawers in my study. To that institution – its administrators, consultants, registrars and junior doctors, perhaps most of all to its nursing staff – I extend my heartfelt thanks.

I am extremely grateful to Hilary Davies, wife of the poet Sebastian Barker, for permission to quote three lines from his sequence *Damnatio Memoriae: Erased from Memory* (Enitharmon Press, 2004), and twelve lines from 'The Ballad of True Regret' from his collection *The Land of Gold* (Enitharmon Press, 2014). I would like to thank my friend Professor Wynn Thomas most warmly for his help with David Ishmael's Welsh. I should further record my debt to the Malinowski Archive at the library of the London School of Economics, Catherine's alma mater, for permission to reproduce the photograph of Bronislaw Malinowski in 1918 with a group of musicians from the

Trobriand Islands. Professor Margret Kenna of the University of Swansea was an invaluable informant about the LSE in the 1960s when Catherine attended it.

Sincere gratitude is also due to the Lakeside Nursing Home where Catherine spent her last few weeks. I would also like to thank the Revd. Lucy Winkett, Father John Pritchard and Canon Andrew Wilson for their moral support, and Kirsty-Ellen Smillie for her sympathetic reception of the text, and the care that she has taken over its production.

Charlbury,
Oxfordshire, May 2018.

PASCAL'S TEARS

or

HOW NOT TO MURDER ONE'S WIFE

An Opened Letter

ROBERT FRASER

To Rona, with very best wishes,
Rabat, November, 2018

CRANTHORPE
MILLNER
PUBLISHERS

A CIP catalogue record for this title is available from the British Library.

ISBN 978-1-9164400-1-2 (Paperback)

www.cranthorpemillner.com

First Published (2018)

Cranthorpe Millner Publishers
18 Soho Square
London
W1D 3QL

FOR BENJO, WHO SHARED THE VIGIL

The greatness of man is that he knows he is miserable. A tree does not know that it is miserable.

It is therefore little to know ourselves little, and it is great to know ourselves little.

Thus his very infirmities prove man's greatness. They are the infirmities of a great lord, of a discrowned king.

Blaise Pascal.

Thou shalt not
  kill; but
  needst not
  strive
Officiously to
  keep alive

Arthur Hugh Clough

CONTENTS

1 PROLOGUE: PASCAL'S TEARS

Tuesday, November 5th, 2013, Thornton Heath

My Lovely Punster, My Delectable Procrastinator and Slowcoach, my ambling, hill roving, bare foot paddling, sea shuffling nymph, my wily wordsmith, my satirical, atheistic, shyly stubborn, utterly Welsh, ardently affectionate, Menthol-tasting Nuisance:

I do not know in what tense to refer to you, whether you are, or what you are. We cannot talk to one another now, because today you do not recognise me. But I shall write you this too long letter that you may never read because it pleases me, and because it eases my pain. I shall refer to you throughout in the second person, though I am not sure that you are any more you, and sometimes I am not even sure whether I am any longer myself.

The doctors refer to you grammatically as "you", and so I shall follow their form. We seldom used to write one another letters. Since the two of us were so constantly together, had become so much the backdrop to one another's lives, there was not that occasion, or that need. Today - and from now on until the edge of time - there is and there will be a need, and I shall make of it an occasion and a celebration. *Namasthe. Namasthe.*

★

This evening in the corridor, whilst they were turning you in bed, we encountered Dr Morag McIvor sauntering along the linoleum of the Blue Zone. We flagged her down in her dedicated progress, and she came to join us on the chairs. Early forties, chestnut hair tied back, sable clothing, full-length skirt, thick specs. An open, committed gaze.

Dr McIvor is a Consultant Neurologist and our Second Opinion on the perplexing, unpredictable riddle of you, and the reasons why we are keeping you alive. She is clear and nuanced in all that she says, earnest in manner, interested in both the practical and philosophical aspects of her profession. We trust her, because there must be someone whom one trusts and because her words, whether reliable or not, carry the conviction that convinces.

Morag appears to respect our intelligence, which at least is reassuring. She possesses besides the sort of precise and pedantic enunciation that our twenty-six-year-old son associates with severity. "I value my intellectual independence" she told us yesterday, and she has almost the bearing of a swot. Yet she is compassionate, receptive, an accomplished listener, wearing - I hazard to guess - a professional mask or demeanour during working hours: in the evenings and at weekends, she will probably comb her air out, add makeup and substitute contact lenses for the specs. She will attend parties in Coulsdon, at which she will dispense gossip mixed with neuroscience.

She asks me "What do you do?"

I say "I am a Professor of English."

Then she asks our son "What do you do?"

He replies "I am a Physicist, a String Theorist".

Then she asks us both "And Catherine, what does she do?"

I say, "She is – she was – a lawyer".

This sleek and dedicated professional has ordered an MRI scan of your head. Our son has explained to me what this is. Each atom in your brain has a nucleus which behaves much as a bar-magnet does. Each nucleus has a magnetic "moment" or torque set in motion when exposed to an electromagnetic field. When this happens, the nuclei line up and the poles gyrate and alternate direction very rapidly, leaving a distinctive mark or trace. A second magnetic field is then superimposed on the first, after which the mathematics of the Fourier transform are deployed to clarify the results. By this means they can chart the various sorts of matter that compose your mind, what's in working order and what is not, what has been eradicated by the organic shock a month ago and what of you - above and beyond the brain stem that keeps you breathing and your heart ticking - somehow manages to survive. She wants to know, for example, whether your language centres have been "stroked out". Were that the case, you would not understand anything said to you, and you would be very difficult to rehabilitate. This is a clinician's way of putting it. But Sweets, Jane Austen- adoring Sweets, what would you be without words? You are, and always were, irony itself. Without access to language, would you even vaguely be you?

Dr McIvor rises to her feet, talking of "Medical Humanities". Should we, I idly inquire, perhaps write a book together? "I would love to write a book, except that I am rubbish at writing." Should she email me her opinions?

"Yes, we could do that, but I am rubbish at emails." And then she walks off quickly and quietly, sashaying down the corridor as she goes.

My confidence in this efficient medic has turned almost erotic. She's about the same age as you when we first met. I can resist nymphets, models, strippers and centre folds. A dedicated professional woman in her forties finds me without defence. It is good that she and I can speak to one another so frankly. We are in a zone of estimation, where knowledge and judgment preside. But the knowledge is relativistic knowledge, and it is embarrassed by a mesh of values even more elusive than itself. But dear God, what sort of a man is it who, while weighing up the personal and medical destiny of his wife of thirty-one years, allows himself to be thus implicated in the mazes of another woman's mind, drawn by her accent and her personal allure?

⋆

Was that question rhetorical or was it personal? Addressed to you, to myself or to the universe? Is it, I wonder, meaningful to ask you questions any more. Can I put to you - for example - questions in the form of "Do you remember?" A style of inquiry, some would say, meaningless when directed to someone who has lost the gift of speech, a tabula rasa to all intents and purposes, theology's starting point and philosophy's nightmare. The recollections rubbed out, the *hiraeth* wiped clean.

But let us, for formality's sake, begin at the end: with that stinking copy of Pascal. You would recall, if you could recall anything, that moment of alarm, that shelf crammed with books. The bookcase itself a wonky absurdity constructed out of cheap painted boards and crammed precariously into the eighteen-inch-wide alcove between our basement living room and my once coal hole, now pine-panelled, windowless study. On its top shelf there lingered, and still lingers, a selection of my most precious tomes: the Jebb Sophocles, Frazer's *Pausanias and Other Greek Sketches,* a first edition, now almost ruined, of David Gascoyne's *Poems 1937-1942.* Among them there stood the volume I was reaching for that September Saturday afternoon: an 1885 translation of the *Thoughts* of Blaise Pascal, the seventeenth-century French mathematic genius who published a revolutionary treatise on conic sections and then, basing his decision on an early version of game theory, took a personal wager to the effect that God exists. That evening I was searching for his succinct celebration of the supremacy of human intellect over the unconscious world of things:

> Man is but a reed, weakest in nature, but a reed which thinks. It needs not that the whole Universe should arm to crush him. A vapour, a drop of water, is enough to kill him. But were the universe to crush him, man would still be more noble than that which had slain him, because he knows that the Universe has the better of him. The Universe knows nothing of this.

The first time I had read these sentences, my mind had kindled at so bold an expression of its supremacy over mere matter. I recall, if you cannot, the evening I sat reading those words to you from this self-same copy in our four-poster bed in a tasteful hotel called Jeakes House in Mermaid Street in Rye in Sussex, a converted Quaker Meeting house and former home of the American poet, Conrad Aiken. They meant almost as much to me then as they do now, even if subsequent events have led me painfully to question them. If a person is a thinking reed, what manner of thing - I ask you searchingly, just as I ask myself - is a person who, to all external appearance, has ceased altogether to think?

But, as I reached up for the book that evening, a malodorous surprise awaited me, for the maroon boards in which it was bound were half-covered in an evil pink slime that had even got inside the covers and defaced the first few pages with a smudge of rouge. Pascal was visibly weeping. I applied the front of the book to my nostrils and was assaulted by an acrid stench that almost made my stomach turn, so I called up to the first floor kitchen where you stood preparing our supper of corned beef with parsley sauce, asking you to come and take a look, even unthinkingly to take a smell.

You refrained from descending the stairs to examine the damage, and with good reason. Six years previously when we were touring South Africa, you had been seized with acute shortness of breath and, following x-rays at the Christiaan Barnard hospital, had been diagnosed as suffering from chronic asthma. The condition had since come and gone, but was essentially under control, contained by a twice-daily intake from your light blue steroid inhaler, boosted at times of dire distress by what you called your "emergency puffer", a beige and brown dispenser of the B2-adrenergic receptor agonist, muscle relaxant and anti-spasmodic preventer, Salbutamol. At all times you carried quantities of each in your faux leather handbag, many of them superannuated and some of them unused. On a recent visit to that mountain-girt city and pollution trap Florence, whither you had accompanied me complete with a handbag of inhalers, you had experienced one of your most acute attacks to date, and you lived thenceforth in daily dread of any occurrence or exposure that might exacerbate a condition that was fast becoming a way of life.

You are not medically educated, but your nasal instincts told you that you must at all costs avoid mould. My copy of Pascal was now saturated with it. When I examined the adjacent books along the top shelf, they too were infected with the loathsome fungus, the Jebb soppy with slime, the Pausanias dripping with sludge. I respected your wishes to come nowhere near this scene of biological warfare, and carefully sponged the covers of each of these books, removing much of the colour in the process, even destroying a few affected pages. Then I sprayed the alcove with Astonish Mould and Mildew Remover, the bleaching action of which eradicated in a few minutes any sign of the dark grey blotches that had attacked the back wall behind the shelves. But the associated stink remained in the surrounding air for many days.

Aspergillosis, so your medical nephew has since informed me, is an allergic reaction to an invasion of any organ, especially of the lungs, by the spores of certain varieties of fungus. You did not need to know the technical term to dread the occurrence of this particular species of menace, and for days you avoided the basement. But in the middle of the following week, shortly before your seventy-first birthday, I discovered you hunched on the side of our bed complaining of much same symptoms as had dismayed us during and after our brief stay in Italy. I 'phoned the asthma nurse at the surgery at which we were both registered, and obtained an appointment for the following week. It was far too late.

2 OCTOBER: LLANRHIDIAN MARSH

Friday, October 4th

Manchester's Bridgewater Hall had been more impressive than I had expected. From the outside it appeared brutal, almost ugly: sheer concrete walls, stretches of gauche red brick, harsh geometric dimensions, sharp corners, acres of unsympathetic glass. The only human touch was a bust of Sir John Barbirolli, founder and first musical director of the Hallé Orchestra, to the right of the principal entrance. Once inside, however, the harshness dissolved to be replaced by gleaming brass fittings, tiers of soft seats, an auditorium curving inwards and outwards like a woman's waist and hips towards the smooth scrotum of the stage.

I am here to present the biographer Jenny Uglow with a degree, and have written her a glowing citation which reads in part:

> Each and every one of her books is meticulously researched, magnificently written and fundamentally original in its approach. There is no such thing as a formulaic Uglow biogaphy. Instead, she re-thinks each of her subjects from the beginning and tailors her angle of approach accordingly. As a result, each of her books fits its subject as snugly, and as eye-catchingly, as a new coat.

I have written this laudation, but I am not permitted to read it, a task allotted by some new-fangled regulation to a higher official. Instead, I must settle for sitting on the stage as I listen to the text being respectfully delivered by the Dean of the Faculty of Computing. I am kind to the Dean afterwards, and glad to meet Jenny over lunch.

"You don't need to go to Manchester, really, do you?" you'd murmured the previous morning, hunched with your inhaler on the bed. "You're just doing it for the show." Your asthma had shown some signs of worsening, but I am used to these ups and downs, and by common agreement we do not let it stand in my way of anything we are pledged to do. "I'd said I'd go", I remark as kindly as I can, "and I'd like to meet Jenny. And besides they've gone to all the trouble of ordering my robes."

Besides, our son had rushed home for your birthday the previous day, and I could reliably leave him in charge. At the last moment, you said "You'd better go."

After the ceremony and lunch I catch an early afternoon train back to Euston across burnished autumnal countryside. It takes the circuitous route via Crewe, avoiding it seems most towns and following the twisting and turning canal system down to London. Jenny is in the same carriage, and I catch a glimpse of her a few rows forward of mine working at her laptop computer. Around fifteen miles south of Manchester I take out the official photographs that had been handed to me just before leaving, one with Jenny, another with a larger academical group. In both I look stuffy and ridiculous, as I always do in official snaps – "Smile" the photographer had said, and the results were as phoney as a waxwork. Never mind, I think. Soon I'd be at home, laughing at the pomposity with you.

Just to make sure everything is alright in South London, I put through a call to our son's mobile. He answers from the Acute Medical Unit of the hospital. You'd spent most of the previous day and night hunched up on the edge of our bed and then, at seven that morning, had hammered on his door complaining that you had taken the maximum permitted dosage of your usual brown steroid inhaler, after which the emergency blue-green Salbutamol puffer had had no effect. You'd asked him to contact the surgery, where a doctor had informed him that the Salbutamol dosage could go up to ten but that, under these circumstances, it was wise to call for an ambulance. A paramedical team had arrived within five minutes. They'd given you a nebuliser to steady your breathing, and taken you the Resuscitation Unit at Croydon University Hospital, where you'd been tested to make sure you weren't retaining too much carbon dioxide in your lungs. I ask to speak to you over the 'phone, and you weakly reply that you're feeling "shattered" and, I infer, more than a little confused. I tell you I'll be there just as soon as I can.

I pocket the phone and try to concentrate on the flat Midlands countryside pouring past the broad window. In early October, cruelly, England has never looked to me so lovely. The trees just turning, stretches of water like gun metal, canals and curling streams, scattered farmsteads, and flocks of long-necked swans flying purposefully above. All I can think about is you. As we draw into Euston I pass Jenny to my left and tell her what has happened. She looks concerned and wishes us all luck. Then I rush to take the quickest route I can think of, from Victoria by fast link to East Croydon, and then a taxi to Thornton Heath. At the hospital shop I briefly pause to purchase some toiletries you've asked for, then find the first floor and dive into the pale turquoise sea of the Acute Medical Unit where you sit perched on the end of your bed in Bay C like some beached mermaid with an incongruous oxygen mask clamped over your face. Benjo is holding you in his arms. As I stand there on the green lino floor clutching my pathetic gifts of toothpaste and a towel, you throw me a look of mild reproach. "Your son's been wonderful", you wail and throw me another baleful glance, adding "You can kiss me if you like." The top of your head is damp as I brush it with my lips. It is already late, and I stand feeling inadequate as Benjo fills me in with more details of what the doctors said in A and E. How they had tested you for levels of CO_2 and asked about your twenty-year history of smoking ten a day. How they had questioned the diagnosis of asthma, and wondered whether your condition might have been "smoker's lung", or Chronic Obstructive Pulmonary Disease, all along. And my mind races back to a Cambridge night twenty-two years ago when you kept the whole house awake with your coughing and in the morning thanked our exhausted hostess for her concern but refused her offer of an introduction to the clinic to be held that morning round the corner. And how the following month at a lunch for colleagues in the light-flooded living room of our rented residence in the college gardens you had sat listening to a conversation about teaching Greek tragedy to the Greekless, and coughed and coughed and coughed and coughed…

Saturday, October 5th

I am back at the entrance to the Unit at half past nine in the morning, after walking alone along the dull half-mile of the London Road from West Croydon station. I have brought you a new radio hastily acquired to replace your old one with the faulty volume control that delivered only loudness. It is a small late birthday gift to add to the Givenchy 'Mariage' perfume and the red roses for love, the card bearing Tenniel's likeness of the cheshire cat from *Alice's Adventures in Wonderland* with the smile famously like your own ("To keep you grinning on your birthday – and throughout every day of the year, from your Adoring Husband Robert XXXXXX") and the dish I'd invented for your celebratory supper featuring lamb's kidneys in pesto and cream on a bed of Canellini beans, so rich that you almost couldn't eat it. But at the desk I am met by a matron of proverbial sourness who informs me that visiting starts at one. I plead with her, so she relents to the extent of allowing me to put my head round the door briefly to greet you. You are still wearing your stern oxygen mask, and you do not look pleased to see me. "You are not supposed to visit now," you almost snap and then, seeing me looking so pathetic, tell me to put the radio and the comb I've brought for you on the bedside table and promptly leave. "I'll see you this afternoon," you say.

"I'm on at the Festival Hall at four", I explain.

"Well then, I'll see you early this evening"

I walk back along the London Road with its Halal butchers and green grocers, its gap toothed buildings – a ruin that was once a pub then a gym, a late Gothic Revival C. of E. church turned Hindu temple - its interchangeable Dosa restaurants just opening for lunch, its lustreless cafes - and, as I go, I 'phone our son. I briefly discuss cancelling my talk in the afternoon, but I tell him you seem settled and stable, with no apparent cause for alarm. I'll call in at home for a wash and a bite to eat, then set off for the South Bank. After the talks session, only an hour long, I can join you both at the hospital shortly after six.

Since January, you've been watched me contributing fifteen-minute talks in the Festival Hall for their year-long celebration of Twentieth-Century Music and Culture "The Rest Is Noise." Already I've pontificated pithily on nationalism in W.B. Yeats and the role of dialect in D.H. Lawrence. For the Paris weekend I'd covered radical lesbian bookshops and Anais Nin, finishing the second talk by squirting the eponymous scent over the audience. Afterwards, I'd ceded the bottle of perfume to you. In May I'd read my translation of an elegy for Alban Berg by the poet David Gascoyne against two recorded movements of Berg's own Lyric Suite for string quartet. You'd come to that as well, but as I swept away one of my more glamorous postgraduate students for tea in the downstairs riverside café, had got lost on your way down to the lobby from the fourth level of the Green Side, and found your way home alone, standing bemused amid the traffic fumes of Trafalgar Square, waiting for the Number 3 bus.

This weekend, the theme is "The Post-war World" and four of us speakers are on in the St Paul's Pavilion up on the blue side. Lara Feigel, a tall and confident lecturer from King's College London with a husband and small child in tow, speaks incisively about Billy Wilder's period in Berlin, before fleeing with her boisterous family into the afternoon. Sophie Mayer, an extrovert feminist I'd heard some weeks back enthuse about Gertrude Stein, camps it up on bad English translations of the works of Simone de Beauvour.

Then I take the stand and agonise about Albert Camus, the nature of freedom and the absurd, and the significance of moral choice. It was while writing this piece that a few weeks back I had felt the necessity of re-reading Pascal, whom I was determined to quote. The material I've prepared is too much for the allotted slot. Surprisingly so, since to ensure that I keep within the limits prescribed, for once I've typed out my text. For far too long a period, I tell the hundred odd people present in the audience, Albert Camus has been associated on this side of the channel with pessimism, a sort of "nicotine-stained despair". Instead, his work proclaims the positive prerogative of Choice. His hero Sisyphus is so strong:

> because, despite the repetitiveness of his task, he understands what is happening to him. I don't know whether any of you recall a passage in Pascal where he talks about the Greatness and the Littleness of Man. "By space", says Pascal, "the Universe encompasses and swallows me as an atom; by thought I encompass it." For once Camus is in agreement with Pascal. Faced by an indifferent cosmos, the absurd man asserts his superiority over it, since while an inert cosmos cannot contemplate him, he can contemplate the cosmos. What is more, he is at liberty to endow his task with whatever meaning he wishes to confer. Accordingly, the Absurd is not a philosophy of despair, but of creativity and risk. This is what Camus means by rebellion; it is also what he means by freedom.

This, I tell the audience, is a practical philosophy which had enabled Camus himself to make hard moral choices. He had joined the French Resistance in the war; later he did not - despite a lot of fashionable pressure – kowtow to the violent tactics of the FLN in Algeria. In his finest novel *La Peste,* the difficulty yet urgency of such decisions is epitomised by the hard-pressed Doctor Rieux sticking to his unglamorous and stressful vocation of healing in plague-infested Oran. Not all of the other characters possess his lucidity, tenacity or patience. For example:

> Rambert, a French journalist, by contrast, wishes to escape to join his wife in Paris. During one tense interview Rieux asks Rambert why he is so keen to leave. Rambert replies that he has already done his bit fighting for the Republicans in Spain, that in any case he is through with sacrificing himself for an idea. Rieux looks at him with sad understanding and says softly "l'homme n'est pas une idée, Rambert"; people, Rambert, are not an idea.

Then, despite all of my precautions, I run out of time, and have to scramble my account of Camus' last novel, *La Chute.* I sit down feeling a failure and humiliated, barely able to concentrate on the fourth talk by my university colleague Nick Foxton on the Atom Bomb before escaping downstairs for a consolatory beer in the Ground Floor Bar. Then I'm on the train to Croydon again, and with you.

At first I cannot find you. In the Acute Medical Unit the duty nurse does not appear to recognise your name. So I spell it out to her again, wondering whether you have been registered under our married surname or the maiden name to which for most formal purposes you proudly clung. Recognising neither, the nurse checks in the back office where she is told that you were moved this morning. You are now in a specialist respiratory ward called Heathfield 2 in the Orange Zone on the ground floor. So I make my way to the down escalator next to the Oasis Restaurant to find it stuck in useless immobility behind a notice explaining that I must take the stairs. Heathfield 2 when I reach it is large and well equipped. Beside your bed is what looks to me like a sophisticated monitor system measuring your breath and pulse. Our son has been with you for three hours and has accompanied you during the move. Again I am seized with a sense of inadequacy as he and I sit on opposite sides of the bed, each holding one of your hands. We watch and listen as the nebuliser belatedly delivers its shy hiss, and the oxygen from the wall tap strives to reach the critical point at which the salbutamol solution in the ill-fitting mask vaporisers to ease your afflicted lungs. Discomforted and not little alarmed by all this equipment, you struggle and writhe as the healing fumes leak uselessly into the atmosphere of the ward.

In the next bed to yours is a thin and pallid woman from Cardiff called Sylvia with amber bifocals and short, iron grey hair. In the hours of my absence you have, despite your offhand attitude on my appearance this morning, been boasting to her about the lecture that you had hoped to attend. You had even re-read Camus' *L'Etranger* in preparation for it, taking my copy with you on a lone foray to Brighton while I sat at home cursing you for depriving me of an opportunity to quote. On your desk at home there is a copy of Thomas R. Flynn's *Existentialism: A Very Short Introduction* in which you have underlined the quote from Sartre on page 63 that reads "The choice of authenticity appears to be a *moral* decision". You've also underscored the first sentence of Chapter 4 pointing out that "for the Existentialists ethical decisions are paramount." You've been attempting to explain all of this to Sylvia between gasps, but Sylvia is more interested in her own destiny. So she tells us at animated length how she had moved from her native Cardiff to Croydon to be near her daughter, and how after six months an arsonist set fire to her block of flats, depriving her of the heirlooms she had carefully brought with her from Wales, and reducing her to the blackened wreck hardly recognisable as a human being that they brought into A and E. "They had to wash me three times to find what race I was," she tells us with barely disguised glee. That was eighteen months ago, but her chest is still affected by the aftermath of this incident, which is why she lies in the next bed to yours now, two South Walians wagging their tongues over their respective triumphs or woes.

You lie there listening and, as you do so, you impatiently tug at the lead that connects you to the heart monitor. You are uncomfortable and restless, and now you want to go to the loo. So we take the leads off your arms and chest and you lean on our son's arm as he supports you down the corridor. While they are away, I listen through the nylon partition curtain as a couple of orderlies discuss your case. "Admitted for observation", I hear them say. But when you get back Sylvia makes light of the situation, telling you that you will probably be here "at the outside 'til about Wednesday". You roll your eyes in distress, so I promise we will come every day, for just as long as the visiting hours permit. Then you glance at the watch on my arm and grow fretful on our behalf. It is nearly half past nine, "and I don't want you hanging around waiting for a bus at midnight.

Phone for a taxi. Go on, Benjo, tell him." So I kiss you briefly, murmuring "love you" in my wake as we both depart, leaving you looking lonely and forlorn with the monitor leads still lying in futile detachment beside you on the bed.

Sunday, October 6th

I am drifting off to sleep in the myrtle-wall-paper lined grotto of our room when our son enters from his bedroom across the tiny carpeted landing to say that there has been a call to his mobile from the hospital. "The situation", a ward orderly informed him, "has deteriorated". I am disconcerted by this news but, slow to react to the formal understatement, not unduly alarmed: your condition when we said goodbye five hours ago had seemed fragile, but hardly grievous. You were breathing regularly with a little help and you have, after all, only been detained in hospital for checks. We can confidently expect you home within a few days. Nonetheless we 'phone a local cab firm based at Selsdon, and journey the two or three miles to Thornton Heath, arriving at the main entrance to the hospital to find it locked. But there is an intercom next to the glass and chrome door, and we are able to speak to an overnight caretaker. He will admit us remotely, provided we circumnavigate the building beneath the "Yellow Bridge". Our anxiety rising, we turn to our left and, in our panic and fatigue, attempt to locate a bridge of some sort, preferably yellow in colour. None is apparent, so we return to the intercom, through which the night watchman tells us that "bridge" means overhead walkway, and yellow means off-white.

Thus corrected, we find our way to a side door in an obscure corner of the drab brick building that houses the more important wards. A buzzer announces the release of the door, and we enter the Orange Zone and hurry across to Heathfield 2, which is darkened and eerily quiet. In the dim cathedral of the interior I look across to the bay containing your bed and recognise the cardiac arrest trolley like a rolling red enamel filing cabinet with the grey monitor of the defibrillator propped on top of it like a small portable TV. Beneath it are drawers labelled "Airway Management", "IV Access" and "IV fluids", and beneath them a larger drawer holding the Suction Machine. We are invited to sit in a side room where after perhaps ten minutes of tense silence I look up to see the slender figure of Dr Bharati Padmanabha, an alert Registrar from Tamil Nadu in her early thirties, framed in the doorway. "First let me tell you," she is saying, "that your wife is alive". Then she stops herself. Stupidly in the face of the growing evidence I think, well, why wouldn't you be? She sits down next to me and reaches out one skinny and dusky arm, looking approximately into my eyes. At first I have some difficulty taking what she is saying, though the words "cardiac" and "arrest" are clear enough.

Only later am I able to reconstruct what had happened in the early hours of that morning in terms I can appreciate and understand. After we left you at around 9.15, Sylvia had chatted to you intermittently about Wales for the better part of two hours, as your breathing weakened and improved by turns. You kept on complaining "I can't breathe. I can't breathe." She had laid her skeletal hand on your arm and told you not to panic. At eleven the ward lights had gone out. Sylvia was, she later told me, conscious of your anxiety-ridden form sitting hunched up about six feet away on the side of your bed. She had then swallowed her sleeping pills and drifted into a shallow slumber. She had woken up at around ten to one to hear the swish of cubicle curtains near to her and the voice of a male care assistant anxiously repeating “I can’t find a pulse. I can’t find a pulse.”

The cardiac arrest team had arrived from an upstairs ward within two minutes. They had delivered three electric shocks to your chest, and injected one dose of adrenaline. Ten minutes after their arrival, your heart beat had re-appeared. Now, Dr Padmanabha tells us, they are preparing you for admission to the Intensive Therapy Unit, a procedure which will take about two hours.

For a few minutes after she has left, we sit side by side, not knowing what to say. Then we are led to the unit, which is on the same floor as the ward, down a side corridor furnished with stiff backed chairs placed in parallel rows along the ubiquitous orange lino floor. There is, we are told, a guest room where we could possibly spend the rest of the night. But it is small, and when we look through the narrow aperture of its window, is obviously in the early stages of refurbishment. Benjo has brought with him a paperback Penguin of the Selected Stories of Katherine Mansfield and, to alleviate our apprehension, he turns to “The Prelude” and reads a few pages before succumbing to our increasingly sombre mood. We hang around, disinfecting our hands with alcohol-smelling foam from a dispenser in the wall every few minutes, just to give ourselves something to do. An Asiatic Registrar appears to brief us about your progress. You are stable, he says, but they have inserted an intubation to assist with oxygenation, and other tubes or lines to assist with nutrition and the administration of drugs. As yet, you are comatose. Sooner or later, probably in the next few days, they will attempt to wake you. In the meantime, there are some causes for moderate concern. A cardiac arrest can have unpredictable effects on the rest of the system. For example, there is as yet no telling what effect the shock may have had on your kidneys, and so they are monitoring them carefully. In addition, when admitted to the unit, you appeared to be "fitting", subject to spasms of face and limbs. They cannot rule out the possibility that the arrest may have damaged your brain.

The Registrar withdraws to be eventually replaced by Denise, a Trinidadian nurse so expert and calm we initially mistake her for a doctor. She takes us into the side room where you are kept, chilled to several degrees below the rest of the hospital so as to preserve your brain. You are sleeping on your back surrounded by instruments but, Catherine Cariad, why are you smoking? Surely that is not allowed in here. Besides, you gave up on your daily dose of Consulate menthol some fifteen years ago. Then I look again, and what I mistook for the shaft of a cigarette, and the hand holding it, is an inflated white latex glove, supporting between its index and middle fingers the tube that they have inserted down your throat, through which oxygen is administered by a hissing ventilator. Beside you stand the monitors that count the quantities of you, the facts and figures that amount to your measurable life: the flutter of your assisted breath, the continuing hammer of your heart. As we stand perplexed and shamed by our ignorance, our apprehension and a sort of stunned dread, Benjo looks at me, for perhaps the first time with truly adult eyes, and remarks "You don't know what to do with yourself, do you?" It is true. I do not.

Meanwhile, and throughout the rest of the endless night, Denise pads to and fro on her plastic crocs of which she is so proud, taking your measurements, adjusting controls. I have the impression, or perhaps the illusion, that, in all of my sixty-six years, I have not got so quite close to another human being in such a brief accumulation of hours. Denise with her imperfect complexion, and her blond wig slightly askew. Denise with her cockeyed glasses, and her standard blue overalls, worn with such careless, indomitable style. Denise with her sly smile and her reassuring patter of a Trinidadian mother and an Irish father estranged. At eight there is movement outside the door. The twelve-hour night shift is drawing to a close, and the day staff are being updated on all current cases, including yours, by the ward sister. It is high time we left and, besides, as Denise reminds us with a wisdom beyond her thirty-odd years "You must look after yourselves. For your own sakes. But, above all, for hers. Be strong."

We 'phone a local cab firm, and arrive home at about half-past nine. Instinctively, remembering through my confusion that this is Sunday, and responding to an ancient self, at a quarter to ten I ring through the local vicarage and leave a message saying what has happened and requesting that your name be placed on the prayer list for the main morning Eucharist, if there is time to sneak you in. Why, I imagine you asking, stirring in your deep sleep, have I done this atavistic thing? Because, as I dimly recognise, I am already caught up in a process of anticipatory mourning, maybe only for a part, and maybe for the whole of you. And being me, with the temperament and background that I bring to this new challenge, I cannot conceive of mourning outside of a religious framework. Sorry about this, sweetheart. "There's sentimental" is what you would have said.

I'll say more than that. We clashed on religious questions every morning of our lives together, but we never disagreed at base. Fundamentally your views are just the same as mine. The only difference is that you believe in God when you feel like it, and I never feel like it. You're vulnerable now, and so you have started praying. Robert bach, how could you? Not merely praying, but putting moral pressure on others to pray on your behalf. Worst still, to pray on my behalf who have never prayed in my life, and am so loath to be prayed over now. Take my name off that prayer list at once, or I will recover instantly and tell the whole sanctimonious bunch of them just what I think. And just what you think too. When you are not pretending.

But, Catherine mine, you are misconstruing what I have done. You are the stricken one, and it is I, not you, who am mourning. You are simply the subject of my anticipatory grief. As such, you have no rights.

Correction. I am the object - not the subject - of your hysterical, pre-emptive grief. You have converted me into a grief object. Take my name off that list immediately.

Too late now.

3 *CALL ME ISHMAEL*

We were not, and had never been, Romeo and Juliet. We were Punch and Judy, we were *'Til Death Do Us Part,* we were *Commedia dell'arte.* The tragic mode does not suit us quite, though we may yet learn to play a part in it before this present trial is done. We are the lower Shakespeare. We are the light relief.

Each evening I catch the taxi back here from the hospital and let myself into our house – no longer quite our home – a place that has temporarily turned against me, a collection of foreign, familiar-seeming rooms, newly defined by the lack of you: a space in which you do not breathe or move. How odd is this hush, how alien is this silence. Seldom was there silence before. Instead there was an interplay of inhabiting sounds, small, muffled sounds, domestic and funny sounds: the clattering of a tea cup, or of plates being moved to the sink, the dribble of the radio as it played your favourite programmes: 'Just a Minute', 'Claire in the Community', 'The Archers', the impertinent pips presaging the hourly News. Here are your law books piled on your desk next to the Regency front window, here are your diaries stacked and revered. Here is your padded, navy blue autumn jacket slung a little carelessly across the back of the orange-cushioned, unravelling wicker chair. Here hangs the Calendar featuring seascapes of the Gower peninsular, a beach or cove to every month. Watch me turn the page, as Llanrhidian Marches yield to Tears Point.

Beyond stands the upright piano, and the many clues to what we were, or maybe even are. Each morning in the uncharted hush I stand and look at it, and consider the attractive quaintness of our life together. An upright piano is not commonplace furnishing hereabouts: more especially an upright, Welsh-made piano. Some have baby grands in upper rooms, private emporia in which they practice at ease, apprehensive of what the neighbours are making of sonata movements or parlour songs, arpeggios, études and scales. We seldom practised, you almost never. And yet the piano is brazen and visible from the street. Piled with yellowing music, it stands in the front room in full view of the broad window jammed with paint, the short, flag-stoned path and the three granite steps up to the old and newly fashionable street. Families on their way back from Sainsbury's, laden with young children and bulging orange plastic bags, stare brazenly at its gallery of likenesses of the great composers – 'Beethoven 1770 – 1822; Franz Schubert 1797 – 1823, and a sad-looking hook-nosed Mozart - crudely crayoned by our son at the age of four-and-a-half and still sellotaped there twenty-three years later, curled and peeling off the walnut-veneered front of the piano frame. We had never had the heart to take them down. Between these cartoon-like portraits the crazy music rest with one brass clasp broken off and, on it, the score of an anthem in Welsh, "Pris Dwy Geinegg", price two-pence, open at the first page.

Who has a two-penny anthem in Welsh, printed in 1916 in the small mining community of Trelewis, on open display in the front parlour of their Grade Two protected terraced suburban London cottage? And who possesses a shabby, iron-framed upright piano manufactured in the year 1925 in the even smaller mining community of Abertillery by the German-sounding company of Harmston & Co., Piano and

Organ Merchants of Pontypool? Answer: a couple of middle-aged madcaps perennially in love in their incongruous hive of crotchety affection and cherished, tarnished jokes.

Come back again in your full consciousness, cook me your Saturday supper of corned beef, parsley sauce and tinned peas. Mock at me as I adulterate this commonplace yet subtle dish with Coleman's mustard, and we will once more decipher these clues. You who talked so gently in your un-emphatic Rhondda valley lilt, so gently and sometimes so maddeningly when you could talk. Here in our front room, with your cluttered desk facing the paint-blocked window, the bookcases full of early editions of Dickens, the basket crammed with tacky sporting equipment, the photo albums full of pictures of us, the Yugoslavian 'Cello purchased in 1980 from Paul Voigt of Soho and now propped ineptly in one corner, rests the detritus of two cultures in one nation – Welsh Wales, and England in Wales - two languages, two ways of life at ancient war, and the maternal grandfathers who embodied them.

Tell me once more about Ishmael who made the music, his ancient woes, his piety and his brittle pride. Brew me your tea, and I will tell you about Gittins, who bought the piano and survived in his long johns, deaf to all the world.

You spoke to me often of your maternal grandfather David Ishmael in our early days in bed together. For you he epitomised I think a certain vision or possibility of Welshness, immured in a language you speak only imperfectly, but which was his sole means of communication. Born in 1867, he was, you told me, from deepest West Wales: from Pont-rhyd-y-groes – "The Bridge of the Ford of the Cross" in Cardiganshire. The bridge in the village's name stretches across the river Ystwyth, one of three rivers – the others being the Wye and the mighty Severn - which pour off Plynlimon, the loftiest of the Cambrian mountains, the "Green Desert of Wales". From there it flows south-westwards towards its estuary in Aberystwyth. The valley is rich in lead, zinc and silver, and mining had been conducted there since Roman times, in marked contrast to the far more recent coal mining industry, a product of the nineteenth century. Even now the river contains deposits of all three metals.

David's father Thomas Ishmael would have started his working life at Glogfawr Lead Mine about two miles to the north of the town. Mining, however, has always been a seasonal business, drawing personnel backwards and forwards from the lead and zinc mines of West Wales and the Tin Mines of Cornwall. Thomas was working at Glogfawr at the time of his marriage to Catherine, the great grandmother after whom you are named, and the birth of his three children, David, born in 1862, Harriet Ann and Thomas. It was in Glogfawr mine that David started his working life. In his very early twenties, however, he was drawn into the ambit of the burgeoning coal mining industry of Southeast Wales by the sinking of a shaft at Abercynon in the Rhondda Valley to feed steel works in Cardiff, seventeen miles to the south. At the age of twenty-four he was working there as a colliery repairer mending timberwork and machinery underground. Already he had married Ann, by whom he was to have four children, including your mother, born in 1900. The family lived in 55, Lock Street, beside the canal that is drawn off the River Taff just to the north of where it and the River Cynon join.

By the time your mother was eleven, her own mother was dead. David brought in a middle-aged housekeeper called Ann David, worked all day underground and attempted to make do. Already the pulmonary illness he had inherited from his mother had been cruelly exacerbated by his daytime work. He had two recourses in his solitary widowhood. The first was Annibynwyr, the Welsh Independent chapel which he attended on Sundays to be harangued by vernacular preachers intoxicated by *hwyl*, whilst the Elders in the Sedd Fawr , the "Big Seat" beneath the pulpit, bleakly voiced their agreement with re-iterated refrains of "Ie, Ie!!" The second was the male voice choir whose rehearsals David Ishmael attended on weekday evenings. Someone had taught him the tonic sol-far, and the basics of choral harmony. Oppressed by many cares, penned underground throughout the daylight hours, slowly expiring of a wasting disease of the chest, the earth's crust in his lungs, in early middle age this lonely father of four had a vision of pure glory:

Gwyn eu byd y bobl a adwaenant yr hyfryd laise,
Yn llewyrch dy wyneb, O Arglwydd, y rhodiant,
Yn dy enw di y gorfoddelant, ac y llawenychant,
Ac yn dy gyfiawnder yr ymddyrchafant.

Blessed are they who know thy beauteous voice,
Thy face shall ever be their dwelling place.
For ever happy, in thy name they rejoice,
And in thy name they rise in glory.

That hymn of yearning is up on the piano rest now, and our son is playing it. Over and over it goes, the harmony close, the key E flat, amenable to accompaniment by a brass band, perhaps a colliery band. Naturally Grandpa Ishmael knows his Bible, so the text echoes the Beatitudes from St Matthew's Gospel chapter five, in William Morgan's translation of 1588.

Pie in the sky is what Karl Marx would have called such sentiments, and you my dear would have agreed with him. By the time we met, you had little time for religion, but its influence had followed you everywhere, even into your very detestation of liturgical forms. In 2006, the year of the publication of Richard Dawkins' *The God Delusion,* amused by the rumbling battle of belief and non-belief in our household, I packed a copy of this atheistical jeremaiad into the same parcel as *The Good News Bible* - a nice straightforward translation, you'd been told, with few frills - and placed them with a loving message to you under our Christmas tree, in the hope that reading both would furnish your mind, and our jokes. For the following six months you read through the Bible each morning book by book, and cover to cover, from *Genesis* to *Revelation* while I sat downstairs listening to you scoffing aloud at the culinary provisions of Leviticus or the sexual prejudices of Saint Paul. When at length you closed the volume for the last time, I inquired when you intended to start on Dawkins. "No need," you remarked, "No need."

4 *MEWSLADE BAY*

Monday, October 7th

By the time we returned to the hospital early this afternoon, Denise had been replaced by Christabel from Grenada: tall, fiftyish, very black, with spectacles one side of which needed mending. Christabel is decidedly in charge: focussed, authoritative and majestic. Indomitably cheerful, she lives in Mitcham, has five children, and is patently used to her wishes being obeyed. After we have been here for about ten minutes, she announces "I need to take my measurements and I want you outa here". For all that, she has mislaid your dental bridge, which came out during the intubation process. She has put it in a cup, and now she cannot find it. How you would have hated that. About nothing were you so vain as your teeth, one of the few aspects of your life and person, apart from your auburn hair, on which you have always been willing to spend your money.

Dimly, through my anxiety, I begin to take in the details of the room. The large adjustable bed stage centre on which you lie brocaded by attachments and wires. The nurse's station near the glass-panelled door at which, between her routine ministrations, Christabel stands writing up her notes. Behind you stand ranks of equipment, and two monitors, one keeping watch over your pulse, and the oxygen saturation in your blood, the other attached to the ventilator that now supports your breathing.

These undulating and parallel green curves at the top of the upper panel labelled "Beneview T8" recount your heart.

This lone blue trace in the middle of the panel records your oxygen saturation, the yellow line beneath it the amount of carbon dioxide in your respiratory tract. A square in the bottom right hand corner of the screen tells us that your blood pressure currently reads as 147 systolic and 80 diastolic. Beside you, an aluminium stand from which hangs your nutritional bag. Thus are you quantified, accounted for, and fed.

Early today, before we arrived, they attempted for the first time to wake you. Thus far you have been sedated, but early this morning they lifted the anaesthetic so as to ascertain how much of you is still there. As we enter the room I glance furtively at the nurses' notes. "No appropriate response" is written inside the relevant box. Already, concerned by facial seizures which a course of drugs is presently suppressing, they have ordered a CAT scan of your head.

Tuesday, October 8th

We are slowly becoming aware that, parallel to your own, another tragedy is unfolding. The corridor leading from the unit towards the main axis of the other ground-floor wards has become an arcade of communal grief, with comfy chairs provided for the anticipatory mourners. Along it since yesterday morning has been draped a large family who have hogged most of the chairs, drawing our compassion and resentment in equal measure. Since only two visitors are allowed by each bedside at any one time, they take it in turns to disappear through the swing doors for an hour or two, and then to re-appear, wreathed in distress. This afternoon, while waiting outside for you to be turned, we inquire into the reasons for their presence. Beyond those swing doors lies a forty-year old woman who, after a decade or two punishing her body with alcohol, is dying of cirrhosis of the liver. The condition has gradually weakened other of her vital organs. The doctors have given her only days to live.

This family, united with us in pain but divided by culture and by habit, is multitudinous, boisterous and Catholic. South Londoners of Irish extraction is what I suspect, their mutual greetings and departures phrased in the demotic terseness of "See you then", "Till next time", "chin up". Over the hours they become to us as familiar as characters in a nightly soap opera: the strong-armed taciturn brother, a main support to his siblings, the younger sister who regularly re-emerges from the unit with red-rimmed eyes, her sorrow and apprehension as gauche and blatant as a cheap synthetic dress. They ask us in turn about our attendance at the unit every day, and so we tell them about you. From then on, to the ritual phatic repertoire of sign-offs and sign-ons, the comings and the goings, is added the sideways compassionate articulation of "I hope your wife will be alright", "She'll be okay", et cetera.

This family and ourselves maintain a sort of awed, respectful distance from one another, even as we recognise our kinship in suffering. At times when we return after taking a break from our vigil in the café out in the main foyer, we are faced with a decision: either we will join them in the confined space circumscribed by those chairs, sharing their sad tidings and being obliged to share our own, or we will keep apart, standing out in the main axial corridor, further tiring our limbs while running the risk that our discretion will be mistaken for standoffishness. Usually we remain apart.

There are, I realise – and how you might have berated me for the thought - social nuances, even to actions as intimate as the rites of mourning, or the preparations for mourning. Beyond that lours the truth that all grief is both particular and general. Everyone experiences it, but each instance is as variously tinged as the vividly hued leaves that now precariously hang from the lone acacia tree out in the small quadrangle of a garden we glimpse out of the bleak institutional windows, a tree where in an earlier season and year while I was an orthopaedic patient in this same hospital, we sat together holding hands one June.

We have decided to read you back into mental life. Each day into this awful side chapel of silence in which thoughtlessly you lie dying yet not-dying, a space in which you are there and yet not there, we ferry a selection of anthologies containing your favourite poems, which we take it in turns to orate. Benjo has with him Ted Hughes and Seamus Heaney's *The School Bag*, while I have brought along one of the many early twentieth-century editions of Palgrave's *Golden Treasury* in their distinctive Oxford blue covers that you kept in your desk in the front room, each one inscribed by me as, acquiring it for a few pounds from a second-hand bookshop in Lewes, Arundel or Brighton, I brought it home to you at the end of the day as a token of mutual understanding: "To Darling Catherine from her adoring Robert: one more edition".

We begin with your all-time favourites: Wordsworth's "Daffodils" and his "On Westminster Bridge", some Dylan

Thomas, Arnold's "Dover Beach". Then, recalling how you loved the opening evocation of twilight, I launch into Gray's "Elegy", delivering it a little too rhetorically across your recumbent form:

> The boast of heraldry, the pomp of power,
> And all that beauty, all that wealth e'er gave,
> Awaits alike the inevitable hour.
> The paths of glory lead but to the grave.

Then, a little self-consciously, I carry on with:

> Can storied urn or animated bust
> Back to its mansion call the fleeting breath?
> Can Honour's voice provoke the silent dust,
> Or Flattery soothe the dull cold ear of Death?

Wednesday, October 9th

This morning they made another attempt to wake you. Again the box on the nurses' report form is filled in with the words "No appropriate response". What I wonder would be appropriate? That you stood on your two feet, raced to the centre of the room and denounced me publicly for my neglect? As it is, they have re-sedated you, and at ten thirty this morning, before we turned up, they wheeled you upstairs to perform the CAT scan.

Unfamiliar with medical acronyms, I am not quite clear what a CAT scan is. This afternoon, while we were waiting out in the corridor to allow you to be turned, I inquired about its significance to our scientifically sophisticated son. No sooner have I done so but an unfamiliar voice addressed us from in front of the double doors that lead from the unit into the outer corridor. For days we have been remarking the behaviour of a member of the hospital staff unknown by name to either of us, yet evidently welcome wherever he goes. Dr N. is spare, wiry and energetic. In his late fifties perhaps, possibly of Greek or Armenian origin, he obviously occupies a fairly senior position in the hospital hierarchy yet, from what we can work out, he enjoys no particular brief and is allocated to no particular unit. Instead, he stalks everywhere: striding down corridors, bursting through doors, hailing passers-by. Has he a sort of roving, advisory brief? And all the while he appears inspired by an elated feeling of purpose, his face alert and smiling, his limbs and his manner suffused by a committed, almost an ecstatic, appreciation of everything he undertakes. To me, in this place where so many are experts in subjects of which I am ignorant, he has already become the animating spirit of science.

This individual is tipsy with a love of knowhow, drunk on difficulty, on technique, on the complicated, interweaving *haecceity* of things. The this-ness of the valve, the roominess of the ray, the precision of a line, the perspicacity of a lens. How the scientist in Pascal would have loved him: he is thin and pared-down, trim and accurate, passionate about exactitude, randy for the felicitous fashionings of fact. From his position near the doors, having overheard my question, he launches into an enthusiastic explanation of the scientific principles underlying Computerised Axial Tomography. A *tomos*, he explains, is a section or a slice. By rotating around an imaginary axis, a CAT scanner creates two dimensional images across a series of horizontal planes, producing pictures that represent cross-sections of an organ, in this case your brain, which can then be re-composed into a three-dimensional panorama. Thus can the radiographer report on the physical evidence of your inner condition, enabling the doctors to decipher your case.

There is a mood of excitement and revelation as he expounds these essential facts, which must have been familiar to him for decades. Dr N. has never grown tired of explaining them, these - to him - almost platitudinous details untarnished by constant use. They excite him still because they are intricate, and because they are true. Dr N, this bounding and charismatic figure in his regulation green gown, is the revived spirit of the Enlightenment, as significant a cipher of our culture as Thomas Gray was of his. Once again, I am reminded of Blaise Pascal. It was as a sixteen-year-old self-instructed in mathematics that this young Frenchman, this curious and omnivorous prodigy, wrote his first work, his *Treatise On Conic Sections,* defined by the *New Oxford Dictionary of English* as figures discovered by the intersection of individual planes with a circular cone. I know little of them, but our son explains them to my dull, poetically-attuned ears. Depending on the angle of the plane with respect to a cone, I now learn, a conic section may be a circle, an ellipse, a parabola or a hyberbola. Whatever shape it assumes, so the late adolescent genius found out, a conic section invariably has the following, consistent property. If you select six points at random around its circumference, and then join them with lines drawn right across the section from one side to the other, thus forming a hexagon, all of the lines joining pairs of points that lie opposite to one another meet along a common axis, known as Pascal's line. The gifted youth originally wrote this hypothesis out as a note, supplying no proof. Nonetheless, practice proves it to be the case.

Talking with our son, I find out more. Not all cones are circular, but come in a variety of shapes. With a square base, a cone becomes a pyramid, each section of which is also a square. If you tilt the plane, the configuration of each section mutates into a rectangle or into a rhombus. I wonder at the intricacy and complexity of these processes, wonder still more that, simply by treating the organ that houses your mind geometrically, the doctors in this palace to rationality can reconstitute a picture or set of pictures reflecting the parameters and limits of your present consciousness. The priests do not tell me this much.

By early afternoon the results of the scan have reportedly come though. Shortly before tea, Benjo overhears a conversation between two registrars talking together in corridor beyond our glass-panelled door. The team, one of them was telling the other, "now have everything that they need to know". Later we get to see the scans, four in number, which show various cross-sections of your head. The first includes your neck, the whole of your skull seen obliquely from behind, with various attachments dangling from it. The second shows the top of your head as seen from above. A grainy grey sea covers almost the whole area, with few contours or differentiating features. Already the radiographer has delivered his preliminary verdict:

> Sulcal spaces are relatively inconspicuous, particularly in the right parietal area. The appearance is highly suspicious for global oedema. There is also a suggestion of reduced grey-white matter

> differentiation within the base ganglia. Some ill-defined more focal density within the left frontal lobe. No focal lesion with mass effect, and no haemorrhage. The basal cisterns are patent, no tonsillar descent. Retained secretions within the paranasal sinuses are noted. Overall appearances are consistent with global ischemic brain injury.

In other words, you have a blocked nose and you have suffered no stroke, but your upper brain is now one homogeneous ruin.

Later that afternoon, the preliminary report triggers an interview on the ward with the duty consultant. Dr Ahmed is one of the army of learned persons from Pakistan without whom our National Health Service would not be the comprehensive and pliable outfit that it is. As befits someone of his seniority entrusted with the ultimate matter of your care, he is cautious with us, feeling his way from statement to tentative statement. A preliminary survey of the scan, he says, suggests that the cerebral impact of your combined respiratory and cardiac arrest has been extreme. Before he can be sure how extensive the damage has been, however, he will need to lift your sedation a little more so as to assess your neurological state. The team will perform a tracheostomy on you tomorrow to ease your daily care, the removal of your secretions. Once the sedation has been adjusted, he will have a further word with us.

Thursday, October 10th

As we re-enter the sanctum of your side-room this morning, there is change in your appearance that at first we can't account for. Then we look again, and notice that the mouth tube through which you formerly breathed has been replaced by a clump of bandages at the base of your neck. To it is attached a plastic airway leading to the ventilator, removed by the duty nurse several times an hour so that suction can be carried to relieve the pressure on your afflicted throat and lungs.

Looking over the day nurse's shoulders, I catch sight of a note that reads: "10.a.m: TRACHEOSTOMY PERFORMED: Pre-oxygenation. Full monitoring + ETCO2. Pre-sedated and paralysed with atracurium. Horizontal incision + blunt dissection. Tracheostomy size 8.0. 2 x sutures. Sedate one hour, then wake and wean."

Once more they have striven to bring you back into full, responsive life. Once again, they have failed.

This afternoon a message came through that Dr Ahmed wished to speak with us again. We are led out of the main body of the unit down a corridor into a cramped study, where he invites us to sit, then takes his chair in front of a desk. Against a far wall leans a monochrome portrait of a white-haired woman in late middle age. Wanting to endow him with as much common humanity as I can, I wonder briefly whether this is a photo of his wife.

Dr Ahmed possesses an almost leonine appearance, dark brows prominent above his bright, alert eyes. He has a slow and gravely hesitant manner of speaking, his habit one of forming phrases carefully, and letting them fall in a pool of attentive silence. Then he will wait as the ripples of significance spread out. He respects our intelligence, and tailors his approach accordingly. What he has to tell us is grave, but no longer unexpected. In the minutes following your rest, your brain was starved of oxygen for around twelve minutes. After five minutes, brain cells begin to die off, and the whole organ begins to expand, and then to contract. When it settles again, large sections of it will have been compromised. In your case, as far as the radiographic evidence can tell, the injury extends over the whole surface, with results that can be inferred, but not precisely predicted.

The condition to which you have now been reduced, he says, echoing the radiographer's report, and pronouncing the technical terms carefully, is one of "Severe Global Hypoxic Brain Damage." Global because diffused right across the surface and inner parts of the brain, with no particular clusters or lesions, but with a generalised detrimental effect. You will never again be what once you were.

It is, he tells us, hard to predict what the precise effects of this unforeseen accident will have been as far as your mental capacity is concerned, since no localised centre seems to have been affected more than any other. The medical team, he tells us, have now made several attempts to rouse you to no avail. Eventually they will withdraw your sedation completely. When they have done so, they will be able to determine exactly how far you have been impaired. You may, he told us, be in a coma for the rest of your life. He gave no indication, however vague, of how long this might be. Moreover, in cases such as these, the repercussions differ widely from person to person. They range from "some slight memory loss" to the persistent - even a persistent – "vegetative state". Dr Ahmed approaches the last phrase with care, recognising its emotive implications, the nearness lexically speaking of "vegetative" to "vegetable." When he reaches the relevant words, he mumbles them slightly, and his eyes give away his unease. Then he says, directly and as sincerely as he can within the protocol of his role, "I'm sorry."

Catherine Cariad, there is no doubt in our minds as to how you would react to news of this gravity: you would strive to deflect it: into humour, into a healing levity. So, once we are again by your side, I abandon the poetry recital and I reach to the bottom of my shoulder bag to bring out my Kindle, on which, in preparation for the solemnity of a moment such as this, I have downloaded Jane Austen's *Emma.* We read it aloud as a tribute to satire, to a salutary astuteness, to the alert human intelligence, to everything that you have lost. How bottomlessly cynical she is, now unsentimental, and how true:

> The real evils indeed of Emma's situation were the power of having rather too much her own way, and a disposition to think a little too well of herself; these were the disadvantages which threatened to allow her many enjoyments. The danger, however, was at present so unperceived, they did not by any means rank as misfortunes with her.

As I read these lines, I sense the duty nurse moving around the room, making notes, checking the monitors, twiddling with dials. After the conclusion of the first chapter, I ask her idly what her name is. "Emma," she replies. And does she enjoy Jane Austen's book? "I haven't read it," she replies. "I haven't the time. But the film was awesome."

Friday, October 11th

"Each man kills the thing he loves", and as you lie there, moral responsibility seeps into me like rain. Across my vision flash the moments in the last year when I might conceivably have acted to forestall this dilemma, and this tragedy.

The moment last January when panic seized me because of some trivial computer accident that I mistakenly thought had blocked all of my files, sending you as so often before into a sympathetic reflex of distress manifesting itself as a gastric complaint that landed you in bed for five days.

The March evening on the front at Swansea when you were taken with shortness of breath after a glass of chilled white wine at a café. I got you home to our flat after you had taken a couple of breaths from your salbutamol inhaler, but afterwards did far too little to urge medical advice.

The beautiful but freezing morning on Rhossili Down the following week when, descending a steep slope towards the inland village of Llangennith, you were almost swept off your feet by a sudden gust of wind and rain. For almost a minute you stood there teetering on your feet, clutching an umbrella in one hand and trying desperately to steady yourself while I remained at the bottom of the slope looking impatiently back, but never stirred a foot to help you in your plight. How easily I could have rung up the doctor's surgery the following week and booked an appointment to monitor your evidently worsening condition, and yet again I did nothing.

The moment in the piazza of the Duomo in Florence in early July when you clutched my arm in dismay, asphyxiated by the swirling traffic. On our return to London you succumbed to one of your chest infections, and I was spurred at last into booking an appointment for you to consult the asthma nurse, and even accompanied you and watched as you blew into a machine and registered a lung capacity half of what it had been only twelve months before. The Jamaican nurse asked you to return to be re-tested once the infection was over, and in the meantime told you to return that very afternoon so that a general practitioner could treat your chest.

At five I reminded you to go back, but succumbed far too easily to your insistence that this time you walk the hundred odd yards to the surgery alone. Instead of being there to make your case and bear witness to your aggravated symptoms, I stayed and watched a film on the internet. After what seemed like minutes you returned to tell me that, with your usual avoidance of exaggeration or fuss, you had reported your condition as mild. As a consequence, you had been prescribed the lowest strength of antibiotic, practically useless in the circumstances.

In vain do I console myself with a recollection of the trivial steps that I then took on your behalf. After talking for a while with Hilary Davies, wife of the poet Sebastian Barker who is suffering from lung cancer, I recognised that the British Lung Foundation might be able to help, and phoned them up to complain that these totally insufficient antibiotics were not working. At their suggestion I prevailed on the surgery to re-prescribe, and nursed you through the next ten days, making you tasty meals with jokey menus while a course of steroids restored your strength. But why, when this temporary crisis was over, did I not follow up by booking another appointment with the obliging asthma nurse to have your lung capacity re-checked? Not until a week ago did I do this, and by that time a second chest infection had rendered the exercise futile.

I have no notion of Heaven, but I possess a distinct and very vivid notion of Hell. It is a place where we are brought helplessly face to face with our inescapable moral responsibility: naked in a den that is cobwebbed, stinging, utterly cold, without excuse to offer the judge, since the judge is ourselves. There we dwell forever in a comfortless cell the only other occupant of which is an unpitying self who will never avert his accusatory stare, that shivering and culpable self whose righteous indictment we will never be able to evade.

It is true that Existentialists do not properly believe in Hell, though even Sartre was moved to remark "l'enfer, c'est les autres", "Hell is other people". He was too kind on himself, and certainly his judgment is too kind on such as me. "L'enfer, c'est moi." Hell, under circumstances such as these, is none other than Oneself.

Saturday, October 12th

This morning they moved you out of your private side room into the main body of the unit. There you have a bay to yourself with your instruments and monitors re-arranged, next to a small podium like an ecclesiastical reading desk at which the Australian male nurse stands perusing his notes.

You are now almost entirely off sedation, as much you as you are capable of being. As I approach your bed, I greet you, and, for the first time in over a week, am able to look into your eyes. They are beautiful eyes, once described on your passport as "blue", but in reality a sort of aquamarine lightly flecked with gold. Today they gaze up at me with the perfect trust and emptiness of a new born child.

My dear, tell me, tell me, how do I address you now?

"Hello, Catherine", I say and, again, "Hello, Catherine." My voice wavers. Are you any longer the being whom I used fondly to call thus? At what point, I wonder, do you cease being you?

The nurses continue to address you by name, and to request your permission when turning or changing you. I have a sort of faith that their doing so amounts to more than an article of etiquette. Treatment in this merciful place would be meaningless were there no one to treat. I need and want to persuade myself of the persistence or something or someone beyond a transformation even as drastic as this. Do the predicates alter the person or affect the vocative noun? If you were you when you wore your hair long, and you when you wore it short, your selfhood manifestly transcends accidentals such as a haircut. If you were you when behaving gracefully, and you when in a huff, the Catherine-ness of you clearly underlay all such moods. If you were you when well, and you when you were sick, the you-ness of you is patently independent of your health. You were you in a red dress, you in a blue dress or wearing nothing at all, wearing mascara or not, fatter or thinner, richer or poorer, suntanned or pale. Your you-ness was, and is, an essence.

But, the sceptic in you would have insisted, surely there are limits to this rule. We discussed the Sodates argument one morning, do you remember? Of course you do not remember. A sodates is a heap in ancient Greek, a heap let us say of wood shavings. You can add wood shavings to a heap, or subtract them. Is there a moment in the process of subtraction when the heap relinquishes it heap-ness? How ill, an analogous argument would run, do you have to be in order to cease being yourself? By any standards, you are presently unwell. Does this outbreak of unwell-ness fall under the same heading as a headache, a period pain, the herpes of the lower lip that in our early days together so often afflicted you when exposed intemperately to the sun? In the August of 1973 you and a friend were on the island of Santorini to visit your anthropologist friend Margaret Kenna, who had undertaken several years of field work on the then unfrequented Cycladic island of Anafi. A few hours prior to your departure, the habitual scourge struck, and you were holed up for days in the Grand Hotel, Megalochori, nursing your blighted lower lip which, under such circumstances, you always hid as if leprous. You attempted to obliterate yourself, to remain invisible to the world. Yet through it all you remained Catherine.

Catherine, my Catherine, are you any longer there? Tell me why you tremble so. Your arms are shaking and, from certain convulsions beneath the sheets, so I gather are your legs. Why do you yawn thus, and when you do, why do you extend and roll your tongue like a lion in its cage? And why do you clench your hands together with such desperate energy, leaving marks all over your darling, tender palms?

What am I writing to you for but to restore to us both what has been lost: memory, language: all that made you, you? How can I possibly do this but by reaching deep down in my mind to recover the sounds, sights, smells and scents of you in associative succession, so as to make them plain to myself and to the world.

But Robert bach, Robert little darling, your successive perceptions of me are not me. They are what you have made me over the years.

Catherine Cariad, whatever else have I to go by but the sing-song of your voice as I recall it, the gestures of your body as I recall them, our shared past as I cherish it, the reaches of your unique past as you chose to summon it up as opportunity and the changing emotional weather gave you leave?

Forgive me. Forgive me too if I tell you things you already know. Or knew because presently I cannot be sure that you know anything.

Robert, I am at your mercy, then.

Catherine, forgive me. I must talk to you, and somehow imagine your replies. I must speak for both of us, even if the you that responds, the you that resents, that resists or rejects is an imagined or even an imaginary you. Or else a remembered you, though what is memory but a function of the imagination?

I am doubly at your mercy then.

Yes, you are doubly, trebly at my mercy.

Outside in our courtyard garden at home, the white iceberg roses we bought last summer are putting forth their second flush. On our bedside table, your softly ticking Sekonda wristwatch now reads ten to eleven. Yet, about this time last week, your spirit died. Wiped are the ambivalent fondness for Wales, the love of Michaelmas daisies, the hatred of Margaret Thatcher, the distrust of pomp, the memories of the valleys, the partiality for martial sounding hymns, the atheistical opinions, the tales of lesbian teachers and of the school trip to Paris when, sweeping down the Champs Elysées on a party coach with animated friends, you stared out of the back window and observed the driver in the following car expose himself at the wheel. "That's a lovely vehicle, Gwyneth," you screamed above the din, "but what is the man in the Renault *doing*?"

Sunday, October 13th

This afternoon, shortly after three, a convoy of vehicles arrives from Essex, carrying your sister Margaret, your brother–in-law David, a retired lecturer originally from Neath, one nephew with his wife Edina, and one great nephew. We have already hinted to them by 'phone what to expect, and as they enter the great open hangar of the hospital foyer, there is a briskness and friendliness about them that masks their unease. We hang about idly chatting until I gather sufficient courage to take them into the ward. Only two visitors are permitted at any one time, so I accompany Margaret and David, stretching the rule to three.

Margaret is in a wheelchair and, as she approaches the bed, she holds back slightly, terrified at to what she might find. As she draws level with the bed, she just says "Oh, Cath" and looks into your eyes, seeking and praying for some sign of recognition, the barest response. There is nothing, though your lids are now open for most of the day.

I talk as coherently as I can about the course of your treatment and, as tactfully as I can manage, I convey the probable prognoses, beginning with the most favourable and proceeding by tentative degrees to the more drastic. David asks a series of pertinent questions, and Margaret says almost nothing as she holds tightly on to your right hand and continues staring into your lovely, empty eyes. We have Heaney and Hughes' *School Bag* with us, so I turn to page 283, and ask David to read you Dylan Thomas' *Fern Hill*. He is a keen amateur baritone, and once in his Neath schooldays in the late nineteen forties heard Thomas himself read. He now performs a very fair imitation, adopting the poet's BBC voice, and coating his own his habitual rolling Welsh accent with the declamatory projection and civilised articulation Dylan always adopted for public consumption:

> Now as I was young and easy under the apple boughs
> About the lilting house and happy as the grass was green,
> The night above the dingle starry,
> Time let me hail and climb
> Golden in the heydays of his eyes…

Beloved, do you recall our last visit to the Boat House at Laugharne? Mist hung over the great double estuary of the rivers Taf and Towy, and in the distance Llanstefan dimly glowed. Above us, almost unseen, lurked the great hulk of St Nicholas's head where the cormorants once wheeled. Later that week, we got lost in The Grove, Swansea walking to a Sunday lunch appointment with Margaret Kenna, now Emerita Professor of Social Anthropology at the university. Someone had given us the wrong address, and we found ourselves instead outside a gaunt white converted Methodist chapel. During the years of World War Two, it had been a slender, makeshift broadcasting studio, and from it Thomas had read some of his stories and poems, including perhaps this one. Now "Fern Hill" echoes across the drab, whitewashed spaces of a South London hospital ward, disturbing the rest of the Barbadian women opposite as with closed eyes she slumbers on her crisply laundered pillow, ignoring the huddle of anxious relatives gathered just inside the blue plastic partition curtains.

I thank David and commend him on his performance as he falls silent again, regarding with the open basin of his eyes the impeding catastrophe that is you. I had asked him to bring some Austen to read aloud but, seeing that we have already embarked upon *Emma*, he has brought instead James Thurber's *My Life and Hard Times & The Owl in the Attic* in the Hamish Hamilton edition of 1950. His well-leafed copy was purchased from Foyles Second Hand Department, and was a recent Christmas present from his Florida residing son and Colombian daughter in law, fondly inscribed in pencil "We are very happy to find one of your favourite books, Gloria and Michael". Now it lies on your bedside table amid the bottles and the flowers, and so I ask him to open the brick red coloured cover with a sketch of a somnolent poodle in front, and pick just one story to read. More to cheer us up than you, he selects "The Subjunctive Mood" marking the place with a memento of some foreign holiday, a yellowing label that reads "Keo Coomadaria, Cyprus Grape Wine, As Originally Made for the Commanders of the Knights Templars in Cyprus During the Crusades 1096-1291." This is the nearest we can get this afternoon to your favourite American humourist David Sedaris, and David reads it with a sort of rollicking self-conscious whimsy that predictably only intensifies our gloom. It is one of our family's nostrums that no subject is so dire that it cannot be made the subject of humour; wit of an honourable sort, we both believe, frames circumstances in a common sense perspective from which its true dimensions can be judged. We seem to have reached the limits of this particular adage.

5 STONE

Almost by definition, it seems to me, our maternal grandfathers were Christians. One of my most vivid memories, often shared with you, is of sleeping as a child in the loft bedroom of my maternal grandparents' house in Pontypool, in the then Anglophone, anglophile borderland county of Monmouthshire. It was Christmastide and I seven years of age, which identifies the month as December, 1954. I had been put to bed early, at about half-past eight, shortly after supper. At around eleven, I awoke to hear slow footsteps noisily ascending the stairs. The door opened to admit my eighty-two-year-old maternal grandfather, stooping and, as I had long realised, profoundly deaf. He was wearing his charcoal grey three-piece suit, on the right hand pocket of whose jacket hung the receiver for his immense and clumsy hearing aid, as large it seemed to me as a radio set.

I half-closed my eyes, and pretended to be fast asleep as he fumbled towards the other bed and began the Herculean task of undressing. Fascinated and appalled, between deceitful lids, I watched the striptease. Off came the complicated apparatus of the hearing aid – thick brown receiver, thick brown wires, glass earpiece - to be deposited carefully on a shelf. Then the jacket came off, the waistcoat, and the cufflinks. The shoes were unlaced and removed, the worsted socks placed side by side across the back of the chair. The red braces were then loosened from the shoulders as his pants fell to the floor, were folded and deposited on a hanger. The starched white shirt was painfully pulled over my grandfather's head to reveal its wearer clad in nothing except that exotic garment: woollen winter long johns.

I was expecting him immediately to fold back the bedspread, disappear beneath the sheets and turn out the light. Instead, he groped towards the foot of his bed and dropped awkwardly to his knees. He placed his pallid veined hands together, and commenced to pray *extempore* and aloud, oblivious of the fact that I, or anybody else apart from the Godhead, could hear him. His supplications passed though moods and phases, beginning with adoration of the divine attributes: the power, mercy, beauty and magnificence of the creator. His praises exhausted, my grandfather turned inward and examined his sins. There were not many, and for the most part comprised domestic oversights – a failure sufficiently to dampen the evening fire, clumsiness or inaccuracy with his accounts, the occasional snubbing of neighhours or neglect of his duties as a parishioner of the parish church of St John Trevethin at the summit of the lane.

His misdemeanours thus pronounced, my grandfather let loose a torrent of thanksgiving for mercies received: the ministrations of his mother Alice, from St Helens in Lancashire, his childhood and education on Merseyside, his dear wife Ada from the nearby village of Abersychan, his job as a Managing Clerk in the long established law firm of Bythway and Son (established 1717), his classically named sons Horace and Cyril, his daughter Ada and his three grandchildren. My grandfather hunched his shoulders, closed his eyes ever tighter and leant forwards towards the patchwork counterpane of the bed. He paused and proceeded, through long custom, to pray for the needs of others. He held before the bountiful eyes of the Almighty the recently crowned Queen, the leaders of the nations, the officials of the British Empire, of the local town council and the disestablished Welsh church. He implored for divine intervention in national and international disputes, for divine charity in the alleviation of suffering at home and abroad, of the unemployed, the indigent, of those afflicted in body and mind. He prayed for dumb animals and over-loquacious politicians. And then he turned to the family.

One by one he brought them before his rapt inner vision, dead and alive, named and cherished them, and recommended them to God's love. His late mother Thy Servant Alice, daughter of James Pilkington of the prosperous St Helens glass-making firm of Pilkington, whose displeasure she had provoked by absconding with a pauper. Thy Late Servants his brothers and sisters, Thy Servant Ada, his wife of fifty years. His children by her: Thy Servants Horace Alfred and Cyril Pilkington, followed his one daughter and my mother, Thy Servant Ada Alice, present with us this night. They were followed by the spouses and consorts of these same offspring: Thy Servants Betty and Madge, and Thy Servant Harry McKenzie, my father. Last in this procession came his grandchildren: Thy Servant John, only son of Cyril, and his first cousin Thy Servant Malcolm Henry, my brother. Last of all to my astonished ears arrived a fervent intercession of behalf of Thy Servant Robert Hugh, present with us now. My grandfather neglected to pray for himself.

The embroidered style of prayer was part of a long nonconformist tradition, and your own grandfather would surely have recognised it. Yet Alfred Horace Gittins, from whose ardent and slackening mouth I heard this recital, was a committed communicant of the Anglican Church, a church warden and former organist, his loyalty to the English crown not to be questioned or trifled with. The Gittinses were *crachach,* gentry, part of the tiny professional elite that stood between the labouring people of this mining town, their monarch, the government and their God. In one of the photograph albums in the bookcase beside our piano is an image taken from the *South Wales Echo* of 1936 reporting on the visit by King Edward VIII to the depressed mining towns of South Wales during the very depths of the Depression. It was a high profile visit much fanfared by the local and national press, designed to demonstrate the social and political concern of a monarch otherwise better known for his amorous affairs. The public response was orchestrated to illustrate the loyalty of the working, or rather the enforcedly idle, people of South Wales. The Welsh coal pits had been badly affected by the economic downturn.

The point of the coverage was to show that they were indomitable, and indomitably loyal. "So stout of heart are these people that for His Majesty's visit", trumpeted Pathé Newsreel shown in both local and national cinemas, "they can still put on a brave show". The royal train with its plush on-board accommodation had been parked in the sidings at pleasant, river-straddling, Usk. From it the King, soberly dressed against the local rain in mackintosh and bowler hat, made forays into the coal dust and pent up streets of the valleys, and at each and every stop was met by carefully controlled crowds. "Everywhere it is the same story", the Pathé commentary continued, "flags waving above the grime and the decay, cheers breaking the silence where work hooters have long ceased to blow."

At Pontypool, as reported by *The South Wales Echo*, the King was met by a cheering throng in the High Street. The photograph in the album encapsulates that moment. In the very front row, their faces suffused with enthusiasm, two figures loom large: Alfred Horace Gittins, dressed like Edward in a mackintosh against the persistent drizzle, and his high cheek boned, elegant wife, Ada. But, when the King visited the Rhondda valley not seventy miles away, your parents sat in their house and scowled.

What had fed into attitudes so diverse, loyalties so divided, such different conceptions of the nation? Your David was not rich or influential, but neither was my Alfred. Your David spoke only Welsh, perhaps inter-dispersed with a few words of English. My Alfred was in essence a monoglot Welsh Englishman, an Englishman in Wales.

The imperial connection was important to him, increasingly so as a distinguishing mark of identity after he migrated to Pontypool to work for Bythway and Son at the age of twenty-five. Your David probably left school at seven, possessing a modicum of literacy in the Welsh tongue alone. It is possible that his hymn, his one surviving testament to the inner life, was written out for him.

TWO FACES OF WALES: *Above,* Striking coal miners at Tonypandy, Rhondda, in 1910;*Below:* Greeted by his loyal subjects, bowler-hatted King Edward VIII visits genteel Pontypool in November, 1936. Alfred Gittins, sporting a trilby, mittened hand to mouth, is in the far front row; his smiling wife Ada stands two to his right in furs.

What had fed into attitudes so diverse, loyalties so divided, such different conceptions of the nation? Your David was not rich or influential, but neither was my Alfred. Your David spoke only Welsh, perhaps inter-dispersed with a few words of English. My Alfred was in essence a monoglot Welsh Englishman, an Englishman in Wales. The imperial connection was important to him, increasingly so as a distinguishing mark of identity after he migrated to Pontypool to work for Bythway and Son at the age of twenty-five. Your David probably left school at seven, possessing a modicum of literacy in the Welsh tongue alone. It is possible that his hymn, his one surviving testament to the inner life, was written out for him.

But born in Liverpool in 1872, five years younger than your David, my Alfred had been beneficiary of the Forster Education Act providing all children with free elementary schooling up to the age of fourteen. Acutely aware that further educational avenues were closed to him, from the age of thirteen he had paid weekly visits to the booksellers James Wollard by the banks of the Mersey, and invested 3d or 4d a week in successive volumes of Cassell's National Library, edited by Henry Morley, Professor of English Literature at University College, London. This was only one of a number of publishers' series issued at the time aimed at furnishing the mind of the literate lower middle class. I have the volumes before me now, the first fifty-two volumes held in an oak bookcase that Alfred purchased for 31/6d to hold the first year's titles. Lord Macaulay's Life of Warren Hastings, a favourite with liberal imperialists of the period, lies beside the comedies of Richard Brindsley Sheridan, Byron's *Childe Harold,* Edmund Burke's *Thoughts on the*

Present Discontents, The Sorrows of Werther, and Dr Johnson's *A Journey to the Hebrides.* These were just some of the offerings for 1885, duly read and ticked off in the fly-leaf by this thirteen-year-old aspiring bureaucrat and humanitarian, and the year ended in festive mood with Dickens' *A Christmas Carol.*

Words were Alfred's pabulum, words sounded inwardly. At the age of thirty-seven, church organist and church warden, married and already a Senior Clerk, he was entering the house with Ada, whilst a nursemaid attended to Cyril Pilkington, the puking youngest of the breed, upstairs. "Cyril's crying" remarked his wife. Alfred stood still and regarded the stair rail. He had not heard the cry.

Thenceforth, the acoustic world distanced itself. The organ loft in Trevethin church was bestowed on a younger, hearing musician, the practise harmonium at home abandoned beneath the stairs, where I still recall its dusty, superannuated presence. At work, interviews with persistent clients were delegated to clerks more junior, meetings with partners in the venerable firm either semaphored or avoided. Up on the bookcase quixotic strangers rubbed covers with Cassell's tomes: books on Christian Science and Theosophy, manuals on vegetarianism, accounts of Far Eastern religions. Increasing deafness turned Alfred into a religious junkee, an eclectic searcher after superstitions, fabulous cures, anything that might assist in his prayers and alleviate his plight.

At twenty-seven, ten years before the onset of his affliction, and four years after his arrival in Wales, he had been initiated into the Kennard Lodge of the Masonic Province of Monmouthshire. One year later, he had been appointed its Provincial Grand Lodge Organist, a role he gradually abandoned as his impairment gained ground. Isolated by his condition, ever afterwards he rose sonorously in its esteem. The Freemasons became his failsafe, his Rock of Ages and his ladder of tribal ascent. Thus the Worshipful Brother Alfred Horace Gittins is lauded in Masonic Calendar and Directory for the Province for 1939, as Past Grand Standard Bearer, Past Assistant Grand Director of Ceremonies (Supreme Grand Chapter), Provincial Principal Grand Sojourner for 1913, Provincial Grand Scribe for 1914, and Third Provincial Grand Principal for 1932. At monthly meetings at the Lodge headquarters or at the Clarence Hotel he sat in silence as his masonic brothers conferred.

Yet the older faith survived. A legend was conveyed to me by my maternal grandmother shortly before she died. One Sunday morning in the depths of the depression, around the time of the King's well-advertised visit, Alfred was making his way down School Lane after the celebration of Matins at the new church of St John's Trevethin of which he had long been chapel warden. Out in the lane, almost opposite "Sunnyside", the semi-detached house where they lived, he encountered an unemployed miner with ragged trousers and downcast mien. Putting into practice what he had just heard preached, Alfred marched into the hallway, mounted the stairs and entered the master bedroom on the first floor, where he removed his Sunday best and ordered that the pants be presented as a Christian gift to the non-working man outside. I have my doubts about the veracity of this episode: it smacks too much of the philanthropic literature of the period. Be that as it may, it consorts neatly with certain aspects of my grandfather's theatrically devout personality.

And I have a fancy too that the recipient of his gift was none other than your David, coal miner, plaything of fortune and composer of that vernacular hymn of longing. The dates are wrong of course, and since David spoke scarcely a word of English, and Alfred not one word of Welsh, conversation between the two would have been limited, even had Alfred been able to hear. Yet, if there is no truth in this indulgent speculation, the beneficiary of this long ago egregious act of charity stands in every poetical sense as a representative, in Alfred's mind and mine, of that other Wales, the Wales of the pit and the chapels, contiguous with Alfred's more privileged existence, the Anglican church, the lawyer's offices in the municipal park further down the hill. Two grandfathers, two languages, two religious traditions, two nations in one, united and divided by a common love, a mutually sustained concern and mistrust. Two visions of the world. All that inspired our marital talk, and our morning altercations.

In old age, at the time of my infant visitations, after his three children had married and left home, Alfred was left in Sunnyside along with his books, his disused harmonium and his deafness. At length, Ada succumbed to sickness and took to her bed, the cossetted and adored invalid I dimly remember, sacred in her daughter's memory. A heroic figure, cut from resolution and the impressive granite of faith, is how I care to remember him:

STONE

i

Upstairs she lay, the angel in the house
Since taking to her bed in '43.
Strapped to his pin-striped pocket
His hearing aid plays 'Christians Awake!'
While, voiceless as a swimmer in a tank,
The maid drifts past to summon him
To dinner with one mute stroke
Of the brazen, unheard gong.

Slowly he turns the pages, muttering
Aloud, cursing the ineptitude of *King John.*
Above the mantelpiece the volumes speak in rows:
Consolations of Travel, The Advancement of Learning,
Marmion enclose by slow degrees *The Christian Year:*
Weekly instalments, 6d. bound in cloth,
Lovingly pencil-marked - voices he can hear.

Randy for knowledge though ignorant of Greek,
He summons to mind apt synonyms for
Marble. On the shelf the clock mumbles silently,
Dins its silent chimes. The maid waits indulgent,
Then semaphores a gestural cacophony.
No response. She waits for a pause between acts,
Then gently prods his arm. Reluctantly he puts
The histories down: "Well, help me girl!"

ii

For twenty years it’s been like this,
Deafness burgeoning like the loganberries beside his door.
Remedies he's tried by dozens: vegetarian diets,
Months on figs and dates, Theosophy.
Grand Mace-Bearer of the Masonic Lodge of
Wales, his medals glitter in the cupboard dully.

He rises elliptically, accepting the
Plebeian consolation of an arm. Once again
He'll dine alone tonight. Upstairs its
Better, the family silver glitters on a tray
Garnishing her invalid's frugal sumptuousness
As, beyond the drapes, the evening
Turns in and spreads a bolster for the night.

In the hallway the clock ticks on. In the grate
Ashes shuffle and briefly spit. In the bookcase
Old Age and Friendship's covers muffle
The Taming of the Shrew. He staggers
To his feet and waves the scraps away then,
Passing his pensioned-off harmonium
Beneath the stairs, climbs up to render,
As to the Lord, his nightly account.

Between its papered walls the room is
Darkened like a volume shut. From her chaste
Marriage bed, her jaw-bone gleams
Surveying her Pontypuddlian Combray.
The journals and the curates swept away, she beams,
Fastidious but merciful. 'Alright, pet?'

Uxoriously he pecks her on the cheek,
Then withdraws, passing the dusted
Effigies of offspring as he goes.

iii

And I too received his rendered testimony.
One Christmas Eve, aged seven, I heard him
Pray for all of us. Intent and half-awake,
Two hours past bedtime, I feigned
True sleep and heard him mount the steps
Towards me. A festival of undressing
Revealed the ancient and complicated underwear,
Exotic long-johns gave way to pyjamas;

Then the slow, noble declension
Towards the bedside, the hands clasped fervent
In the lamp-light before, loud and sure,
The inventory of names as if in 'Deuteronomy':
"Thy servant, my wife Ada; Thy servant my
daughter Ada", side by side like double entry
Book-keeping until, listened for and unbelieved,
"Thy servant my grandson", illuminated and bold,
I was blazoned into scripture, as though into some
Ledger of faith or glass-cased testament.

iv

To me he always seemed cut in stone.
In Trevethin churchyard the wind blows
Over him, the old verities and the
Old struggles worry him no more.

Where now *Holy Living*?
Where now *The Lady of the Lake*?
Are Herodotus and Cowper's *Table Talk* food for
worms?

Stone-deaf, the volumes answer me.
Their husks huddle above my fireside,
Tome by tome held in an oakwood case
Purchased for three and six
"to hold your National Library".
Congregations of the lettered, they
Lecture to autodidacts, all of us,
Expressing like perfume the threadbare
Doubts and certainties of 1885.

All's Well That Ends Well was the
Last one that he read and, reading,
Ticked them off, all two hundred and eight:
All, apparently but Plutarch's *Life of Cimon*.

I take them down and note the dates.
Acquired in youth, these slender books
Served him for a lifetime. Pencil in hand,
I peruse one now, propped up against
A beer can. Beyond the firelight his widowed
Ghost paws the night-dimmed window pane like
rain.

6 TEARS POINT

Monday, October 14th

It is a new week, and the consultancy roster has changed. Dr Butt, the new duty consultant, is another of the formidable contingent from Pakistan; and he is magnanimity and spacious wisdom personified. In the Oasis restaurant on the first floor, where we sometimes take our lunch, he sits at the head of a table peopled by junior colleagues, dispensing pleasantries and mild advice, a huddle of acolytes and admirers taking in every expert word. In the ward he circumambulates in a cloud of Urdu benevolence and jokes – a multicultural update of Sir Lancelot Spratt, the avuncular yet daunting consultant surgeon in the box office hit *Doctor At Sea,* which you saw at the Empire cinema in Pontypridd Road in Porth, just opposite the Western Wales bus stop, in January 1956. ("Dirk Bogarde", you scrawled at the beginning of your diary for that year, "is marvellous"). Big-limbed and loosely trousered, his flannel pants as roomy as pyjamas, he leans over your bed and pronounces over you: "To be frank, all of her systems are slowly closing down. It is important to be frank." Then he moves heavily off to another part of the room.

This morning, puzzled by some commonly occurring nomenclature, I arrested this formidable panjandrum in his progress around the ward and asked him what precisely is meant by the commonplace term "coma", so fuzzy in its general implications, so hackneyed to the uniformed, so comforting to the uninformed. He looked aloof and uncomfortable and replied "Well, it all rather depends on what you mean..." Our confusion on this score is understandable. According to the *New Oxford Dictionary of English*, a coma is a "state of deep unconsciousness that lasts for a long or indefinite period, caused especially by severe injury or illness." But, Catherine, you are not asleep; you are wide awake, with the empty gaze of a new-born child.

At four this afternoon, a message comes through that one of the Registrars who has been working on your treatment wishes to speak to us in confidence. Alice Meyers is an alert woman in her mid-thirties with a complexion of a damask rose and an attitude of palpable compassion. She is very evidently troubled by the news she has to convey. Her articulation is soft and exact, her posture relaxed, tension only given away by the occasional stiff movement of her wrists and hands. The object of our meeting, she tells us, is for us to "revisit" discussions we have already had with Dr Ahmed and Dr Butt. Before we have a chance to do this, I express some concern about the conditions under which your original cardiac arrest took place. The nocturnal incident was, to say the least, unexpected. If possible we would like to know its likely causes. Dr Myers replies that she cannot comment on the level of ward care before you entered the unit. In any case a Pulseless Electrical Activity Arrest may be secondary to a hypoxic event. We may never know.

I am careful to tell her of our satisfaction with your treatment since your arrival in the unit. She acknowledges my appreciation, but then the mood grows gloomy. It is now, she tells us bleakly, nine days since the event, and three days since sedation was lifted. By now one would have expected some evidence of neurological improvement if that is ever going to occur. She re-iterates the conclusions already derived from the CAT scan. They have since performed an electroencephalogram test in which flat electrodes were attached to the surface of your skull to assess the electrical activity in your brain. This has detected no independent and reversible reason why you should not have woken up. In short, the outlook is pretty grim, since the damage appears to be irreversible.

They can, however, not be sure until they have subjected you to a series of behavioural tests to assess the real extent of your awareness of the outside world. With this end in view your case has been referred to the Neurological Department. Soon you will be visited by one of the two departmental consultants whose job it is to assess cases of severe neural impairment, and given a series of tests to grade the extent of your damage, and the likelihood of restoring you to some form of awareness.

We ask about the shivering and jerking we have observed. She answers that is probably related to poor central control. Since you have no cough reflex, there is a continuing need to keep the tracheostomy in place. In the meantime, they are slowly weaning you off respiratory support. Twenty four hours after you are capable of breathing by yourself, they will attempt to transfer you to a general ward. Should support again be necessary, they will make no attempt to reinstate it, in view of the extent of your brain injury. Should you experience a further heart attack, there will be no attempt to revive you. "Not for resus" has been written on the relevant form.

The colour in Dr Myers' countenance comes and goes, her face an open indicator of her concern. It is, she says, always in these cases difficult to give an exact prognosis. The team will be in a better position to say once proper neurological tests have been carried out. In the best possible scenario, you could conceivably be restored to something approaching normality. In the worst, you will prove beyond medical redemption. In that case, she tells us with some unease, it would be hard to know how long you will survive. A sudden event could carry you off within the next twenty-four hours. On the other hand, you could survive for several months with the tracheostomy in place: eventually you could be transferred to a nursing home where you are likely to perish from one of the chest infections to which you will be prone from now on. Dr Myers then pauses. "I'm afraid that Catherine will probably not be coming home."

Two and half hours later, we meet her in the corridor. She blushes, and we talk of other things. I ask her about her career plans, and she tells us that she wishes to specialise in intensive care. There will therefore in future years be many occasions on which she has to conduct uncomfortable interviews of the sort that we have just had. I much appreciated both her candour and her tact, and I tell her so.

Wednesday, October 16th

We spend seven or eight hours a day on this open ward, reading aloud to you, playing you music through headphones, and chatting to the staff. We have now given up on Emma, who is too bossy even for us, and have embarked on your favourite Austen novel, *Pride and Prejudice,* accessing the text a chapter a time from my

Kindle and declaiming it a little too melodramatically, as if the whole ward – patients, doctors and visitors – were the audience at some private rehearsal. I read the odd chapters, and Benjo the even ones. I have been wondering at the wisdom of this: will not someone object? But just now, as we were making our way back from the Costa Coffee Shop in the foyer, a relative of the West Indian women in the opposite bed to yours stopped us in the corridor and congratulated us on our performance. "It is a pleasure", he announced, "to hear the Queen's English delivered with such conviction."

Meanwhile Greg, the Australian male nurse allocated to us today, has been telling us his life story, which includes periods as a labourer. He takes immense professional pride in what he does, and – within the parameters of your set regime of treatment – enjoys considerable leeway for personal initiative. He is determined to get to the bottom of your persistent trembling and, with that end in view, is injecting regular doses of liquid Paracetamol. They do not seem to do the trick, and thus you tremble all the while. Noticing this, one of the female Registrars has separately ordered a blood sample to be sent off to the laboratory to check if you are suffering from any sort of secondary infection. The results, when they arrive several hours later, are negative.

The clenching of your fists is a different problem. Earlier this week, a junior doctor advised us to bring along "stress balls" for you to hold on to. So we fetched from home a couple of yellow tennis balls, which promptly fell out of your hands and dribbled inanely across the floor. This morning we tried an attractive substitute: multi-coloured juggling balls – striped red, blue and green - which fit neatly into the declivities of each palm. You lie there with one in each hand staring up at the ceiling like a juggler who has forgotten how to begin.

You will be amused to learn that a dispute has arisen concerning your religious orientation. The doctors have already asked about this, so I told them "My wife has a Welsh non-conformist background. Not that she practises it much. As for me, I'm best described as some sort of wishy-washy Anglo-Catholic." These refinements were duly inserted into the notes, but the nuances involved have proved too much for the bureaucrats. Tonight, as we were about to leave, a staff nurse asked us what your exact devotional affiliation is, so that she could enter this detail into the mandatory place on her form. Caught unawares, I ventured "Catherine's best described as a sceptic", and watched as she started to write the word "septic" in the space provided. Then I asked her to change your description to "Humanist", which she did, thus placing your religious identity or non-identity in a category the hospital authorities more or less recognise. Like all classifications of this sort, it is at best an approximation, at worst a lie.

Thursday, October 17th

Grief is mostly an inarticulate condition, and condolences are for the most part clumsy devices, well-intended but frequently misjudged. One does not know how to address the bereaved any more than one knows how to address the dead. But how does one speak of - or indeed to – one who is, and yet is not, there? This afternoon our son mildly upbraided me for absentmindedly referring to you in the past tense. But I am not in this dialogue of sensibilities speaking of you, but to you, and so there can be no mistake. Grammatically at least, you are present, and you are present in my mind always, even if I am not present in yours. Do you, as you lie helpless there, dream of me? Over the last few months you have, as you told me each morning on waking by my side, dreamed every night: principally and horribly, you said, about people who are no longer here: your parents in Wales, your psychiatrist brother, felled by a heart attack eighteen months ago, whom we used to visit in his spacious white clapboarded house outside New York each long summer.

Today we learned why you have been have moved into the outer ward. Your bed now looks onto an enfilade of rooms which leads to the main entrance of the unit. Through the glass panel of the plywood door connecting your bay to this corridor, in a private room off which you once slept, we observe a small commotion and drama that are busily in progress. In the passageway stand a staff sister and a Roman Catholic priest, the one instructing the other. The Priest is youngish, balding and bespectacled, and he is very eager for employment. He has a toothy grin, an air of great eagerness, and in his right hand he carries a missal with a black floppy faux leather cover, emblazoned with a gilt-imitation cross. As he stands there impatient to begin his assigned task, the sister is showing him how to fasten onto his clerical personage a standard issue, disposable plastic apron. The titular father follows her instructions neatly, a little too neatly, a little dapperly, with a suggestion of professional and perhaps also of personal vanity, knotting the protective garment carefully behind his back, just above the waist band of his charcoal grey cotton and polyester flannels. He is evidently very proud to be a priest. Perhaps he is a mother's darling; in any case there is something gawkily camp about him, a willingness to be looked at, to attract the approving glances of the hospital staff, especially of the nurse who is now opening the door into the inner sanctum where once you slept. The door closes and a huddle of mourners wait outside it, suing for admittance. We recognise them: they are the grief stricken family whom we encountered so often in the axial corridor last week, the red-eyed sister at the head, the stern and responsible brother behind. They are here for their middle-aged relative's Last Rites. Twenty minutes later the priest and the family re-emerge, the former looking fulfilled and a little self-satisfied, the latter subdued, their tears wiped clean. Then somebody draws a blue serge curtain across the window pane of the connecting door.

Friday, October 18th

This afternoon a stocky middle-aged Iraqi turned up, dressed in a smart navy suit and striped tie. Dr Noori is in his late fifties, and he worked until comparatively recently as a senior brain surgeon in another hospital in South London. Nowadays he prefers the quieter role of a consultant in Neurological Rehabilitation, dividing his working week between this hospital and St George's in Tooting. He has the slightly dour air of the typical phlegmatic personality, in his case contained by a certain persistent sadness, a mixture of battered wisdom and knowing resignation. For all that, he is evidently much involved in his work, and he is very keen to tell us his life story. His task now, he tells us, is to discover how much of you is still there, and now much if anything can he restored. We talk a little about your treatment so far, and then Dr Noori walks over to the bed. Your eyes, for once, are closed. He asks if you ever open them. Yes, I say, whenever anybody flexes your arm at the elbow. He takes your left hand in his right one, and with his other arm he carefully bends the forearm upwards as instructed. Immediately you open your eyes. Dr Noori then rescues from his plastic brief case the single sheet of an A4 form, and from his inner pocket of his blue jacket a green biro. The form is known as the JFK Coma Chart, used since 1991 to assess cases of brain injury. His verdict will depend on your score.

Bending over you, he points the tip of the pen at each of your wide open eyes in turn, and makes as if to jab straight into the pupil, stopping just short of the eyeball. Neither eye flinches, and your face remains trusting and calm. Dr Noori looks meaningful, and smooths out the surface of his form. He has, he tells us, just been testing what under normal circumstances is a particularly tenacious reflex, one to which above a modest level most patients might be expected to respond. Its absence in your case does not bode particularly well. Dr Noori steps back a little, takes a deep breath, and shouts. No response. He sniffs (Dr Noori is a great sniffer; also perhaps he has a cold. For all that I know, it might even be an aspect of the test.) He claps his hands. Do I detect a slight blink? He completes the form and signs it with a flourish. Your score is five out of twenty-five. He notes it solemnly down on his chart, adding at the bottom the words "On anti-convulsant plus morphine."

Dr Noori then stands a little apart, and draws us after him, out of your hearing zone. He adopts an air of mixed detachment and engagement. Dr Noori is a feeling man, but he is no sentimentalist. He does not wish to leave us without hope. Hopelessness does not effect cures. Instead he spells out a kind of prognostic calculus ranging from daydream to disaster. He knows that the odds of any significant recovery are very slim, and he knows that we know. Carefully, in his foreign inflected English, he spells out the alternatives. Your score on the chart this morning is low, but he cannot be sure that it has not been affected by the medications that are still being administered to treat your other symptoms: the trembling, the occasional wince of pain. They will continue testing you every few days. Should your score ever rise appreciably, say to twelve, you might be sent off to a rehabilitation centre in a specialist hospital, where you would be submitted to a smart twelve-week course designed to bring you up to a certain level of responsiveness. But there are certain pre-requisites. You would, for example, have to be in a condition to obey certain commands or requests. Which means that you would have to be able to hear (we are assuming that this basic sense is still there, since we have repeatedly been told that it is the last to go. Besides, this is why we are standing apart). You would also have to be able to make sense of what you heard, and make an attempt both to follow it, and to put instructions into albeit difficult effect. In your case, the connection between sound and sense appears not to be there. There is no point in sending you off to be treated in this way, since you are in a state of limited responsiveness, or what used to be called a vegetative state. Dr Noori then introduces a distinction. Should you survive for six months and manifest slow but steady signs of improvement, your condition would be earmarked as "pervasive", long-term but not hopeless. Beyond that time limit, the chances of your improving at all sink until they read Nil, in which case your condition is deemed to be "permanent."

Then he departs, telling us that he will return, always supposing that in any sense you are still here.

Saturday, October 19th

This morning it occurs to me that the doctors are assessing your condition in two different ways, ways so divergent that they almost amount to two distinct senses or applications of the task of diagnosis. The electronic scans to which you have been subjected have reported on your brain viewed as a physical organ; the simple behavioural challenges with which you have been confronted since waking are crude attempts to describe and grade the current state of your consciousness, call it your mind.

Seldom is the mind-body problem more vividly illustrated than by this divide. Recognising the difficulty, the physicians are manifestly dissatisfied with the results of one kind of test alone. Thus they perform both, and draw their conclusions through cross-reference or comparison.

Yet neither of them amounts to a comprehensive account of you. To draw on the terminology employed by the later Wittgenstein, they amount to two self-sufficient "language games". In W.'s *Philosophical Investigations* there is a passage concerning the conditional mood. It runs "does a person never have the if-feeling when he is not uttering the word 'if'?" By the same token, supposing the scan images present a blank, and supposing that being awake you make no sign and utter no single word, are we thenceforth entitled to infer that, down there, there is no part of you that is aware and thinking "What if I could spring out of my hospital bed and communicate with these people? What if I could speak, get up, run around, gather my small family in my arms?"

It is this sense of the conditional as invoked by us that legitimises our continuing to address you out loud as a person. You are a hypothesis now or, to put it another way, you are a fiction (in much the same way as the jurists sometimes refer to a "legal fiction"). To put it a third way, our continuing commitment to you amounts to a sustained act of faith. It is to the credit of the hospital authorities that, conceding the appeal of any or all three of these arguments, they continue to treat you as they would any other patient.

Or are the medical establishment simply acting on the basis of a very low probability? A possibility is a very low probability in the third and fourth senses provided by *the Oxford English Dictionary:* "As a measurable quantity: the amount of antecedent likelihood of a particular event as measured by the relative frequency of occurrence of events of the same kind in the whole course of experience, estimated by the ratio of the number of successful cases to the whole number of possible cases". It is in these senses that we refer to a probability curve, calculus or distribution. It is in these senses, too, my darling, your continuing existence, and the prospects of your physical and mental survival, are subject to a calculation of probability, even if the resulting ratio is nought, or something approaching very close to nought.

If the probability of your continuing existence dwindles towards absolute zero, does it thereby bring into being the certainty of your non-existence? There is, it seems to me, an analogy here with religious belief. The existence of an omnipotent and omniscient Deity is, you always felt, highly improbable. So improbable is it, indeed, that at times the mere thought of it, in your eyes, sometimes teetered on the absurd. Could this degree of improbability, as some atheists affirm, amount to an absolute, or near absolute, certainty that no such being exists?

I ask our Physicist son what difference Quantum Theory, about which he knows a lot more than either of us, makes to such thoughts. Indeterminacy as invoked by the theory posits that outcomes cannot be predicted; however, their probability, as set out in the above definitions, may be calculated. We are currently bidding on the indeterminacy of you. Not merely attempting to estimate the likelihood of your survival (which, in medical terms, is equivalent to salvation) but your present and future existence as a distinct person, in other words as "you". Does our vigil by your bedside eight hours a day every day amount to a bet?

Pascal too laid bets. After devising Pascal's triangle, in which each cross section figure is the sum of the two above it, his line, a calculating machine – in acknowledgement of which there exists at present a computer language known as Pascal – and a device for weighing air, he turned his attention to the matter of God. Was this an emotional or a calculated reflex, or was it both? Is there finally any difference? The evidence is mixed. In 1654, Pascal was a passenger in a coach that missed the entrance to the narrow Pont Neuf across the Seine, just to the south of Notre

Dame. The carriage plunged into the icy waters of the river, but Pascal was uninjured and shed tears of gratitude, relief or joy. On November 23rd of the same year, he sewed into the lining of his coat a declaration that began "Fire. God of Abraham, God of Isaac, God of Jacob, not of the philosophers and the scholars." Had Pascal, the exemplary mathematician, renounced the use of his reason? Have we renounced ours in continuing to turn and feed you, and to address you by endearments you are unlikely to be able to understand, or even to hear?

Sunday, October 20th

Today they have exiled you to an outer annex known as the High Dependency Unit. It is a half-way house between Intensive Care and the general wards. No longer is each patient allocated a personal nurse: instead there is a permanently manned nurse's station at the end of the room at which sits a sister, who seems to spend much of her time on the telephone. Here there is more bustle, and less individual care. Visitors pass to and fro along the aisle between the two rows of beds and, as they do so, some of them spare us a glance of commiseration, occasionally even a word. You are regularly checked, monitored and turned. But they have lost one of your stress balls, which seems to have rolled out of sight beneath a neighbouring bed. We have brought this fact to the attention of the nursing staff, but what is the loss of a stress ball? In any case, nobody seems to be able to find it. (We later discovered it in a bag). Somehow the intensity of you has been diluted: for the first time since entering the unit you feel like one patient among many, and our distress at your condition must be constrained by the public gaze. One of your oldest and most trusted colleagues, Dilys Bullivant, turns up mid-afternoon. With her she brings a photograph of her and me taken thirty-two years ago in her Clapham garden. It was shortly after I met you, but you do not appear in it. Can you have taken it? Dilys is lying on her back on a folding camp bed laughing into my face as I lean over her, enacting some farcical charade. I have placed my plate of food on the calf of one of her long and slender legs, evidently stirred by her physical presence and anxious to show off. You were always tolerant of my foolishness and wandering fancies, but why this snap of my young and fickle self outrageously flirting with one of your most trusted friends?

Monday, October 21st

Each Monday a fresh countenance presides, a different mood, and distinctly different priorities. It is like the accession of a new headmaster, or the election of a differently constituted parliament or of a new Head of State. A revised regime, an individually nuanced outlook, a decided if subtle policy change, prevails. Existing challenges are inevitably regarded in an altered light. Practicalities loom large. Besides, bed space is scarce, emergencies are forever arising, and there is a perennial need to clear the ward.

Dr Stanley Glover, the presiding consultant for the new week, is I guess in his early 'forties, and a specialist in both anaesthetics and intensive care. There a mug shot of him on the noticeboard in the unit's foyer, beaming at the camera and occupying his skin like a well-fed capon. He has since, it would appear, taken himself in hand, and now represents a sleeker version of himself. He looks young for a consultant, and has evidently prospered in his profession. On the ward he is a popular figure, sharing jokes with colleagues behind the nurse station. Very much a Stan, as distinct from a solemn Stanley. He is serious about his business, and brisk in the dispatch of it. And still he beams.

This afternoon he sought a conference with us, the fourth to which we have been called into the same Spartan multi-purpose office, off the same inner corridor. His manner is scrupulously judged. Conveying the direst of news, confronting total strangers with the most exacting of existential decisions, he communicates a decent and equitable concern that does not dent his confidence in the least. He is nothing if not fair: "Your wife and mother is unlikely to improve much. Her coughing and gag responses are minimal, and she is totally dependent for the clearing of her secretions on the tracheostomy that we have inserted. This treatment is life-prolonging. Without it, she would die. There are nursing homes that will take patients in her condition. She could eventually be released into one, after a period of preparation on the wards. But she would then be permanently dependent on the tracheostomy. She would not be able to speak, even if she showed an inclination for speech, which at present she does not. Is that what you would like us to do?"

A tense pause extends between the chair and the desk. His statement has been phrased as a question: not a rhetorical one. It is a query that is meaningless unless there are genuine alternatives. After a thought-filled interval, I inquire "And if we do not?"

The pause is shorter this time. After two or three seconds he replies with simple honesty "Well, we could take the tracheostomy out."

"What will happen if you do?"

"Your wife would in all probability last a very few hours. She might possibly survive for two or three days, but it is rather unlikely." Then he sits back and waits.

There is no disguising the fact that Dr Glover is confronting us - confronting me in particular - with a choice. I am free to decide on your future: free as Camus's Dr Rieux was free to stay in his pestilence infected city or to leave. Free like Pascal to believe, or not to believe, in God. Free in my case to let you live on in a manner of speaking, or else – cruelly or kindly – to allow you to die.

With a permanent tracheostomy in place, you would be unable to express your thoughts, would not recognisably be you. I look at our son and say "This is a decision I can hardly take on my own. I have an approximate sense of what Catherine herself would have wanted. At least, I think that I do. But in all fairness we must consult other members of her family. There are quite a few of them, and they are widely spread. Some are in this country, others in the States. It will take a little time."

"How long?"

"If I can contact the American contingent tonight, I should have a clearer idea tomorrow."

"Can we meet then? Say in the afternoon. About three o'clock?"

"I will try. I will honestly try."

In a slightly dazed state I leave the room and make for the foyer where the Nigerian assistant in the Baguette Company has taken pity on us and, for days now, has been slipping us free treats – a cake here, a biscuit there – with our purchased teas. I am too upset to explain to her the latest development, though every afternoon since you arrived in the hospital she has been asking about your progress. Benjo and I sit in silence for a while amid the munchers and the mourners, and then we make plans. On his mobile Benjo 'phones the Essex battalion straightaway, and arranges to speak to them later tonight, after they have absorbed the news. Then we check on the American contact numbers. It is still mid-morning there and your relations - a nephew who works as an anaesthetist in a large Pennsylvania hospital, a niece who's a senior nurse in Bloomington Indiana, a second niece who works as a supply teacher on the fringes of New York - will all be out at work. There is no point in phoning them until we get back late tonight. On our way back to the unit we meet a second long-established colleague of yours, Elizabeth Fannin. She has been by your bedside, and is coming out to find us. We explain our dilemma to her as calmly as we can. She asks what we are going to do. I say I do not know.

We reach home around seven, warm up a hasty dinner from last night's leftovers, and then phone Essex again. Your sister and brother-in-law have rigged up the phones in their nineteen-sixties terraced house so that they can both speak to us on different extensions. They have had time now to consider the difficult question of you, and are of one mind. You would not wish to survive without the capacity to speak, and would be loath to live in a state of mental diminishment. On the understanding that this would probably bring about your fairly rapid demise, in their opinion the tracheostomy should come out. If it would help they will come down tomorrow, and we will speak to Dr Glover together. I thank them, and ask if they can be in Croydon by three. They say that they will make every effort: though both are in poor health, their elder son – a road haulier - will drive them. Then we try the States. We catch the younger of your two American nieces, who has just returned to her home in Suffern, N.Y. after a hard day in the classroom. She takes in what we have to tell her and replies that, though the decision is technically ours, on balance she feels you would prefer a quiet release. "But I will be happy with whatever you decide." We then ask about her anaesthetist brother. She informs us that he is presently on vacation, and is on his way back from his beach hut in North Carolina. He should reach his farm in Pennsylvania in a couple of hours; in the mean time she will leave him a message asking him to communicate with us just as soon as he can.

He phones us after midnight our time, half an hour after we have retired to bed. His voice is grave but relaxed, with the slight Yankee accent he has always had, lightly laced with the Southern drawl he seems to have picked up during his years in the navy and as a student at the University of Maryland. The quandary we outline across the Atlantic link is hard for him to contemplate as a member of our dispersed family, but it is all too dreadfully familiar to him as a doctor.

As he patiently expounds his own experience, the vocabulary is more polysyllabic than the British one, but the ethical questions are the same. He refers to your condition as "Hypoxic Ischemic Encephalopathy." On the operating table, a surgical team not infrequently lose a patient's heart beat. If they can, they restore it by any and every means at their disposal. If an interval of more than ten minutes elapses, as a general rule in his hospital they cease to try. The rationale is clear, and it is compassionate on several counts. After ten minutes of oxygen starvation, brain cells die off at a violent rate. There as here, should the patient pull through after a certain period of time, the doctors and the family are inevitably faced with a harrowing predicament, even series of predicaments. In his view, which coincides with the balance of opinion in the American medical profession as a whole, the family in particular should be spared such additional pain. In our case, if we allow you to stagger on, we will be faced with a whole succession of medical and moral dilemmas, and a serious burden on our freedom and our finances. You would never have wanted this. While the decision is ultimately mine, in his considered opinion you should permitted to die with dignity.

I thank him, put down the phone and attempt to sleep, intensely aware that across all of these difficult family consultations tonight has fallen a recognisable shadow: the presence, or should I say the absence, of Big Ben.

Ben was perhaps your favourite nephew – albeit a nephew by marriage - and he was in every sense Big: tall and brawny with light, sand-coloured hair and soft, white, freckled skin. Ben was a gentle giant with a coaxing voice, a compassionate smile, a winning manner and an instinctual though always understated munificence and grace. We once got into a pickle together whilst making pancakes in the kitchen because he was American and I am British and what to me should have been thin crepes to adorn with lemon and sugar, to him needed to be spongy slabs to have with maple syrup or bacon. He was very careful in small matters, and the misunderstanding riled him until the semantic and cultural divergence had been explained. In the yawning garage adjoining your brother's nineteenth-century white clapboard house, a onetime senator's residence outside Suffern, NY, he helped set up scientific demonstrations for our son, pumping electrons up the vertical stack of a Tesla Coil so that sparks burst out at the top end in a furious pyrotechnic display that put Versailles in the shade.

Ben was a scientist and a lover of facts, an enthusiast for Apple computers who named his serious son Mac. As yet the elegant and shy boy is a Small Mac, but in less than a decade he will be a Big Mac, and in either case he has, and will have, no father. Ben was a physicist who went to the University of California to do his doctoral research on the problem of "Nothing". He wrote a couple of papers, but ultimately the Nothing went nowhere so, sometime after wedding your niece, he moved to Indiana and turned radiologist, manning one of the new proton beam machines. Guided by reason more than faith, though perhaps by faith in reason, he guided the little particles from the big machine to invade obdurate cancers so that, gathering energy as they went, they imploded into the targeted tumour and there expended themselves, arrested and most potent at the precise point where they could best perform their healing work. It is called the Bragg Effect.

I never said Goodbye to Big Ben because the last time we were over there I was called away to correct proofs before he could arrive with Small Mac and Small Mac's mum. You went up Bear Mountain and into the National Park beyond while I was far away. Then the snow descended blocking the road and you only just made it through and back to me in London, intensely regretful because I had not been there, and Big Ben was under sentence, the agony-inducing two-year sentence of Motor Neurone Disease. First his co-ordination went, then his ability to feed independently, and finally even his capacity to speak. But he still played chess with Mac.

Ben was big and he was brave, and he wished to leave Small Mac with happy memories. So he waited until Mac was eight, playing chess with him all the while and, shortly after his son's birthday, he entered a hospice and wrote to all of us friends on Facebook to announce that he was refusing nutriment. Ben passed away in the early hours late last year, and I went upstairs to tell you. His last message consoled us, though we knew that he had now merged with the Big Nothing, and that the research project of a lifetime had been fulfilled. You mourned him with silent intensity, and after a while your niece wrote to you to say that nowadays she would sometimes drive into Bloomington half blinded with tears, and that occasionally she needed to disappear into the shower so that she could scream to herself and Small Mac could not hear her.

Ben was Big and he was noble. In thinking through our present quandary, all of us have his example before us. How can I ignore his example; none of us can or want to do that. The onus is mine, and I will act for all of us, for Big and

Little Ben, for you and for reason and for our physicist son. I will say what you cannot say, what Ben has said, and what anyone would say with half a respect for dignity and the wholeness of existence. Tomorrow I will tell them.

Tuesday, October 22nd

It is my decision. Or is it? Surely it is, or should be, yours.

We are functioning in a conditional - or more strictly in a hypothetical - tense. If you are currently a fiction, a hypothesis, even if you represent an act of faith, we are obliged imaginatively to construct, or re-construct, your ethical will. The only way in which we can do this is to recall your stated opinion in other cases. You have left no written will or testament of any sort, any textual indication of your wishes in circumstances that were predicted by none of us. There is nothing for us to rely on except a delicate sense of you that shifts hour by hour as memory, fear or nostalgia dictate. And we do not have many hours.

Robert, why do you hesitate?

Because I want to make sure that I am right.

There is no right, and there is no wrong.

Yet you have rights.

Then exercise them on my behalf. Kill me. Remember Ben.

I cannot bring myself to kill you. In my mind, whatever the circumstances, that would amount to murder.

But if I give you my permission?

Then the act amounts to suicide. Besides, Cariad, you have given me no permission, except insofar as I imagine you now.

Robert, I want to die.

Catherine, you do not have the right to die.

(Widening your dear eyes): *Robert, I want to die.*

I dreamed of fucking you as you sit with legs apart on the edge of a desk before me. My penis bent slightly as I entered you. As we fucked, I kissed you full on the mouth, as I did on the very first evening on which we met. I said, "You are my wife."

Then we were on the campus at Cape Coast, the African university where decades ago I taught. There were minutes to go before the coach left. There was rubbish to dispose of after a picnic, so I said "I'll find the bins." You said, "Robert, I do not trust you." I replied "Catherine, I know this campus like the back of my hand." I was proceeding downhill to where the bins were stored at the back of a hall of residence, when you shouted across to me "Robert, you don't know the back of your hand." I walked back briskly, and retorted "Catherine, once again, your sarcasm has let you down."

Margaret and David arrived about twenty minutes ago. We are sitting in the now familiar narrow office, with Stanley Glover with all his professional equanimity on his swivel chair before us. Equanimity, but concern. Self-assured (a little too much maybe but justifiably so, for he is an excellent physician), and utterly focussed. Assurance is in the eye of the beholder.

He asks, "Well, what have you decided?"

The others have given me their permission to speak for them. In my mind, his afternoon, I am the spokesperson for a general consensus.

A little self- consciously, and resenting the sound of my own voice, I announce "David and Margaret here have discussed this matter with us, and we've also had a chance to consult our folks in America. We all agree that Catherine would not want to live on in this condition. We believe that the tracheostomy should be removed."

In my left ear you are whispering to me. Your paternal grandmother, née Spens, you are telling me for perhaps the fifth time, went back to her Orkney island home every summer. When she returned home to Barry bearing handicrafts as gifts, people asked her what the Orkneys were like. Every year she returned the same reply: "No trays."

Dr Glover asks us "When would you like this to happen?"

I look round at the others and continue "We think she would like the family, or as many members of it as possible, to be present when she passes away. There are four of us here."

"We could give you the side room where she was treated when she entered the unit. It will be available later this afternoon. You may have it as long as you need it, and you'll have a nurse."

It will take time to prepare the room. We remain in the corridor in a frightened, awestruck group not knowing what to say to one another. Incredibly the business of the unit carries on around us, regardless. Nurses are taking readings, sisters are 'phoning and checking charts. Behind the high desk of the nurses' station, registrars and junior doctors are sharing gossip and laughing. Then the door swings open and we are asked to enter. You are lying on your back staring up at the bland ceiling. You have fewer attachments than before, and the bundle of bandages just above your thorax has been removed to be replaced by a simple strip of sticking plaster, just visible above the neckline of your light blue, standard issue, nylon nightie. By way of compensation, you now have a clear plastic bugle in your left nostril intended we are told to open up your airways, assist with your breathing. We remain in silence looking down at you, and then a male Filipino student nurse enters behind us and politely takes his stand near the door next to the tall writing desk. We have encountered him before, days before when you still, in our minds at least, retained a glimmer of hope. He is in his early twenties and carries around with him an aura of youthful enthusiasm and wide-eyed hope. Naively I wonder if he is embarrassed by this particular assignment, but if so he shows no sign of it. To ease the atmosphere, we ask him about himself. He is touchingly proud to have landed this attachment in Croydon as part of his general nursing training at St George's Hospital Tooting and Kingston Hospital which, he has just been telling us, have recently joined up to form a single trust. He tells us all of this in his idiomatic though American-inflected English, as if the organisational framework of his career were somehow relevant to your fate.

David is looking solemn and consulting his watch. They have been driven here from Pitsea by a kindly neighbour called Peter who has hardly met you, but is performing this office to ease our family's pain. Peter is drinking coffee at the Costa coffee stall out in the main corridor next to the roaring, impersonal stretches of the London Road. He will stay there calmly reading his evening newspaper until it is time for his friends to leave. If necessary, he will stay there all night. There is no apparent change in your condition. Defying the doctors, as you always defied the confident generalisations of authority, you are still breathing regularly without your tube.

With a gravitas born of a sense of the momentousness of this occasion only slightly offset by an inevitable sense of melodrama, David is reading the Keats sonnet "When I have fears that I may cease to be." He is acutely aware of the futility this performance, even as we all participate in the ceremoniousness of the gesture. Your sister asks me if she can cut a lock of your spun gold hair before they take their leave. I say "Of course", though I am not sure that it is my prerogative to give or to withhold permission for so simple, yet so meaningful, an act. She cuts one lock with a pair of scissors she is carrying in her handbag, saying as she does so "It's a lovely colour. It's probably what attracted you to Catherine in the first place." I almost reply "No, it was her thighs, but you can't take those away". Then she places the curling strand in a small, transparent plastic bag she has brought with her for the purpose. I ask her to cut me one as well. When she has done so, I place it in a side pocket of my leather shoulder bag. (Later that night I think I have lost it, agonising until I discover it concealed by an obscure zip). They say "We have to leave now. Peter will be waiting." Then David helps to wheel Margaret round in her chair, steering her towards the door, then swinging her round so that she can take one last, soulful look at you. Then he wheels her round again and guides her through the door into the dark, Catherineless world beyond.

Benjo asks "Shall we continue reading?" There seems to be little point, and then there seems to be every point. You would have wanted to sweep out of your whimsical and serious life on a tide of Jane Austen. So I switch on the Kindle, which as usual finds my place for me. We have reached the moment in *Pride and Prejudice* when Lady Catherine de Burgh confronts Elizabeth as to her intentions concerning her nephew Darcy. She is defiant; Elizabeth is defiant, refusing to be cowed by the aristocratic grandeur of her interlocutor. How you always responded to this passage, the modest but plucky young woman outfacing the presumption and thoughtless arrogance of the great. How you always relished the linguistic irony of the Rev Mr Collins actively enjoying the "condescension" of his patroness, the said Ladyship, a whole social history implicit in the shift of meaning behind the use of this one word.

Do you remember, as you lie there still breathing, our afternoon at Austen's small house in Chawton? Upstairs we found ourselves in the chamber she once shared with her sister Cassandra. In the same room stood two middle-aged visitors, one of whom turned to her friend and exclaimed "Oh, what a pity she never married!"

Your brand new bugle is now descanting on an atonal downward scale, as if some miniature bugler were practising his nightly exercises over and over again, and mostly getting them wrong. Patiently, with the forbearance of complete love, we are waiting for you to die. This was your first death.

7 *CYMRU IN ETRURIA*

That mellow morning in Italy, the ancient site had breathed a peace. In Ceveteri we found nothing of the imposing grandeur of the forum, or the self-advertisement in death, the architectural intimidation, that we had experienced back in Rome. Most of the tombs were of the same size, lacked any element of boasting and, as far as we could see, external ornaments of any kind. The Roman tombs had faced outwards; they had been attempts to impress the world. These Etruscan cemeteries, if that was the right term for such homely places, were domestic. Their street plan was as small in scale, as unpretentious in its self-presentation, as Eastwood, the huddled, affectionate, gossipy and perhaps rather bitchy, town in which D.H. Lawrence, whose book of the Etruscan people had drawn us to this place, had grown up. They must have reminded him of the mining villages of his youth. They reminded you of the closeness and claustrophobia of the towns of the Rhondda valley.

Lawrence had seen Ceveteri in the spring when asphodels were in bloom. We went in the Autumn, as the trees were turning. Etruscan cypresses of the sort Lawrence had described in a famous poem rose all around. The site was criss-crossed by paths divided from each other by bee-hive shaped tumuli, many with thatched roofs, like the medieval cottages preserved in St Fagans on the outskirts of Cardiff. Like Lawrence, we were struck by how little the atmosphere resembled other resting places for the dead. It seemed, in fact, less like a cemetery than a village, and the individual tombs when we walked down into them by stairways cut into the living tufo were like dwellings stripped of their ornaments. Many of the tombs were set out in rows like terraces of cottages, so familiar and homely in their appearance behind their stone lintels that you felt like dropping in. At home we have a photo of you poised on the threshold of one of them, as if you had thought of visiting one of your parents' neighbours in Porth, and wondering whether to knock. When we entered, we found each of them divided into chambers connected by doorways through which ran a passage flanked by bunk-like shelves on which, Lawrence thought, the slaves of the household must have rested, their ashes preserved in large, urn-like jars, while their masters were laid out full-length. It was a continuation into death of domestic arrangements that, in Lawrence's view, the Etruscans must have enjoyed in life.

The following week we visited ancient Sutreum, modern Sutri, a city which, early in the Roman period, had concluded a truce with its imperial rulers. The town had then become the focus of a series of attacks by the Etruscan league aimed at returning it to its abandoned roots. Our album holds three photographs of you standing before a sarcophagus in the town centre, wearing your elusive smile, your light blue blouse, and the leather handbag that we have stacked by your hospital bed now. The inscription, clearly visible in each of these frames, quotes the ninth book of Livy's *History of Rome* in reference to an episode in 365 BC, and is crowned by an allusion to Pliny the Elder:

SUTREUM
ETRURIAE CLAUSTRA
URBS SOCIA ROMANIS
COLONIA CONIUNCTA IULIA

SUTRI
THE GATEWAY TO ETRURIA
A CITY IN ALLIANCE WITH THE ROMANS
A COLONY CONJOINED BY THE JULIAN LAW

Unsurprisingly, Lawrence had viewed the Etruscans as a peasant people who had been brutalised, and then assimilated, by their conquerors. In that respect, they reminded you, and increasingly me, of the Welsh. Later, back in London, I was preparing an article on our expedition. I conceived the fancy, or perhaps the fantasy, of turning the opening sentence of Lawrence's *Sketches of Etruscan Places* round, applying it to the children of Cymru:

> The Welsh, as everyone knows, were the people who occupied the middle of Britain in early Roman days and whom the English, in their usually neighbourly fashion, wiped out entirely in order to make way for England with a capital E. They couldn't have wiped them all out, there were too many of them. But they did wipe out the Welsh existence as a nation and a people. However, this seems to be the inevitable result of expansion with a big E, which is the sole *raison d'etre* of people like the English.

You always kindled to mountainous places, seeking them out. For you were as capricious as a Welsh spring, as ordinary and quite as surprising. Thirty-two years ago, our courtship was all three. We were introduced on the last Sunday evening that October in the Mother Goose Wine Bar in Lordship Lane in South London. "Do be careful," read your diary later that night, adding between brackets the rider "promise + threat." The following weekend, you invited me to share your Sunday dinner of cod mediterranée with valpolicella, and afterwards I stayed on, officially to watch *Barchester Towers* on your colour TV. Two months later, with mild astonishment, you inquired "*Barchester Towers* is over now. Why are you still here?" "I enjoy the view," I replied. Besides, I had fallen for your childhood tales of a Rhondda culture exotic to me: tales of 14, Grawen Street, your parents' home in Porth, of Billy the Shop; Evans the Pop, James the Co-op and Morgan the Coal, of a rabbit called George Bernard Shaw, of the self-taught miner next door with his primers of ancient Greek, of the radio which only played when struck – in a particular spot too - and of the single light bulb that served all three rooms of the upper floor, transported between them on its long flex, then draped on a cup-hook over the bed. And I had learned to appreciate your Cheshire cat grin, your menthol-laced caresses, your russet-corn tresses, your flesh of clotted cream, the single mole on your neck, the bunions on both of your ticklish feet, even the way in which you sprawled on the shaggy brown carpet of your living room, kicking me over and over in the ribs while demanding. "I love you to pieces, Robert *bach*. But where, I might ask, is your integrity?"

Slowly, from hints, I began to reconstruct the geography of your childhood. If Sutri was the gateway to Etruria, Porth was gateway to the Rhondda valley. There the likeness ends, since the people of Rhondda would not have struck a truce with any supervisory power. For all that, Porth was - and is - an ungainly little town. Even now, it possesses the air, as so many places on the earth have, of somewhere that has been expunged. Like Ceveteri, the Porth of your youth was proud, but it was a huddle, even a muddle. It possessed, besides, a closeness that bred amity and animosity in almost equal measure. No wonder you loved it, no wonder you escaped it. Throughout the more than thirty years we were together, the Rhondda held you by the short and curlies. It would not let you go, much as you wished to relinquish it. It was in the lilt of your voice, it was in the peculiar intimacy of your affection, it was in your passion, it was in your politics, it was in your blood.

The town had a physical geography and a social and political geography, both typical and utterly its own. The physical was easily described. The railway up from Cardiff, connecting the Rhondda with the world. The mess of streets around the station, the two cinemas at opposite ends of Hannah Street, the Central and the Empire, near the second of which stood the town's sole claim to architectural pre-eminence: the largest public gentleman's lavatory in the valleys dubbed, in reference to its Puginesque superstructure, "The Houses of Parliament". In the town centre the Rhondda river split into two: Rhondda Fawr (The Big Rhondda) and Rhondda Fach (The Little Rhondda). During your childhood, both ran black with coal dust from four local mines. Up the Rhondda Fawr lay Treherbert,

Treorchy and Llwynyria, where seventy-one years ago you were born. Up the Rhondda Fach stood Maerdy, known as "Little Moscow" after the radical resoluteness of its inhabitants and the fierceness of its winters, and Ferndale. In between the angle made by these two grimy tributaries, and to the North of Rhondda Fawr, rose Mount Pleasant; beyond and above it, Cym Rhondda, the composite Rhondda Valley formed by these two river basins, the muse of John Hughes' hymn tune: "Guide me, O thou Great Redeemer."

Across the lower slopes of the Mount ran Cemetery Road, the Ceveteri of the place. Cemetery Road formed the base line of your childhood, and on it, at number 101, lived your bosom companion, Gillian Edmunds. To the north of that rose Mount Pleasant Road towards the head of the valley. A third of the way up its slope stretched Grawen Street; further up, between Davies Street and an open field, the least prepossessing place of worship in the whole Western world, stood Bethlehem chapel, Baptist and English-speaking, seat both of your conformity and your rebellion.

The chapel was a squat and ungainly whitewashed edifice that clung to the side of the hill, with two grim side aisles and a central nave capped by the triangular black tiled roof like a witch's hat. Every Sunday evening you attended it with Gill, after doing your homework and washing your hair. From its pulpit poured a torrent of pure *hwyl*: bucket loads of adjectives, streams of nouns, waterfalls of adverbs. Certainty and invective rained down in equal measure. Between them, flooding the narrow temple, rose the hymns:

When upon life's billows you are tempest-tossed,
When you are discouraged, thinking all is lost,
Count your blessings, name them one by one,
And it will surprise you what the Lord has done.

Refrain:

Count your blessings, name them one by one,
Count your blessings, see what God has done!
Count your blessings, name them one by one,
And it will surprise you what the Lord hath done.

And what forms of magnanimity, pray, had this bounteous deity bestowed? What had been his precise gifts, except principally those same adjectives, nouns and adverbs, weapons in the battle against Satan, the world and the Establishment? As in Ancient Rome, so in modern Britain, those who are suppressed fight their way upwards through the word. So you grew up in a place where expression defined the private, the religious and the political self. It was poetry that joined us, and prose that fed those permutations and causes that had fretted the garden of your growing life: the Labour Movement, the Trades Union Movement, the Co-operative movement, the National Health Service, Aneurin Bevan's lasting legacy that is caring for you now: secular applications of a vanishing heavenly creed. Those endless periods of poetry and prose, that swell that rose and rose and rose. Dylan Thomas, whose sound sometimes defied sense. The Socialist Utopia just out of sight, but perpetually evoked like a collapsing vanilla ice cream. The

Welsh nation perennially plighting its faith, not in the best, but in the most eloquent cause: a polity where rhetoric often prevailed over logic. The teachers, the preachers and the politicians. And, above and beyond them all, a limitless and soaring eloquence.

8 *LANGLAND BAY*

Wednesday, October 23rd

At nine o' clock this morning, after we had spent the night slumped in chairs on opposite sides of your bed watching over your still breathing form, I became conscious of a presence by my side. It was Dr Glover in mildly apologetic mood. He looked as jocund as ever, though a little crestfallen. "When I arrived early this morning," he told us, "I fully expected to hear that your wife had gently passed away. But you never can tell…"

Well done, Catherine.

"We've been here all night," I say. "What do you propose to do now?"

"There are various alternatives. I'm afraid we're going require the use of this room for another patient now. I can either return your wife to the main body of the unit, or I can release her onto one of the general wards. I'll try to make sure that she has a private room there."

"Which do you advise?"

"On balance I'd recommend the second course of action. If we put her back in the outer ward here, she will have to be transferred later in any case, which would involve two moves. But the choice is yours. I'm off on my rounds now. Can you have a little think about it, and let us know just as soon as you can?"

Once again, mine is the sole prerogative of making decision on your behalf. No matter of life and death this, rather perhaps a choice between two styles of dying. In Intensive Care, the treatment is surely of a finer calibre. Your chances of survival in any recognisable form are now pretty slim, but they are surely higher here among specialists, attended individually by solicitous nurses, than in the hurly burly and medical scrum of the general wards. I look through the thick glass at the top of the connecting door across the main corridor and onto the nurse's station where as ever the staff are chatting and exchanging jokes, and wonder if I have the moral courage to countermand what appears to be a general consensus. Eventually I convey my misgivings to our son, who briskly leaves the room and has a word with the ward sister. Within an hour, word comes back that an *en suite* private room has been found for you on a ward on the first floor. Then the ward sister herself arrives and explains that such rooms are not often made available. If we turn it down, she can give no guarantee that another can be found before your inevitable eventual transfer. We are urged to agree to the prepared plan. With some reluctance - and mostly out of physical and mental exhaustion - I do.

It is early evening, and the porters have arrived to collect you. Everything you own in this place is piled on top of your bed in plastic carrier bags together with your notes, and we are off as you are wheeled into an outer corridor and into a spacious but spartan lift. Then we are in the room, which seems stark and bare, bereft of any personality because it must accommodate so many. A male care assistant hangs the Nutricia feed bag on one of the curling steel hooks at the top of your bedside stand – and trails the flexible plastic tubing through the enteric feeding pump and the rotating hexagonal joint powered by its slow internal motor. After several turns, the third light on the vertical panel blazes and the mechanism delivers a peremptory beep next to an instruction that reads "Occlusion to Flow." He calls a nurse who soon arrives to explain that this has happened several times before on this outlying ward. She attempts to flush the blocked tubing with a syringe, then she restarts the motor, which runs for several seconds before it jams again. She seems unfazed by this – "These machines" she says "are very sensitive." – Any obstruction or sluggishness will automatically cause the system to freeze. Eventually she gets it to work, and we sit in rueful silence watching the robotic pump delivering your tardy meal.

A message arrives from the female junior doctor in charge of the ward this evening. No consultants are perpetually on duty here, though I am informed that a senior doctor is on call day and night if need be. In any case, the consultant to whose care you have been assigned will be available for consultation in the morning. In the meantime, the house physician wants to know about your history and your medications. They appear temporarily to have lost your notes during the move. Perhaps they fell off your bed while we were in the lift, perhaps they have been returned to Intensive Care in error. I tell her all that she wants to know, then she asks if you are due for resuscitation in the case of a recurrence of a PEA arrest. It has already been agreed that you are not, and I tell her so. Soon after, she leaves for the night, abandoning us to the tender mercies of the nocturnal care staff.

Here, it is manifest, we are in a lesser medical world, a sort of peripheral wilderness. Two of the lights in your room do not work, so that at night we may either leave you in full floodlight or else in a liminal gloom fitfully illuminated by the strip lights out in the corridor. A television hangs limp and useless from its wall bracket, offering programmes that you will never watch.

No complex monitors or dials here, no green statistics spelling out your pulse. When I ask about this, a care assistant returns, takes hold of one of your limp arms, and counts out your heartbeat by his wristwatch. Regarding this primitive display with disquiet, I exchange knowing glances with Penny Hyde-Smith, a lawyer friend of yours and fellow graduate of the LSE, who has just joined us. After the care assistant has withdrawn, I pick her brains about the legal position. You have survived the removal of the tracheostomy, but none of us is in any illusion as to your hypothetical wishes in this situation. You would not have wished to survive like this, nor would any of us wish to inflict this half-life on you.

Logically and morally, it seems to me, I should be in a position to prevent it, so I quiz Penny about "Power of Attorney", only to learn to my astonishment that, technically speaking, no such unitary condition now exists. Until October 1, 2007 there was in English law a provision known as an Enduring Power of Attorney which, had you bestowed it on me in advance, would have enabled me to assume control of your financial affairs once you had "lost capacity", that is once you were in no longer in a position to make such decisions for yourself. Since the Mental Capacity Act of that year, this has been replaced by something called a

Lasting Power of Attorney, which operates on two levels: one affecting your property, and another your medical welfare. Had you foreseen the present state of affairs, had there for example been an incremental diminution in your mental powers sufficiently gradual for us to persuade you of the wisdom of such a step, you could have entrusted me with either power or both, subject to the oversight of the Office of Public Guardian entitled to intervene should they ever have reason to suspect I was acting for my own benefit rather than yours. In a circumstance such as the present one, when a catastrophic and sudden cessation of capacity has occurred, an advance consultation of that sort is much less likely. None of us had any inkling of a tragedy such as this. Nor, exercising unusual foresight, did you leave any written indication informing us of how you would wish us to act should an accident of any kind render you incapable of making a rational choice or your own behalf.

It thus appears that I possess no Power of Attorney of either, or indeed any, kind. I am your next of kin and beloved husband, and no more.

Robert bach, I could have told you all of this.

Then, Catherine dearest, why didn't you?

Robert, at the time where was the need?

There's an urgent present need, now it is too late. Even you lawyers get it wrong. Witness an instance: two friends of ours, barristers, married to one another, both in early middle life, both healthy, with two teenage sons, living in a large house in Solihull. Georgie is 53, a top QC, his wife Lydia a literature graduate and barrister and member of the Middle Temple. Very much in love, they seemed to have everything to look forward to, everything to hope for. One morning in the early hours of an April day in 2007, Lydia woke up in the marital bedroom to discover her husband hunched up in a chair in evident pain. A paramedical team was called. They found no pulse, and so they applied the defibrillator, the boom, boom, boom of which, six and a half years later, Lydia can still hear in her dreams. After seven minutes, circulation was restored and the unconscious Georgie was taken to the local hospital, where his afflicted heart was operated on. "I waited in a side room while it happened", she told me over the 'phone. "It was like being stuck in a broom cupboard." Afterwards she had a meeting with the surgical team. "Your husband's heart was re-started after seven minutes," they told her. "Regrettably, how much remaining brain function is it realistic to expect after that?" "We've tested Georgie's. It's around two per cent."

They induced a coma, though in effect he was in one already. Daily his wife attended him in his private room, playing him Mozart as loudly as the regulations permitted, reading to him, pleading with him to come round. She looked into his eyes and there was nothing, just a blank stare. A letter had arrived at their home announcing that Georgie had just been appointed a Junior High Court judge; she leant over the bed and conveyed to him this welcome, but under the circumstances now fairly meaningless news. He did not, he could not, respond. And then the realisation started: she had no rights. Georgie had always felt himself to be in robust good health. As recently as a month prior to the attack, the family had acquired a second home in the country. He had returned after the completion of a medical test producing the paperwork announcing he was as fit as ever. Highly successful QCs in their mid-fifties do not usually make provision against catastrophic brain damage. They are in the full flood of competence and enjoyment, and plan the rest of their and their family's lives on that basis. They make no living wills, they convey no written wishes as to how they would wish their nearest and dearest to act should their minds suddenly fail.

Now Georgie was in what the doctors referred to as a "persistent vegetative state." Nothing she or the medical team did seemed to make any difference. The patient's heart was beating independently, and he was breathing on his own. Since none of his vital functions was being supported mechanically, drastic intervention was out of the question. Contrary to the mythology of medical soap operas, there was no machine to switch off. Lydia had the ear, and the confidence, of one compassionate and patently honest consultant. He told her frankly "It is our sworn duty to keep your husband alive. We cannot in all honestly withhold treatment. We are doing everything which, as doctors, we are sworn and obliged to do." Then he looked at her between the eyes. "But I am telling you - and I'd prefer this went no further than this room - I am withdrawing nutrition. If I was you, I'd pray for pneumonia." Lydia's prayer was granted. In the July of 2007, Georgie died.

Thursday, October 24th

We stay all day by your bedside and, in the evening, Benjo leaves to enjoy a night's uninterrupted sleep at home. There is a large blue faux leather arm chair to the left of your bed. I snuggle into it all night, looking down into your empty eyes, and occasionally taking and caressing your hand. It is the first time we have been alone together for three long weeks. How have I known and loved this face - for so many nights and decades past: the high hair-line, the prominent, slightly puffy ear-lobes, the lightly freckled, slightly wrinkling skin. How we quarrelled when I mentioned those slight wrinkles.

Catherine, if you wished to die, why didn't you? We have given you every opportunity, and yet you hang stubbornly on.

Robert, if I wish to die, then I will die. If I am scheduled to die, then I will continue to live.

Catherine, are you that contrary?

Yes, Robert bach. I am me. I will die, if I choose to, in my own time. I will not be tidied away.

Catherine Cariad, I cannot possibly live without you.

You'll manage.

I wake in my armchair, strangely refreshed. After a shower in your *en suite* bathroom with its immaculate tiles and careful air of non-occupancy, I take the non-functioning escalator down to the ground floor for breakfast in the Costa Coffee Shop, and buy a copy of *The Guardian* from Amigo's, ferrying it upstairs where I read excerpts aloud over your recumbent form. We have long avoided *The Guardian* as too predictably Left Wing, but for weeks now it has constituted our weekly sustenance, ever since taking a joint tactical decision to avoid Rupert Murdoch and all of his works. For years the unctuous hedonism of *The Sunday Times* has riled. Following a poor review of one of my books, *The Times Literary Supplement* appears to be looking on me with disfavour, and has stopped answering my friendly emails. After the death of your brother in America last year, his annual gift of a subscription to the *TLS* has likewise lapsed. Now there is nothing for it but to brave the *Guardian's* ethical campaigns, its rectitude and air of slight moral self-satisfaction.

As usual they are in a pother about something or other, and are congratulating themselves on their solicitude. This morning it is international mobile phone correspondence between Washington and Berlin. "The furore over the scale of American mass surveillance revealed by Edward Snowden," I indignantly orate to the silent room, pronouncing *furore* the Italian way, "shifted to a new level last night when Angela Merkel, the German chancellor called Barrack Obama to demand satisfaction over reports that the US National Security Agency was monitoring her mobile 'phone." There is a colour photograph of Merkel using this favourite device on the front page, which I hold before your new-born baby gaze, displaying the aforesaid politician holding an instrument as dark as your mascara to her left ear, frowning beneath her dyed hair as she does so. "They call her 'die Handy-Kanzlerein'", the report continues, helpfully explaining that "Handy" is German for a cell phone.

We have left your cell phone in its lime green bag in the kitchen at home, and we have left your mascara in the white cabinet near the bathroom door. Tomorrow I will bring the mascara as tribute and as gift, and dab it around your empty eyes. You will not resist, any more than you do now as I spray your Cacherel's *Anais* eau de toilette around your dear neck, moistening its folds and pervading the atmosphere of your room with sickly, sweet perfume, blend of Madonna lily, hyacinth, blackcurrant, jasmine, rose and orange blossom. Do you remember when we bought this scent? It was on February 8th this year, the day before my Festival Hall talk on "Sex, Bitchiness and Anais Nin". You attended, watching from the back of room as I described the aroma, then Nin's meretricious life and work, before my scripted *coup de théâtre* of squirting *Anais* all over the front row as I delivered the sentence "She so fictionalised and mythologised her life she seems as elusive as Proust's Albertine. She is perhaps a character in a yet-to-be-written novel to be entitled *Anais Disparue*."

Catherine Disparue, do you hear? You are a crumbling star, and I am staring straight into the brown dwarf of you.

A gentle knock on the door announces the arrival of the slight and brisk form of Ann Smith, who introduces herself as one of a three-strong Macmillan Palliative Care Team attached to the Trust. She hands me a folded A4 leaflet that explains "Palliative Care is the active total care of any patient whose illness cannot be cured. Our aim is to achieve the best quality of life for patients and their carers." She does not mention death, though the implication is that you are indeed dying, albeit more slowly than the well intentioned Dr Glover supposed. Her object now is to keep you as comfortable as possible until the inevitable occurs. It could take hours, days, even weeks, the team simply do not know. In the interval, however long that might be, their sworn duty is to apply Tender Loving Care. For once she uses the whole phrase: no acronym, thank God, no "TLC". The ethically nuanced language lets me know that here, in the inner sanctum of the very last thing, for once I am in the presence of something profoundly and reassuringly traditional, amid all of the impersonal charts and machines. For all that, she enunciates the phrase with a dry precision, as if it amounted to a medical term. In your case, the team has decided to order a cocktail of three drugs: Morphine, the sedative and anticonvulsant Midazolam, and the anti-secretion agent Glycopyrronium. They are to be delivered at a rate of 0.87 millilitres per hour via a small pump that is connected intravenously to your right arm. The pump is housed in a clear Perspex case through which we can see the three squat syringes sitting side by side. At this rate their contents last for a little under twenty-four hours, at the end of which a shrill beep sounds. By that time the nursing team are expected to have prepared the contents of next pump that should immediately replace the last. This, as we are soon to learn, works better in theory than in practice.

At around four the beeper sounds again on your feeding pump. So far, the twining tube with its nutritious sludge has been curling quite satisfactorily around the hexagonal joint on its stand, a pivot albeit as delicate as our consciences, and as liable to fail. When it stops, a signal is being sent of some blockage further up the flow, in the naso gastric tube itself. Syringing can help, but for how long?

In the evening I return to find an email on my machine. It has arrived from Essex at half past ten this morning, and it pleads: "We cannot stop thinking about Catherine's state. It has occurred to us that we, in consultation with the specialist, and having the unanimous opinion of the family both here and in America, agreed to let Catherine slip away peacefully. By continuing to support her breathing and by feeding her instead of allowing her to die, the hospital is prolonging her life indefinitely, which is a contradiction of the agreed decision. Surely there could be a way of increasing the morphine injections and withdrawing sustenance which will achieve the end we all – not least Catherine – would wish. In other instances patients have, by agreement of all concerned, had their life-support systems turned off. The hospital should undertake this act of common humanity." Its concern is understandable, but in the circumstances it seems a little inaccurate and unjust. Somehow I distrust the logical force of statements prefaced by the rhetorical adverb "surely". Besides, there is no life support machine to turn off.

Before I retire to bed, I talk to our son. While I have been agonising by your bedside, he has had our Welsh piano retuned by his girlfriend's grandfather, a retired Congregationalist minister and organist who lives down the hill from us in Elmers Grove. The E below middle C had slipped, converting the major common chord into a muddy version of the minor. To test out the result, I strike a perfect cadence from the dominant to the tonic. It comes out perfectly, unlike practically everything else at present in our lives.

Friday, October 25th

As we entered the room this morning for our usual six-hour stint, we were met by an unfamiliar starkness. Gone were the attachments connecting you to food and fluid, gone were the complicated wires and leads in which you lay enmeshed. You lay in bed gently breathing beneath the sheets. Outside in the corridor a hush prevailed. Within, and more especially within me, panic slowly rose: a sensation in the solar plexus of desolation, helplessness and fear.

Do not leave me behind, beloved, do not abandon me to this dread.

At mid-morning a junior doctor called Isobel asked to see us. She evidently had something of importance to communicate. Once settled in her seat next to mine, she started slowly and gently to explain the difficulties the team are having coping with your blocked naso gastric tube. To replace it would necessitate yet another X-ray and a complicated procedure that might well shorten, rather than extend your life. Since the sands of your existence seem to be drifting away in any case, the arguments for so drastic and potentially uncomfortable an intervention seem slender. Under the circumstances, there would seem to be as strong case for letting the natural consequences of withholding feeding take their course. Unless we express any strong objection, this is what the doctors on balance have now decided to do.

In communicating so bleak a decision, this excellent and conscientious young medic had far less of the acquired immunity from overt displays of feeling available to her seniors. She was very obviously distressed by our plight. In future, she told us, she wishes to specialise in palliative care. I sense this is a difficult task that she will have to perform many times before she becomes a consultant. For now she is too young not to be affected by our predicament, and too young not to show that she cares. Her very compassion was attractive: it existed at the point where moral sensations stir the nerves: the pulse of pity, the tincture and the texture of concern. The news evidently pained her deeply, and her face and manner showed it. Speaking as she does for the whole medical team, the course of action she set out struck me as responsible and pragmatic. As she put the case, it also appeared stringently – if not abstractly – ethical. True, this is no absolute rightness, but we are all caught in a relativistic - and inexorably changing - situation in which ultimate principles carry less and less weight. Nudged by circumstances – a blocked piece of equipment - we have, so the argument runs, to do what is humane and appropriate, rather than what is - or might be - ideal. As Camus' Doctor Rieux put it "People are not an idea". You are not an idea.

We sat in silence for a while, absorbing what we had just been told. There are further concerns. We are being told a lot, but are we being told everything? When you were moved to this ward, saline drip was being delivered to your arm at a rate of 83.333 millilitres an hour over a period of twelve hours, a litre every twelve hours. Now the dose is being delivered at 20 millilitres an hour: 240 millilitres in total over the same period. My school maths tells me you are getting one quarter of the fluids you were getting before. Is your liquid intake being slowly reduced to nothing?

Now it is early afternoon, and a team of doctors led by a registrar has just called round. They reiterated what we had already heard, adding that your kidneys are now deemed too delicate to cope with the previous intake of saline drip. Taken together with the absence of nutrition, the unspoken implication is that they are winding you down, starving you out of existence slowly. Let us face it, girl. They have already stopped feeding you and now it would appear they are not even giving you fluids, eventually perhaps not even a salty drop to ease you out of life. If matters continue on this downward course, we will have to witness this gradual decline from your bedside, waiting for its inevitable conclusion, and powerless to arrest it.

Advise me, beloved. You with your Cheshire cat grin, go on advise me. Pour me a cup of coffee from the cafetière and make me see sense.

This was your second death.

Sunday, October 27th

Catherine, you could always sleep for Wales, but even for you this slumber is excessive. Twenty-one days and nights, and you still snoring? Whatever can you mean by it? Wake up. Wake up. I know that you're in there somewhere. You were always slow in leaving: it is quite predictable, I suppose, that you should take a long time a-dying.

Monday, October 28th

Hospitals are the least anonymous of places. People have praised the sociability and human variety of airports, but to me the main corridor joining the general wards on the first floor of a teaching hospital is quite exotic enough. A hospital corridor is the *vade mecum* of feeling. Because of that, it is full of human interest: the elegant girl in a wheelchair who propels herself forward with lean, tattooed arms. Behind her comes a middle-aged waddler of a man who cries openly "O Lord, O Lord, O Lordy-o!", for all the world to hear. The

Rastafarian with a Jamaican accent who ranges down the linoleum intoning, over and over again, the words "I am nat decent, I am nat decent." Drawing level with me, he creases with appreciative laughter as I respond "Thank God for that!" People understand one another here. The barriers come down.

Today, the Ghanaian nurse said that you opened both eyes as they were cleansing your mouth. She added reassuringly "She is there. She is resisting us." Small mercies. Small mercies.

Tuesday, October 29th:

Dr Noori is here again with his JFK chart and his solemnly suave manner. At the foot of the page he carefully notes the medication that you are on: Midazolam for sedation and against fitting, and morphine for residual pain. Then he smacks his hands together, pokes within an inch of your eyes, and rolls a rubber ball down the length of your right arm before he applies himself to the grid. And what is its verdict this morning?

Auditory Response: Nil
Visual Function Scale: Nil
Motor Function Scale: Nil
Oromotor/Verbal Function Scale: One
Communication Scale: Nil
Arousal Scale: Nil
Total Score: One out of twenty-five.

But how much of this is you, and how much Midazolam?

Timidly, I inquire about the future. Can you hear us down there on the bed and, if so, how much of this can you take in? Is there even a "you" down there to weigh the cost, or to feel the pain? How long, I ask him, can you hang on like this? "Well," he answers, "technically for a very long time. Her condition is not in that sense terminal, as long as she is watered and fed." "How long" I ask him once more, "can this go on? With his serious professional manner he explains that, recumbent as you are, and with no input of calories, your metabolism has by now slowed down drastically. You are not using much energy, and all your systems are working at half cock. This process - if process it be - will take some time. So if we do let things go on like this and do nothing? You have, he tells me, two, maybe three weeks of weakening existence before you, after which your heart will succumb to the strain. And we must stand by and watch all of this? I pause, look significant, and inquire what will happen if they reinstate feeding? Oh, he repeats quite blithely, then you could go on for ever.

So once again the choice is mine, mine alone to decide whether you live or die.

Wednesday, October 30th

By coincidence, the Registrar attached to this ward is the very same doctor who headed the resuscitation team that restored your heartbeat slightly less than a month ago. She remembers us, and we remember her. There is a mutual trust and, I reassure myself, even a mutual liking between us. For all that, she does not mince her words. You have, she is explaining to us, merely motor responses now: you are, she said, like – then paused and chose her words – "let us put it as gently as we can – like a bird." I think she had wanted to say like a reptile, even like a snake. Well, certainly your lustreless eyes possess a certain Lamia-like hardness as they stare uncomprehendingly up at me. "All of the higher faculties characteristic of human beings" she expanded, "have gone."

We mention the conversation we had yesterday with Dr Noori. "That" she says, "is how matters stand. But we can always revisit decisions, you know. No decision is irreversible."

Thursday, October 31st

Each morning you would listen to "Thought for the Day", BBC Radio 4's two-minute slot conceded to multi-faith devotion, with a mixture of fascinated horror and Voltaire-like scorn. Then one day a preacher overstepped the mark. You leant across the yellow Formica working surface of our kitchenette and remarked, wide-eyed and with a sort of mystic, sardonic bewilderment, "Whatever happened to the Enlightenment?"

Seldom was there anyone so fixedly anti-clerical, so contemptuous of the structures and devices of religion, as you. And yet this very afternoon we have witnessed two merry vicars in this small room of yours, conveying their regard. Fathers John and Andrew are the Ant and Bee of the spiritual world. They are benign and understanding, the very best sort of Anglican. There has been besides a Scandinavian Protestant chaplain oozing her respects, and a South London nonconformist minister who sat at the foot of your hospital bed and orated for several hours on the history of his particular denomination whilst scarcely shedding a glance in your direction. And now, courtesy of a Romanian ex-girlfriend of our son's, we gather that they are offering up orisons for you at St Paul's Cathedral.

Send them away, Robert bach.

Lastly my friend and doctoral supervisee Elizabeth Ingrams has shown us a Buddhist chant that we might choose to recite aloud over the long hours of our vigil, though whether to fortify ourselves or revive you we are not sure. It runs: "Nam-myoho-renge-kyo" and she tells us that its origins are ancient and Indian, and that it has migrated by sundry Buddhist pathways through China to Japan. Then she carefully explains what it means, making gestures as she goes. "Nam" appears to be an abbreviation of "Namasthe", a traditional Eastern greeting meaning I dedicate myself or devote myself, usually accompanied by a folding together of the hands and a slight declension of the head. I am slightly familiar with this, since my great friend Dr William Radice, scholar of Bengali and translator of the works of Rabindranath Tagore, often greets myself and others thus. "Myo" means open or pure, and "ho" is its manifestation. "Renge" is the lotus flower which, I now learn, blossoms and fruits at the same time, and hence signifies the simultaneity of cause and effect. "Kyo" is a textile, or by extension a text. Hence the ensemble seems to mean "I open myself to the wonderful law of endless possibilities present in the text of you." I have now declaimed it thirty times, which makes me feel better, even if it has no effect on you.

What is there in you that has inadvertently released this torrent of ecumenical supplication?

Send them all away, Robert. Send them all away. What are you all doing to me?

Catherine, you are the focus of our care. You had no great liking for honorifics, but now, according to a notice at the head of your bed, you are CATHERINE FRASER NBM: Catherine Fraser Nil By Mouth, or perhaps No Bloody Maries in deference to our favourite in-flight tipple. And your Coma Recovery Scale is initialled after your favourite American president, JFK. Or is this a reference to the one New York airport for which you had little use after it ceased to be Idlewild? It was, you said, simply too inconvenient for our regular vacation destination of Suffern in New York State.

Soon, during that brief, inconsequential East Coast spring, the daffodils will be sprouting out in the drive of that white, clapboard house from the bulbs that you planted there two falls ago, never to see them burst into flower. Your eyes are open. Why do you growl at me? Why this insatiable moaning? Moaner, moaner, Mona Lisa, Gioconda of the Pumps.

9 SINNERS AND SAINTS

Thursday, October 31st

Of only one thing am I certain. Whatever the pressures on me at the moment, I need to feel free. Only in a condition of personal liberty will any decision I take on your behalf possess meaning or validity.

Today is our wedding anniversary, and it is All Hallow E'en. I spent the early evening with our son in the Saints and Sinners pub – "Premium Beers. Quality Food Served Daily. Evening Entertainment" - just down the drab London Road from the main hospital block, at the corner of Mayday Road. Two steps up on a dais with laminate flooring surrounded by a kind of dark-varnished altar rail, we sat on plastic-covered cubes shaped like overblown pouffes. Against the driven muzak, we discussed you, our marriage, Big Ben and the practical puzzle of death. As we sipped our pints of John Smith's, the alternatives appeared to be clear. If we did nothing, you would die in a very short while. If we chose to intervene by means of some as-yet-to-be decided course of action, you – or some version of you – might linger on in a diminished state. Or you might not. I had a dim sense of your presence throughout, though whether that coaxing voice in my left ear belonged to you, to my recollection of you, my reconstruction of you, or to some persistent legacy of you physically and mentally present in our boy, I was never quite sure.

"I don't know what to do," I said.

"Do you actually have to *do* anything?" asks our son.

"Yes, because under circumstances such as these, to do nothing itself constitutes a course of action. Officially we have all agreed to the status quo. If we fail to intervene, we have in effect become accessories to a mercy killing. Yet the question 'Do you wish us to stop feeding her?' has never directly been put to either of us. We have been sprung into a *fait accompli* by a hitch in some faulty piece of equipment."

"Given that, there is nothing actively wrong with the plan the doctors have laid out. Arguably, it is the most practical course of action available to them. They are simply employing common sense."

"But, realistic as it seems, their decision has foreshortened all the philosophical arguments. In the process they have deprived us - have deprived me - of all agency. I have to wrestle with the roots of this dilemma, or I am nothing, and Catherine too is nothing. What kind of a moral eunuch permits his ethical choices to be dictated to him by a naso gastric tube?"

"Yet you were quite reconciled to the removal of her tracheostomy two weeks back. You were reconciled to it because back then – not so long ago – you seemed certain what Catherine herself would have wished."

You were absolutely right, Robert bach, you know that you were. So why are you in two minds now? Why are you hunched over your drink in such a state of equivocal misery?

"Because last time I was given a choice. This time my hand is apparently being forced, not so much by the doctors as by circumstances. If the feeding tube had not become clogged, this state of affairs would never have arisen. Nor has the question been put to me as to whether I agree to my wife being starved to death slowly. Even if we hope she will not suffer the pangs of hunger in the process, how are we to be sure one way or the other? Besides, we are not in the same position as before. The withdrawal of treatment and the withholding of sustenance are two different paths, and they involve quite separate issues. The providing of nutriment is an obligation, only set aside if likely to compromise a patient's prospects of survival, as here. Nor is this all. On the earlier occasion we were faced with a clear-cut decision, yes or no. The tracheostomy did not fall out of its own accord. We were specifically consulted as to whether we wanted it removed. For all sorts of reasons, the present decision seems a lot harder, principally perhaps because the events that have led up to it have been more protracted and complicated. We are being invited to bring about the termination of her life as a by-product of merciful non-intervention. To murder her by refusing a helping hand, to assassinate her with a lovingly restrained caress. I keep on having visions of her standing at a street corner fumbling in her handbag and appealing to me for help, but I can't make out what she is saying."

Around us the textured wallpaper was lined with cheap reproduction abstracts like mass-produced Mondrians. In the corner next to the side door to my left, a Barcrest fruit machine was flashing yellow and red, the dials on its raised face eerily reminiscent of the monitor keeping watch and ward beside your bed. On its lower trunk, a notice in bold capitals read MACHINE EMPTIED AND DEFLOATED

DAILY. The word Emptied was underlined, but I had no idea what De-floated meant. Are you being de-floated?

"You know what she would have done if she had been present to speak for herself," Benjo said. "She'd have followed Ben's example."

"But she is not Ben, and neither am I. Again there is no equivalence. Ben's mind was whole; it was his body that was going. Catherine's body is now more or less intact. It is her mind that has been wiped clean. Ben was free to choose on his own behalf, while I have to make a choice for Catherine. We may believe we know what she would have wanted, but any provision we make for her hypothetical wishes will of necessity represent a form of imaginative reconstruction. Even if we remember what she once said about other cases, this is not of itself an accurate guide as to what she would now be feeling in her own case, supposing – and it is a very big supposition – she was able to experience her own incapacity. As I understand it, this is the very reason the law at present limits the role of relatives in decisions such as this. The lawyers want to restrain flights of speculative or wishful thinking."

No sooner had I said all this, than I wondered if the differences were clear as I had made out. Were they perhaps more a matter of degree than of kind? Maybe the life-or-death question seemed more the agonising to me this evening, simply because it has now been posed twice. And am I perhaps saving myself from one sort of ordeal, only to invite another? The mode of your likely departure lately outlined to us is likely to be much more harrowing to watch than last time, its effects on you more difficult to gauge.

Your life will be over in a matter, not of hours but of weeks. I doubt I can stand by your bedside and watch this spectacle. Nobody can possibly know what it feels like, to someone even in a state of very low awareness, to be starved and parched to death.

I was staring out of the side window towards the side street and the Coughlin Bakery where we have been buying jumbo sausages for our daily lunches. There was a large scroll over the shop front boasting "Hand crafted quality since 1937." I tried to sum up: "In effect, it seems to me, the medical authorities have presented us with a compassionate opportunity to end Catherine's life while keeping within our sense of what is best for her, and the provisions for such cases enshrined within the law. What they are telling us is that the re-insertion of her naso gastric tube would have caused her unnecessary distress and, what is more, that it was more likely to have shortened her life than to have extended it. Against the background of their certainty that her existence is ebbing away, and must sooner or later come to an end whatever is done or not done, they have reconciled themselves – and have attempted to reconcile us – to the prospect that the withholding of food and liquid will terminate her life within a couple of weeks. The declared intention behind this provision, however, is not to kill her. Any such result will be a bye-product of a humane course of inaction aimed at avoiding her short-term discomfort. In the upshot, they will have finished her off, as it were, by accident.

I went to the bar to refresh our drinks. Behind a row of upturned spirit bottles there was a flat television screen showing the six o'clock weather report. One of four in the pub, it hung between twin recesses, each lit from behind through stained glass panels depicting identical stylised suns, the beams of each rendered as triangular shares of primary yellow, gold and green. Returning to our table, I asked "You don't think that the doctors may be doing this, partly at least, so as to cut their costs?"

Benjo took a sip from his beer, then added "Possibly, but also because they sincerely believe that we too are seeking a way out for ourselves, and for our mother and wife."

"So then, are we?"

After a pause he continued, "Catherine was always selfless. She would not have wanted us to lead a drastically curtailed existence, as we must do if she pulls through this episode. Then again, realising this, arguably it is our duty to counteract her instinctive selflessness. Perhaps we should give her a fighting chance, even if she doesn't want one. Dad, which decision do you think you would be happier with in ten years' time?"

Dimly I recalled the philosopher Mary Warnock's summation of the Existentialist view of futurity. "Conscious beings" she wrote, paraphrasing Sartre, "are able to conceive both of past and future; things which are not at the present moment. It is out of this ability that the freedom of such beings arises. They can envisage, imagine and create, by deliberate 'projection' or choice, a future which is their own."

In imagination I found myself staring back through a long enfilade of rooms as down the corridor of a hospital, and saw my dwindling self, hunched by a burden of retrospective responsibility, about to seize the knife in mercy, or else return it murderously to its sheath. To whom, I wondered, will I then feel a need to justify my decision: to myself, to some notion of God, or to you? Groping for familiar but meaningful language, suddenly I heard myself say "Whatever I will have done, or will not have done then, it will have amounted to an act of Faith."

Ancient terms were beginning to enter this argument. Benjo said he agreed with me, so I asked him, in that case, what Faith meant. He answered that the word did not necessarily have to be used in a religious sense. "There is also a secular application, if we understand faith as the assurance that, if we act honourably and truthfully, things will turn out for the best. All of us must take decisions in the light of that perception. Otherwise we cannot act at all, or at least cannot act with any clarity."

"So it is a secular form of Providence?" I asked.

"Something like that. And it also amounts to a non-religious understanding of the doctrine of Redemption. You remember Silas Marner? He takes a young baby into his safekeeping, and is symbolically redeemed by a trove of gold. Life sometimes turns out like that."

"And so may ours. Though I would add that this reading of 'faith' and 'redemption', if I understand them aright, are not inconsistent with those qualities as viewed in a religious light."

"What makes you say that?"

I was staring ahead of me to where a Sound Surfer Digital Audio juke box sat solemn and square, like a squat judge on the bench.

"Because, as I am slowly coming to realise, I am more religious than I used to think. Which maybe entails a reverence for all human life, however minimal and however reduced."

"If you take the religious view," says our son, "the course of action we now take is irrelevant in the long run. What is immortal in Catherine, even if it is just the idea of her, will survive in any event, whatever we choose to do or not to do."

"And so, you believe in the soul?" I asked this young scientist in some surprise.

Visible to me just above his head, a pensioned-off euphonium was leaning drunkenly against a jar of Crispo hand-made sugar cones. It appeared to be the centre piece of a retro collage of *objets trouvés,* garish as cast-off beliefs.

"In one sense all of us, even the doctors - perhaps them most of all - must give due weight to the idea of the soul. If we and they did not, none of us would be conducting this particular argument. The soul is the abiding presence of someone, the self to which we defer when we discuss their welfare. In that understanding of the word, only the soul has rights."

In that sense too, I added silently, you still exist back there on the hospital ward. It is your soul the nurses address when they call you by name as they begin each and every shift, your soul that they consider when, several times each day, they ask your permission to turn you.

You are still there in your stricken body, Catherine cariad, you are still there.

"I don't want to lose her," I heard myself announce.

"In one sense, we have already lost her. In one sense, she is already dead. So what *are* you going to do?"

"Whatever I choose, I'm convinced now that I can in the last resort only act for myself. Nobody can make this choice for me. Nor can I allow myself to be swayed by another's logic. The position I eventually reach will in no way be prescriptive. It need not entail the opinion that others in a similar predicament should act in an equivalent way. Anyway, our situation - even if it echoes those faced by many other people - strikes me as possessing features almost unique to itself. In the end, the only possible choice is one that is right for me. It will derive its justification from that aptness, maybe from that alone." There was perhaps a half minute of silence before I added, "As long as there is a flicker of hope, I'm going to try keep her by me."

And so, sweetheart, I heard you softly demur, *you would be prepared to privilege your moral sentimentality above my agnostic certainty, my craving for closure and for peace?*

So it would appear.

I fear I must protest.

Sit down, soul!

10 NOVEMBER: THE WAGER

Friday, November 1st

Today to add to our problems our next door neighbour has caused two huts to be erected in her garden that overlook ours with their large, gaping voyeuristic windows. We are not sure that she has planning permission for this, or needs it. You would have fought this intrusion, and so shall we. How you would have relished the fight. Before we set off for our daily stint at the hospital, I fire off a letter to the council inquiring what the legal position is.

Yesterday, I was full of doubt. Today I am full of resolve. As soon as we reach the hospital, I ask to see Dr Padmanabha. When she arrives shortly after lunch, I tell her that I have come to a state of modest decision. I cannot stand by and watch you waste away without lifting a hand to help. There are two very small actions that I would like the team to consider. I understand the reasons why your NG tube has not been restored. Weaning you off liquids, however, seems to me to be unnecessary, and in my uneducated eyes even callous. I therefore ask that, gradually and in the most practical manner possible, fluids be re-instated. Secondly I say, that while we have every faith in the processes of neurological assessment that we have observed, we have at present only spoken with one neurologist. We think we owe it to you that your condition should be subjected to a second expert opinion.

The first request meets with a readier response than the second. There is no way in which the doctors can resist the re-administration of saline drip. We are immediately told that liquids will be restored just as soon as they can, subcutaneously but without glucose. On the second point, she demurs. It is true that we have only spoken with just one member of the neurological team. He has been asked to see you because he is the hospital's specialist in neurological rehabilitation, and it was with a view to assessing your suitability for this that the team was contacted in the first instance. Moreover, on each occasion that he has seen you, he has reported back to the three-person team responsible for neurological cases. Your case has been reviewed by them on a daily basis, and your treatment has been directed by these discussions. If we insist that another member of the team see you, however, they will see what can be done.

In the evening a group of our son's fellow students turn up and sit round your bed. They include one of his former girlfriends, a darkly glamorous psychology student from Romania, who has arrived bearing a bunch of red roses. After she has left, we are joined by his present companion, a lively law student from Swansea, and we all pile into a taxi and come back to the house to feast on pizzas and red wine. I am full of relief and pride at my moderate decisiveness, and towards the end of the evening hear myself making an intemperate speech. I am, I say, fed up with listening to others think, fed up with consulting the family. From now on I will rely on my moral instincts. I believe in you, and I believe in our future. Towards the end of this slightly absurd oration, one of the party cheers.

Saturday November 2nd

As our son works in the downstairs study, I am seized by a sudden fit of weeping. I am gushing Pascal's tears, but whether of sorrow or of relief, I am not quite clear. Suddenly and unaccountably, I have a vision of you on the pavement before me opening your faux leather handbag and fiddling with the loose change in your purse. You often did this, especially overseas when confused by the currency. To my shame I would sometimes intervene peremptorily and impatiently count out the money for you. Now you look vulnerable, naïve, a bit lost, one of the many attitudes that drew from me a poignant mixture of affection and pity. To love, to have loved. People are moved by all kinds of qualities in their nearest and dearest. But for me there was one quality that invariably drew from me the authentic attraction and pain: the reality – or more lethally the appearance - of innocence. Faced by such vulnerability, four lines of T. S. Eliot's always come to mind:

> I am moved by fancies that are curled
> Around these images, and cling:
> The notion of some infinitely gentle
> Infinitely suffering thing.

And now my shoulders are heaving uncontrollably and I am whimpering aloud, over and over again in a tremulous voice I hardly recognise, "She is dying, she is dying, she is dying." You are appealing for my help with those blue-grey eyes of yours, and I truly do not know what to do. Our son comes forward from the back room study, and gathers me in his arms as I repeat the words "She is dying, dying, dying."

Sunday, November 3rd

It is the Feast of All Saints and, in conformity with my newly found piety, I decide to go to church. The vicar, a

Welshman from Swansea who distrusts Wales, preaches a sermon about the company of saints, which include representatives of very virtue and every vice known to humanity. He invokes Saint Catherine on her wheel of pain. And then he mentions a saint I have not heard of, who is surely tailor-made for you. The patron saint of procrastinators, so it would appear, is a certain Saint Expeditus. He was a Roman centurion stationed in Armenia who converted to Christianity in around 303 AD. His feast day is April 19th. According to one version of his legend, on the morning of his conversion the devil visited him in the form of a crow, who advised him to postpone his conversion until the following day. But Expeditus stamped on the bird, declaring "I'll be a Christian today, or I never shall."

Less heroically, his name is sometimes attributed to the arrival in North Africa of a packet containing his bones. The envelope was stamped with the words "Expedite", or "For Urgent Delivery", which thenceforth became his title. I think I prefer the second story, and I am sure you would have as well.

Monday, November 4th

Late this afternoon, our request for a second opinion bears fruit. Whilst our son is fetching tea from the café downstairs, there is a flurry of movement outside the door, and the trim shape of a female consultant enters your room. Brisk, business-like, intelligent, focused, in a bit of a rush. Instantly I seem to sense a kind of affinity with her. I am saying to myself "Our specialisations may be different, but we two are of a kind. You are a bright research scientist in early middle age, and you probably give papers at seminars. In another existence you might be my junior colleague. I might be your greying mentor, and I might well be unconscionably proud of – as well as mildly stirred by - you. I will listen to you because I respect what you stand for, your ever-so-definite judgement, as well as your clear manner of delivering it. This is essentially what we both believe in: the play of the mind, never more effective than when its subject is the temporary – or possible the permanent – absence of mind. She extends her hand and says "Morag. Morag McIvor."

After introducing herself, she says "I gather that you've already had a fairly pessimistic prognosis". Then she turns down your bed sheets, taps at your limbs, shines a torch briefly into each of your eyes, and rolls a rubber ball down each of your legs. At that moment our son comes back with the two plastic cups of tea, and she asks to speak to us both outside, so you will be out of earshot. A good sign, I think.

There she announces "Well, there's one thing I can tell you. Catherine is not a vegetative case. Judging from her reactions, I put the chance of her recovery to some degree of meaningful consciousness at about one in four. Recovery to some form of mental capacity, that is. She wouldn't be quite the lively lady you knew before. Even so, there's an almost hypothetical three per cent in which patients in her state come back to a remarkable extent and are almost, if not quite, their old selves again." She pauses for perhaps three seconds and looks at us frankly. "I'm sorry to supply you with so divergent an opinion. The fact is that we - that you - are faced with a choice, and you'll have to decide fairly quickly. It's easy for someone like me to pontificate. I'm a professional, and I've been aware of the ramifications of cases such as this since I started studying medicine at the age of seventeen. I also value my own intellectual independence highly, and I wouldn't want to live on in circumstances in which it was severely compromised. I sense you two both value mental clarity as well. You wouldn't wish to be dictated to in this matter by anyone. What do you think?"

The open question hovers in the air between us, but not for very long. Dr McIvor needs to know what we, what I, truly want: not what I might say I want, might opine after lengthy consideration, or can plausibly justify in the eyes of others. After perhaps three seconds she puts a direct question: a question blunt yet sharp: "Are either of you two gentlemen religious?"

"Well, I'm not", our son truthfully replies. "And Catherine is not either."

Her eyes have yet not turned towards me, yet from a very great distance, and with something of a detached astonishment, I hear some ancient part of myself declare "I'm afraid to say that I am."

Even as I make it, I am not clear to me what I mean by this statement, but I nonetheless recognise that in some sense it represents the most authentic sentiment I have expressed over the last few irksome weeks. Dr McIvor does not give me an opportunity to expand on my thoughts. She is trained to detect instinctual reactions, and by some process of osmosis she has picked up from me something I have not yet explicitly articulated: an overwhelming desire for your survival, whatever the consequences. Scarcely are the unexpected words out of my mouth, than she sets off in the direction of the office, saying "I'll order an MRI scan so that we can get a more precise picture of what exactly is going on inside your wife's head. In the meantime, it is my opinion that the hospital has a moral duty to resume feeding Catherine. And that's what I am going to say."

Dr McIvor has walked off smartly down the corridor. Soon she is out of sight. Verbally maybe, but more likely through some refinement of body language, some obliquely conveyed preference or inexplicable process of osmosis, I have indicated my consent. So I stand in this bleak institutional corridor wondering what or who has prevailed. We have it seems turned a corner, and even now I am not certain how or why. Attrition has played a part, of course, the wearing down and eventual exhaustion of intellection and preparedness. As a result of a long and gruelling process, I am no longer exactly reasonable: I am just me. I've heard all of the common sense arguments in favour of a compassionate letting of nature take its course, and in the last resort I am not convinced. Against the unambiguous counsel of many - perhaps most- who wish you well, I appear to have made a gesture of faith: in you, in medicine, in destiny, in the universe or God, I am not sure. But something in me has stood up and indirectly asserted that I do not wish you to die, however sensible it might appear to allow you to do so. As Pascal once famously said, "The heart has it reasons, which reason does not know at all."

Overriding all other considerations, two overwhelming factors have made themselves felt: a need, and a sort of act of faith. The need was, and is, my abiding love of you and determination, whatever happens, to hold on to that bit of you that remains. The act of faith has been a hunch concerning your continuing existence at some level or another, the persistence of one towards whom I feel an eternal tenderness.

Tuesday, November 5th

Tonight I am invited to St Paul's Girls School in Hammersmith to hear my friend Sebastian Barker, one-time editor of *The London Magazine*, former chair of the Poetry Society and son of my one-time biographical subject, the forties poet George Barker, read from his new volume *The Land of Gold.* I am not going for two reasons. On September 15th this year I attended a moving event in the crypt of Canterbury Cathedral at which sixth formers from his old school recited his long sequence *Damnatio Memoriae* or Lost to Memory. The poem was both a summation of all that the West, what used to be known as Christendom, has lost by relinquishing its historic faith, and a triumphant declaration of the poet's own. Several months back, Sebastian had been diagnosed with cancer, which had left him much weakened. He sat in his wheelchair listening intently in that candle lit space as from a distant chapel the choir sang Byrd's *Ave Verum* and Tallis' hymn *Te lucis ante terminum,* and bright seventeen-year-olds from the King's School read out his words:

> I believe the notion of God essential to the mind.
> I believe divine power lifts the hand
> Working visible things invisibly.

Nothing, I feel, could possibly trump that experience. Besides, I am sitting here late at night in the subdued lighting of a suburban Indian restaurant eating Chicken

Biryani as Guy Fawkes revellers set off sparklers against the grim night outside, like forlorn beacons of hope. I am thinking about those words that I heard in September, I am thinking about Pascal, about science and religion, and I am thinking about you.

Both Sebastian and Pascal were scientists, and both became – or have become – people of faith. Because of this, Bertrand Russell in his *History of Western Philosophy* accuses Pascal of betraying his own impressive mathematical intelligence. There, however, the similarity seems to stop. Pascal for one did not consider that "the notion of God" to be essential to his – or indeed to anybody else's – mind. Instead, he took a bet. God, he thought, was unknowable, but to decide whether he existed or not was a necessity. So he wagered, putting his life on the table. In this act of risky decision-making, he thought, the odds were stacked in favour of belief. If God existed, Pascal would be rewarded by an eternity of happiness; if God did not, he would have lost very little, apart possibly from his reputation and intellectual self-respect.

I too now have made a wager, in which you are the stakes. I have implicitly agreed that the hospital authorities resume feeding you. If you survive in consequence, then I will have been rewarded by a continuation or restoration of you, or more probably a very small part of you.

The disadvantage is that you may well as a result be subjected to confusion or suffering, and I will have no way of knowing whether you are or not, since I cannot speak with you.

Had I, on the other hand, not agreed implicitly to this request, then you would most assuredly have died, after an interval that will probably be painful for both of us. There would then have been an end to your suffering, but not to mine.

We have, in any case, been pitting finitudes and certainties against infinitudes and doubts. All I am certain of is, had there been no intervention, you must have died within a very few days. During that period you would subliminally have suffered, and I will never have the means of knowing how much.

Nor do I know, having assented to the doctors reinstating your nutrition, for how long you will survive, or precisely in what condition. In neither case, do I know how much suffering your existence for a longer or shorter time will have entailed, for you, or indeed for me.

However, this evening I do find myself in the quaint position of envying Pascal, in that, considering the odds of his bet, he apparently felt the need to put only one being's happiness into the equation: namely, his own. "Considering your happiness," he writes in Paragraph 233 of *Pensées,* "Let us weigh the gain and the loss in wagering that God is…If you gain, you gain all. If you lose, you lose nothing." There is, it now seems to me, to be an essential element missing in this account of the terms of this choice. At no point does Pascal calculate the likely effects of his decision on God, who may be delighted, disappointed, or even cruelly hurt, by the outcome.

In this respect my predicament has been more complex than Pascal's. If I lose, I will have lost, not nothing, but something or someone immensely precious, namely you. Moreover, I have had to consider, not merely my own happiness – not even principally that – but your peace of mind, always assuming that you still have a mind, and that unresolved question is itself part of the bet. Besides, Pascal was convinced that, if the coin span in the right direction, he had a chance of eternal felicity. Whichever way my own coin spins, I seem to be in for a spell – or more than a spell - of profound wretchedness. As my old maths master Vincent Paton would often say, with the exaggerated enunciation of his calling – he was skeletal, hatchet-jawed and balding and resembled nobody as much as Chalky, the merciless schoolteacher who once featured in Giles cartoons in *The Daily Express* – "We are in a cleft stick."

Wednesday, November 6th

Our friend Adelaide – an experimental psychologist – talks in the most sanguine way of herself as a material object. I ask her about decision-making, and she points decisively at an area of her skull about a third of the way back on the right side. It all happens inside there, she says.

But there are elements of uncertainly in this account. The community of her colleagues, she tells us, cannot decide on the question of precedence: is decision-making an up-down process or a "bottom-up" one? Do alternatives give rise to thoughts, or do thoughts give rise to alternative? Do we envisage divergent paths, then stand at the crossroads cogitating which route to take, or do the roads converge at the point at which we decide?

Nobody in any case, or so it appears, can work out where it is that thoughts exactly come from. You can detect their physical presence when they make their appearance: the origin is a bit of a mystery. Despite which, Adelaide claims that she is a materialist. Until, that is, I introduce into the conversation the quandary of Free Will. Then she insists that she has freely chosen whether to be a materialist or not. By the same token, I am free to decide about you. Were it not so, I would not feel so empowered. Were it not so, I would not feel so oppressed.

In vain does my contemporary the philosopher Galen Strawson insist that each decision that I take is a direct and ineluctable consequence of the sort of person I am. Since I have no control over my nature, so he would claim, I have no autonomous control over my own decisions, the interventions stemming from them, and the results that they incur. Part of me would like to feel this – it absolves me of any indulgent feeling of regret – but I cannot in all conscience reconcile myself with this logic. I am stuck in the mire of personal responsibility, like it or not.

Thursday, November 7th

The porter calls to take you for your scan at 11.30. You go with fluids and oxygen, but your feed has again temporarily been stopped. Morphine has been discontinued as from today, but your anti-secretion medicine is still in place. We proceed in a solemn procession via the lift. There are forms I have to sign, pretending to be you. Once in the MRI suite itself, I am divested of all metals: my watch and keys, the loose change in my pockets and even my credit cards. I anxiously inquire about my brass signet ring, and the titanium inserted ten years ago to bind a broken ankle. At the last moment I remember and remove my belt.

The scanning bay is like nothing so much as a broadcasting studio: plush, serene, with a single pane of glass giving onto an operations room where the radiographers sit and preside like sound technicians. The centre of the room is dominated by the vast, open-lidded aperture of the pale blue scanning machine, with a pattern of chrysanthemums and fluttering butterflies decorating its skin. From it emanates the subtle and syncopated rhythm of a rap beat. I ask what the throbbing means, and am told it is the cooler. My loosened trousers are beginning to sink down my thighs.

I hold onto your stocking feet and whisper fond nonsense into your left ear as you are shifted from hardboard onto the scanner slide and into the gaping abdomen of the machine. Once inside, you are a babe in the womb, or in the neck of the vagina waiting to be delivered, you are a chrysalis longing to emerge, you are a cicada in your fourteen-year sleep, an astronaut on some intergalactic mission primed to awake on some distant moon of an uncharted star. You are like the space fiction travellers of *Alien 1* bound for unknown perils, a futuristic corpse in some cryonic state of sleep. Across your face a plastic mask like a grid, around your unhearing ears the rapper pulse of the cooler. I hold and massage your feet as successive waves of sound crowd around your head: the grind of a drill, the thud of a disco beat, the insistent bleat of a siren, the fluttering of some demented moth. From the control room a disembodied female voice prepares us for the final assault: "This is the last one, and I'm afraid it will be rather loud." As the grinding barrage of impure noise attacks our senses, you stir and suddenly flip your head from side to side in dissent. We signal to the radiologists beyond the window, but already your ordeal is over. After fifteen minutes of electromagnetic prodding, you are mapped, possibly and impossibly known.

Once you are back in the ward, I am handed yet another form to give my permission for a Percutaneous Endoscopic Gastrostomy tube to be inserted to facilitate feeding. The tube will enter your body through an aperture in the abdomen wall and go directly into your stomach. You are to be taken down to the endoscopic unit on the ground floor of the hospital for the procedure tomorrow. There is, I am told, a small but finite risk of complications. With some misgiving, I sign.

Friday, November 8th

This morning they inserted the PEG into your stomach wall. When we arrive for our daily visit, you are hopelessly groaning and grimacing down on the bed. I reach down and smooth your arm, but nothing that I can do can ease your distress, and I am powerless to help you, powerless to explain to you what is happening, even to ask the location and nature of your unease. You are abandoned, an animal caught in a trap. And I consented to this monstrosity. I signed the assent form for this contrivance without which, I was told, no care home would accept you. As I look down on your discomforted body, for the third time I ask you - and ask myself -"Would you not rather have died?"

Could there be a moral justification for this? The logic with which I have been presented is practical. It is, to use one of your own favourite French aphorisms, a case of "réculer pour mieux sauter". But you have no English, let alone French, words now in which we could discuss your predicament. "Partir est mourir un peu", and you are now both departing and dying, if a little more slowly than before, resolved at some level to take your leave if only we would let you.

Yesterday I could not bear the thought of watching you die. Today I cannot stand the spectacle of watching you live. I had a choice of torments and chose the softer option – softer, at least, for me. Once again, my love, you are the unwilling victim of my sentimentality and selfishness. I cannot ask anybody else, cannot with any conclusiveness even inquire of myself, "Have I taken the right course?" As the American contingent lately informed me, there is no right and no wrong path. Both lead through jungles of one sort or another and neither, from where I am standing, offers an ultimate panacea of peace.

I chose to listen to an optimist, but the pessimists may have been kinder to you, as well as closer to moral and medical truth.

Saturday, November 9th

All day you have been wincing and whingeing in pain. Despite the upturn in your circumstances, I am still in a black mood. In the evening I return to the house and at ten minutes past eight turn on the radio for comfort. The programme on Radio 3 is "Discovering Music" and the speaker is the music critic and broadcaster Stephen Johnson, with whom I shared a session earlier this year during the "The Rest is Noise" Festival on the South Bank. Then he was talking about Holst, and I was speaking about W.B. Yeats. This evening his theme is the reliance of the mature Tchaikovsky on the music of the Russian Orthodox Church, which he illustrates by the recurrence in The Sixth Symphony, the great and sombre "Pathétique", of 'The Kontakion of the Dead', a hymn traditionally performed at Orthodox funeral services. The symphony was first performed in St Petersburg one hundred and twenty years ago, on October 28th 1893, one week before the composer's own death, and the coincidence of the timing rapidly gave rise to the rumour that he had intended it as a sort of suicide note. The Kontakion first appears intoned by the low brass during a calm in the middle of the first movement's "hurricane-like" development section. Its principal melodic feature is a descending scale, which is then taken up in later movements as "an idea of mortality distilled in a basic melodic pattern" which the composer immediately contrasts with a rising scale suggestive of hope. As a result, the whole work, the organic unity of which Stephen was arguing for, is torn between two countervailing tendencies, a "downward tug" and an "upward aspiration." The symphony ends with "one long, disconsolate, unmistakeably dying fall" and gutters out on a "dying heart beat," but the countervailing aspiration is never absent, even in these closing moments. Predictably, as I listen to this patient explanation of a magnificent musical tableau, I am thinking throughout of you.

Sunday, November 10th

A beautiful, sunny autumn day such as you always relished. After a rare five-and-a-half-hour bout of uninterrupted sleep, I wake to see the brownish leaves dancing on the louring sycamore beyond the double Regency arch of our bedroom window. I turn to tell you about it, but you are not there. For two hours I luxuriate in this late year calm, only occasionally lapsing into the dread of our predicament. At the last moment I throw back our duvet, hastily dress, forget to shave, brew a perfunctory cup of tea, half of which I pour down the kitchen sink, then totter out into the sunshine and downhill on my way to church. You, of course, had no time for my beliefs, or half-beliefs, attributing my perfunctory attendance at High Anglican mass to habit, nostalgia, and an unfortunate upbringing. "But you sing in the choir and you enjoy that. I don't mind you going, really."

So you will not mind this morning, as I grope downhill towards consolation and the conventional commiserations of the faithful. But, half way down the slope I pass huddles of children in formal green shirts, red and green scarves secured with *faux* leather toggles, and recall that this, after all, is Remembrance Sunday. Do I, I wonder, wish to participate in this solemn and patriotic commemoration of sacrifice whilst you are lying in your condition of suspended life a nine pound taxi ride away? You whose most abiding memory is of cinemas in South Wales in the fifties and the audience packed into the smelly stalls booing when Winston Churchill strolled onto the screen, their collective memory still smarting from his dispatch as Home Secretary of troops to Tonypandy during the miners' strike of 1910? And of the bar of the London School of Economics ("The London School of Comics") on January 30th, 1965 where your friends held an all-night party to celebrate the great man's committal to Bladon soil?

Once I'm on level ground, there are groups of service men and women, all bound for the same destination, Isaac Watts' "Oh God Our Help in Ages Past", the bugle call and the ceremonial silence. Assisted by you, my misgiving grows. Now I am at the very door of the choir chantry. I can just make out the faint strains of the 'Agnus Dei' from the Fauré Requiem – the most lugubrious and, I suspect, insincere - of the standard settings of the Mass for the Dead - percolating through the heavy vestry door. In a Hardyesque gesture that you would recognise and perhaps commend, I turn on my heels and walk away. I stroll back towards the sunshine and up the dapple-shaded woodland walk, back up to the top of our hill, treading heaps of sodden leaves as I go. Could I have faced "Abide with me" this morning? You for one could not abide it. There is, it strikes me as I wade though drifts of multicoloured leaves towards our Oxford blue front door, more truth and raw honesty to be found in these stripped branches, these drifts of decaying foliage, than in half the creeds.

Monday, November 11th

At twenty past three this morning our time, a compassionate intervention from Indiana reads:

> Well, I think Catherine would be smiling a teary eyed ear to ear grin over your acts of love these last few weeks. She is one of my favourite people and so I am hoping that the MRI results bring positive news. If it definitively shows extensive damage I think she would want as Ben did, not to "live" in a shell from which she could merely observe life. It is

> difficult for me to write this of course, I am trying to be helpful, not hurtful.

At tea time we sit in the corridor beyond the wards and ruefully discuss Locke's theories of the mind. We have been reading this to one another during the long hours of our vigil, and have just reached the celebrated passage in Book II in which the philosopher attempts to refute the idea that there exist in the mind any "innate ideas" lodged in us when, or before, we were born. The mind at birth, Locke insists, is more like a blank sheet:

> Let us then suppose the mind to be, as we say, white paper, void of all characters without any ideas; how comes it to be furnished? Whence comes it by that vast store, which the busy and boundless fancy of man has painted on it with an almost endless variety? Whence has it all the materials of reason and knowledge? To this I answer, in one word, from experience: in that all our knowledge is founded, and from that it ultimately derives itself. Our observation, employed either about external sensible objects, or about the internal operations of our minds, perceived and reflected on by ourselves is that which supplies our understandings with all the materials of thinking. These two are the fountains of knowledge, from whence all the ideas we have, or can naturally have, do spring.

According to this of view, your mind, when it emerged on October 2nd 1942 into the external world in the maternity hospital at Llwynapia on the outskirts of Porth, was as blank as the A4 page on which I write these words.

As you grew, words, phrases and sentences came to be inscribed upon it, impressions from the world of sense that lodged themselves as ideas: ideas of the solidity of objects (such as your rattle), ideas – again stemming from sensations – of pleasure and pain, ideas eventually of cause and effect, of the words and languages (English, Welsh and French) you learned to speak, ideas concerning judgment, probability, assent and dissent, reason, error, and even of the God whom you came to reject. Eventually this congeries of thoughts and beliefs was recognisable as you: as the compliant but animated "snob" from Porth County Grammar School, as the lively, party-going undergraduate at the London School of Economics, as the Careers Advisor in Chiswick, the administrative assistant in Rockland County, New York, the lecturer, the lover, the wife.

This was your identity, far more demonstrable an indicator of the essence of you, as I and you recognised it, than any supposed "soul" underlying and propping up the mass of your sensations and thoughts. By means of these continuities of memory and thought, you became a person.

And what is a person? Well, for Locke, she or he is "a thinking intelligent being that has reason and reflection, and can consider itself the same thinking thing in different times, which it does only by the consciousness which is inseparable from thinking, and essential to it."

My one and true only love, no longer, so far as we can see, are you intelligent. No longer do you reason or reflect. No longer do you possess consciousness, as we understand consciousness. As Locke would understand the matter then, you are no longer a person. No longer, in any but a grammatical sense, are you *you.*

So, why do the doctors continue to honour the grammar of the third person singular ("Catherine is doing better today"), I wonder. And why do I persist in addressing you by employing the second person? Is it pure etiquette that constrains us from writing you off as a mere organism, or is it something else?

Last week, in our deliberations concerning your future, our scientifically educated son fell back on the notion of your soul. On the face of it, this was a rather unempirical stance to adopt. As Locke would have insisted, a soul cannot experimentally be located, or even defined. Locke himself was fairly indifferent to the notion of soul, so integral to the Christian faith and to several other religious systems, and he was dismissive of the immateriality of the self. For him, the empiricist and Enlightenment Christian, were you to survive your predicted death to be recreated in a condition of eternity, you would be provided with another, differently constituted body, onto which would be grafted the complex of thoughts, feelings and memories whom I have loved so long. You would become a sort of photocopy of yourself, taken from the document located here on earth.

The doctors seem not to think like this. For them, from a moral and practical perspective, you are still a person, with a person's rights to dignity and respectful address. The nurses ask your permission before they turn you. From whence do they derive this etiquette and this loving respect? Truly, I do not know.

At this point in the discussion, I become quite angry with Locke, through mere puzzlement. If thoughts are located in bodies, and if your body is here while your thoughts - indeed your entire personality - have evaporated, where does that leave the notion of the materiality of the soul? And if the soul is material, where is yours now, since it appears not to exist in that private room beyond the corridor in which we sit, worrying over these possibilities? Is your soul, as it were, held in suspense?

*

As we think these problems through, a familiar figure floats into sight: Dr McIvor in severe medical mode, walking slowly and looking straight ahead. We flag her down, and myopically she recognises us, altering course so as to park her bum on an adjacent seat. When I ask her what she makes of the results from the MRI scan, she looks at us in some confusion as if barely recalling this one case among the many others with which she must deal this busy Monday afternoon. "Have the results come through?" she asks. "I have seen no results. I will go and check at once. Remind me of your wife's name." She stands up and sets off down the side corridor towards the ward.

After a decent interval we follow her. As we reach the nurses' station, we spot her in an office behind, efficiently flicking between bright images on a screen: the magnetic traces of your mind. The first shows a side-section of your head, the whole skull and, within it, a cloudy blob that floats there like a frog-spawn. The second is your skull viewed from behind, with the joint between your spinal column and brain stem clearly visible as a dark nucleus towards the top of the screen. The twenty-three images that follow are taken from the same angle and show the organ that houses what remains of your mind plumbed at different layers of depth. Like a gallery of Surrealist paintings they flash past, one by one. A pebble-shaped eye in the centre of the screen expands to become a bird-like formation, a glider moth with mottled wings and a snout. The wings open and darken. They flow outwards, expanding into a humanoid face, lightly bearded and with a cavity in place of a nose, flutter into a fulsome rainbow span, then separate into the halves of a walnut, dilate into veined marble, close into a compact tangerine, grow testicular cysts which in turn dilate and splay to suggest a Siamese foetus joined at the hip, flatten, sprout butterfly pennants, shrink into mere glares, disappear into convoluted darkness, reappear and shrink again, flood and divagate into traces of blue-black ink, thence into calligraphic squiggles, Egyptian hieroglyphs.

On the next screen, the Siamese twins turn negroid, then hunch themselves into smears, flounder into smoke trails, split and propagate, dance and gyrate, smoulder into spectres, don kimonos and gracefully bow. The central image cluster acquires the annex of a snow drift, then a beak, flattens into sauté potato, opens the tonsils of its throat, boasts a white beard, a meteorological swirl, a cyclone of mist, a gangrenous cyst, a legal bib and tucker morphing into half kiwi. Then a Macedonian helmet smooth as an egg spreads itself into a toaster, squares into a rack, shudders into a sea, opens its eyes, grows startled, stares in fixed alarm, yawns, then sneers, hollas, then jeers, dons Machiavelli's hat, contracts, shrugs, stares bog-faced, takes the huff, takes deeper offence, affects discretion, skips and fades, merges into an amoeba, then into a snow-flake.

A hyena appears followed by a fossil snail, the Sutton Hoo mask cringes to Kubla Khan, to the Buddha, then a rhesus monkey, Madam Butterfly, Darth Veder, then the Time Lord, ET, ET's horse, ET's pet slug, ET's pet mouse, ET asleep, ET alarmed, Munch's *Scream*, Picasso's pain, Chagall's pose, a Micronesian sponge, a tumorous plum, a pomegranate aflame, a solar eclipse, a galaxy afar, the Horseshoe Nebula, an X-rayed liver floating in wax, pendulum of frost, an aerial shot of Everest, an Inca mask, eagle's perch, swarming bee-hive, beacon flames, forests of flame, a swami on his head, half an orange, a graphic cough barely suppressed, a blotting paper sneeze, a chorister's ruff, stained table mat, a wilting badge, beetle juice squash, a Black Hole, a celestial dog, fatsia japonica slightly propped, a cistern of chalk, strata of grey clay, argentine trace, solar flares, Mercator's hemisphere, rippling silks, a worshipper at prayer, a waking chrysalis, a gormless sheep, kidney's disclosed, a sorbet slice, a peacock's egg, a cloacal smudge, maiden's prayer, Spinoza's God, the Holy Ghost, a simmering storm, gherkins in a jar, a cod-piece of sleet, barn dance of snot, an Empress's fan, a papaya slice…

After about ten minutes, Morag emerges from her cubby-hole looking calm. At first she does not see us, until we fall into step with her and tentatively ask, "Is there anything you can tell?"

"Quite a lot."

"Well?"

"Some of it is good news. I had feared that her language centres might have been stroked out, in which case she'd never speak again, nor understand when spoken to. But there's no sign of that. If she'd suffered a haemorrhage in the relevant area, it would immediately have become apparent from a concentrated blotch on the screen. I can now confidently rule that out. But otherwise the damage is fairly extensive. Global means global. The tissue has been affected more or less everywhere."

By this time we are out in the corridor once more. I settle her on the plastic chair next to mine, and continue my interrogation.

"What does this actually mean? In terms of her likely future, that is."

"Prognosis is an approximate art at best, and it's particularly difficult in cases such as this. The brain is a versatile organ with unpredictable powers of recovery. There have been patients in a similar condition who have come back almost completely, but they are very much in the minority, a tiny number. Others get better slowly and gradually re-acquire some of the mental capacity that they had lost. In any case, it's a very long haul. She'll have to go into a nursing home for an indeterminate period. It could be six months, but is more likely to stretch into one or even two years…"

"And…?"

"It's very, very expensive."

"I don't mean that."

"Professor Fraser, I am no prophet. All I can say is that, if you get the right sort of placement, then at least we're giving her a chance. How obstinate is she?"

"How what?"

"Is she stubborn at all?"

"She never went to the doctor if she could help it. That's partly why we're in this mess in the first place."

"Good. I suspected as much."

"But doesn't that mean that she'll resist treatment?"

"Quite the contrary. She's a fighter. So she'll fight to recover her strength if she can. It's the tenacious ones who come through in the end."

I am staring at the linoleum floor as she says this. Then bravely I raise my eyes and ask "So where does this leave us?"

"In an area of uncertainty, perhaps of hope, perhaps of trust. You are in for a very long ordeal, I'm afraid. There are no short cuts, and the outcome is very far from being clear at this stage. It may become clearer later on, but I can't shed much light on that right now. In six months we may be in a better position to tell. I said *may.*"

I think for a few moments, glance back towards our son, and ask. "And what's the best we can hope for?"

"Nothing is probable but, then again, nothing is absolutely impossible."

"It is possible that I may talk to her again? That she might somehow communicate?"

She pauses, looks at me in the eyes and says, very slowly "To some degree perhaps. Yes, it is not totally impossible."

Suddenly my gratitude for this hypothetical reassurance grows rhapsodic. Clumsily I lurch forward in my chair, gather her in my arms, and give Dr McIvor a kiss on her left cheek. It is the first time I have kissed a neurologist. She is thin to the touch. She rises to her feet and says "I must be on my way. It's almost half past five, nearly the end of my shift. And I've other patients to see."

I'm still seated, so she looks down at me as she says, "I've looked at you on your website".

"And I've looked at yours."

Mutual respect is sometimes akin to mutual affection. She walks onwards down the corridor, looks back over her shoulder and repeats "It's going to be a long trial of strength. I'm sorry for your loss."

I look after her retreating form and say "We haven't lost her."

"It's still a loss." Then the neurologist lady has gone.

11 THE WELSH WOUND

For you and your people, language – that which you have now lost – was everything. How am I to explain this to the doctors: not simply a neurological, but a political maiming?

Just as Porth led to the valley, so language had its portal in instruction. Every morning of the school year at around eight-thirty, at the junction between Cemetery Road and Mount Pleasant Road, a bus would arrive from the lower town and disgorge the elements of the social geography of the municipality. They were called "Snobs", "Sardines" and "Toads", and between these three groups existed something like war. The heart of the Rhondda was its mining industry; its soul was its schools. The Snobs were those who at eleven had passed a public exam admitting them to the uppermost rung of the local system: the segregated county grammar school. The Sardines were the tiddlers who had not passed quite as well. Well enough, however, to swim into the co-educational secondary grammar school that lay at the other end of the same street. The Toads were the rejects banished to the Secondary Modern School further down the slope.

Your childhood was bounded by these divisions, since the two grammar schools stood at opposite ends of Grawen Street. You had no need to take the bus. Your father taught at the co-educational two grammar school at the Eastern extremity of the road, and in 1953 when you took the eleven plus you performed well enough to gain admittance to Porth County Girls. Three years later, in 1956, your diary is full of exam results, and school routine broken only by visits to the cinema and Sunday attendances at Bethlehem

Chapel with Gill. The films include most of the box office hits of the period: "A Star is Born" you saw in April, "The Road to Denver" in June, and "The Desperate Hours" in October. You ranked them respectively as "Good", "V. Good" and, most damning of all "Not bad".

You were for ever telling me about the films. The reactions that stuck in your mind, though, were those of cinema audiences of that time and place to something shown between features: the Pathé Newsreels. If all visited the chapel, few then had televisions. During the elections of 1945, 1950 and 1951 a principal source of political information had been weekly visits to the flicks. In the teeth of the ubiquitous socialism of the valley communities, all three were contested by the Conservative Party under Winston Churchill. Churchill would never have dared show his face in the towns of the Rhondda, where at each election the Conservative candidate invariably lost his deposit. Even Cardiff, when he attended the hustings in 1950, he was met with such a barrage of opposition that he was forced to interrupt his speech to justify his earlier political career. In the cinemas of Porth, his reputations as Hitler's victorious foe and the champion of the free world were powerless to save him. The appearance of his jocular black-and-white image striding onto the screen was met by hissing and catcalls, bespeaking a sense of outraged undimmed since the dark days of November 1910.

What had happened in that distant month was perhaps less significant than what was supposed to have happened. It is the latter version, bolstered by seventy years of collective indignation, that you have always related to me: a version unquestioned and unquestionable: a perpetually stoked occasion of patriotic offence. What does your birth certificate read? "Born Llwynyria, Glamorgan, October 2nd, 1942?" What is Llwyneria but the site of the Rhondda's only maternity wing, and the site of the last colliery to remain open and almost operational during the Miners' Strike of late 1910.

The pit had been sunk in 1863; ten years later it was taken over by the Glamorgan Coal Company, later merged into the Cambrian Combine Company. That autumn the Combine, having accused the workers at a newly opened seam of purposeful malignancy and reduced productivity, was in open dispute with the South Wales Miners' Federation. On November 1st, the Federation ballotted its membership; 12,000 men downed tools.

On November 8th the striking miners had picketed the Llywnyria mine to prevent strike breakers entering it. That night, the pump house was attacked. The management, who claimed to be concerned about the effects of the cessation of the pump on the mine horses below, appealed to Asquith's Liberal Government, and requested troops. The matter was brought to the attention of Home Secretary Churchill, who had earlier deserted the Conservatives in protest against tariff restrictions. Churchill, it appears, had demurred. In 1950, as Leader of the Opposition against Attlee's post-war Labour government, he was to tell the voters of Cardiff that he had harboured a secret sympathy with the miners. At length he had dispatched to South Wales a detachment of the Metropolitan Police, together with a squadron of the 18th Hussars, telling the latter to stop short at Cardiff.

In the early hours of the 8th, a demonstration at Tonypandy was dispersed by local police employing truncheons. The following day, the police being felt unequal to the task, an order was sent to Cardiff that the cavalry should assist. They arrived at Pontypridd on the evening of the 9th, and in nearby Porth they found a riot in progress, which they contained for several hours until the Metropolitan Police could relieve them. Not a shot was fired, not one fatality was recorded. But 500 demonstrators and several bystanders received treatment for injuries great and small, and a widespread impression was created that the intervention had delayed negotiations with the employers, and thus a favourable solution to the conflict. For better or worse, Churchill stood condemned. On the one side, the *Times*, who had got wind of his restraining order on the hussars, had thundered "The vacillation shown by those who are responsible for the absence of troops during the present crisis cannot easily be excused." On the other, popular opinion painted him in lurid colours as the Castlereagh of the hour, the instigator of a twentieth-century Peterloo Massacre, the callous military demagogue, the mower-down of the hungry and the helpless.

In vain did I argue the respective merits of these two opinions. In September 1965, when the bogeyman of Tonypandy passed away, you had joined your fellow students in the bar of the London School of Economics in carousing at his demise. You were not going to entertain doubts about the appropriateness of such celebration with me. In May 1984, eighteen months after I moved into your tiny one-bedroom flat, the Tory government of the day announced an end to mining subsidies that had been honoured since Attlee's day, and a phased closure of 200 pits in Yorkshire, Nottinghamshire and the Rhondda. It was opposed by the National Union of Mineworkers and, once again, the police were brought in. In South Wales, where support for the resulting strike was almost universal, memories of 1910 were still livid among the grandchildren of those whose heads had been bruised in your birthplace of Llwynyria. Thatcher, the bulldog of the moment, was cast into the role of a latter-day Churchill, her assumed and elocutionist-acquired gruffness proof of her tendency and her provenance. The newspaper cartoons of the day endorsed the likeness.

You sat in front of our colour television in a state of anamnesis and scurrilous rage. Your father Jo had been an honoured teacher, later a Headmaster, in the Valleys. A plumber's son from Barry, as a young man he had gone to work in the pits. Like Lawrence, therefore, you were a miner's child. Never did you forget it. Can I restore in the telling what cerebral accident has wiped clean: the private history that which, after loving, you would convey to me through the small hours? How much of it, I have sometimes wondered, was true? What is accuracy? What is history? Had Jo Birkett really been the last employee after the General Strike of 1926, to make his peace with the employers? Had he ceased his protest only when the Union offered him the peace-offering of an academic scholarship to Ruskin College in Oxford, where he was to study Economics? Had he commuted this bursary to a place at Cardiff University, where he was the first of his erudite family to gain a degree? The remainder of the story at least was in the public domain: his successive junior posts in South Wales, his marriage to

Catherine Ishmael, a miner's daughter, his involvement with the Labour and Co-operative movements, his familiarity with local socialist politicians, his three children. As you narrated them, certain episodes possessed the uncertain power of myth. In the eleven-plus examination of 1946, the second to be held, his son Peter had come top of the entire Rhondda valley. Jo, then a teacher in the lesser of the town's two grammar schools, refused what his son was later to consider to have been his right, a place in the more prestigious establishment down the road. His son would go to the co-educational Port Sec., where he himself taught. A Pyrrhic victory was won.

Pride of that understated sort was a seam running through your temperament. You and your generation were caught between the three paradigms of hierarchy, meritocracy and a gut-felt egalitarianism. Your father's ploy was to interpret the second in the light of the third so as to evade any suspicion of complicity with the first. You saw him as a champion of authenticity and decent achievement in the face privileges to which the *crachach* clung.

In 1956, aged twenty-two, Peter, who had just qualified as a doctor, wrote a story called "The Last Wood" about a retired miner who took solace in the activities of the local bowls club. He submitted it to the BBC in Cardiff, who broadcast it in October. It was a Monday evening, and you were form captain. After school the whole family deserted the temperamental radio set in Grawen Street and took the bus down to Pontypridd, to the house of your Uncle Ambrose – owner of a chain of optician's shops and a freemason - who possessed, not merely a Rover car, but a wireless set that dependably worked. The miracle of your brother's prose poured forth. "Peter's story on", your diary for that day reads. "We went."

As ever afterwards, you were to tell me. Father and brother, they were masters of instruction, and hence masters of language. In the Senate of political and educational justice, silver-tongued Etruscans putting the Patricians to temporary shame.

12 CASWELL BAY

Tuesday, November 12th

When we arrive in the morning, there is a message from the palliative consultant Debbie Swann saying that she and a group of colleagues would like to see us. We are led into a side room the size of a reasonably proportioned gym, around the walls of which I recognise Doctors Padmanabha and Swann, plus a junior doctor in spectacles called Anna Cobb, and a couple of nurses. Dr Swann is in charge and asks us how much we have been told. This is about the fourth time this question has been put to us. We recite the order of events as we have understood them, culminating with our conversation in the corridor with Dr McIvor. Debbie confirms that the emphasis has changed in the official neurological diagnosis. As a matter of fact, the nursing staff have already begun to notice a change. You are somewhat more responsive when turned, and there has been an increase in your eye movement. As a result of both of these developments, your feeding has been restored by means of the PEG tube. My signing of the form indicated that I was aware of the minor risks involved in this procedure, though this did not amount to an official granting of permission, since in the light of an absence of any power of attorney, I am in no position to direct what is to happen in this regard or not. From now on, you will be monitored while funding is applied for to finance your care in a nursing home of our choice. If the ward sisters word this correctly, certifying your complete helplessness, the likelihood is that you will be granted Continuing Care, meaning that the entire cost will be met, with no contribution from us. We are asked if we have any questions and reply that we have none.

In the afternoon I dispatch to the family a round-robin email of wild jubilation and worrying disingenuousness. It says what it means, but it does not exactly mean what it says:

> Spent part of yesterday going through the MRI results with Megan McIvor, the neurologist who was our second opinion. The long and the short of it is that, while there has been some generalised swelling and then shrinkage of the brain, there has been comparatively little damage to local centres that control specific functions. No thromboses or strokes as such occurred during the process. In particular "she has not stroked out her language centres" so that her ability to communicate is likely to be unimpaired. Prognosis is an inexact art, but it looks as if there might be a return to something approaching normality in six months to a year.
>
> We have seen a distinct if undramatic improvement in Catherine in the last few days. Though most sedation has now been withdrawn, there has been no return to fitting or shaking. Her breathing, heartbeat and blood pressure are all stable and constant. She now opens her eyes a lot, especially when her name is called. She looks around the room a lot, and responds to stimuli such as noise, caresses and the like. Since they started re-feeding her she has plumped out and looks tremendously well. Her skin is as lovely as ever and has a healthy

> sheen. She is yet to comment on Northanger Abbey, but I am sure she has been enjoying it.
>
> On the basis of all of which we have now had a plenary meeting, fully minuted, with two consultants, the registrar and several junior doctors and the matron and sister from the ward. A full plan has been put in place to restore her to health, featuring the temporary insertion of a PEG in her stomach through which nutrition and vital drugs are administered. They expect to have her on the ward for a few weeks, after which continuous nursing care will be provided. We are there every day. It looks as if Catherine is coming through.

I have doubled the number of consultants, trebled the total of registrars, and quadrupled the number of nurses. The optimism conveyed is calculatedly wild. Apart from its understandable but self-important hyperbole, like all communications these words moreover are partly text, and partly sub-text. The surface says "Rejoice. She is given back to us – if very slowly." The troubled depths read; "I have been torn on a bed of nails of anxiety and now, just for an instant, I am relieved of my pain. I have been fed hope, albeit possibly a false hope. I need this hope to sustain my sanity and self-respect." More sinister, and deeper down still, a sub-sub text runs "This mood, and these slight possibilities, are the fruit of brief decisiveness. I have taken this step, and there is no going back. Retreat, you counsellors of doom, you harbingers of difficult mercy. Ultimately I cannot speak for you, or be controlled by your consensus. She is mine, even if she does not want to be." In other words, this is a none-too-subtle rejoinder to helpful interventions from afar, and its bold but inconvenient message reads 'Shove off!"

Robert bach, why are you trying to save me?

Because, I now realise, I need you after all.

I never doubted that you needed me. Far more, we used to agree, than I needed you. Though, of course, I did need you. Remember your definition of a home. It ran "Where you are."

Where are you now, Catherine cariad?

Where do you think I am?

I think at the moment that you are nowhere. So now I have no home? Answer me.

Robert, are you going through this charade just because you wish to hang on to the illusion of a place where you will always belong? I cannot help you. I cannot help you.

Wednesday, November 13th

Too late perhaps, the thought occurs to me that two weeks ago the authorities on this ward presented us with a compassionate opportunity to end your life while keeping well within the bounds of what we might feel to be in your best interests, and a sense of that purpose as enshrined within the law. For a matter of a few days, the re-insertion of your naso gastric tube appeared more likely to shorten your life than to extend it. Bearing in mind their and our shared understanding that your life was slowly ebbing away in any case, whatever we did or did not do, it seemed expeditious as well as kind to ensure that eventual escape whilst appearing to avoid it. The official, declared intention behind that now forestalled action was not to kill you, since any such eventual effect would have been a by-product of an intervention aimed at sparing you temporary discomfort, and preventing your more immediate decease. We would have killed you as it were by accident, whilst acting to avoid you suffering or perishing during an unwelcome and unnecessarily procedure aimed at extending your life.

These alternatives were never exactly spelled out, at least in my hearing, though the doctors may well have discussed them between themselves. They amount to an application of what is known in ethical philosophy as the Doctrine of Double Effect, as set out by Saint Thomas Aquinas in his *Summa Theologiae.* "Nothing," declares the Angelic Doctor, "hinders one act from having two effects, only one of which is intended, while the other is beside the intention. Now moral acts take their species according to what is intended, and not according to what is beside the intention, since this is accidental." If we had, as tacitly invited, walked through the window of ethical opportunity presented to us by these concerned health professionals, we would not therefore have borne the responsibilities pertaining to murderers, or even those applying to mercy killers. Considered from the point of view of intention, their consciences and ours would have every reason to remain clear. We knew this, and the doctors knew that we knew it. At no point, however, was anything said about the matter on either side. The moral implications of this most thorny of moral dilemmas wrestled themselves out in a condition of discreet, mutually respectful, and characteristically British, silence.

Thursday, November 14th

For the last three years I have been working with colleagues on the official *History of the Oxford University Press,* an immense and copiously documented account that will eventually stretch to four fat volumes. The History, which – unhelpfully perhaps from the point of view of its purported objectivity, has been published by the Press itself - begins with its foundation in 1478 and continues almost to the present day. The first three volumes, taking the story up to 1970, the year of the Warnock Commission, are to be launched tonight at a reception in Great Clarendon Street. I have researched and written one hefty chapter on the distribution of the Press's books overseas in the nineteenth century – that is prior to the establishment of its many worldwide branches – and an equally substantial, but I hope not ponderous, one on textbook production up to 1970. In order to prepare myself, I have spent much of the last few years toiling in the bowels of the earth in the Press's underground archives, which are labyrinthine, dusty and not especially well lit. Altogether I feel a need to celebrate the results of all this application, and a much more primitive need for some sort of personal acknowledgment. Besides, it will give me a break from this interminable vigil and a breath of fresh air on the way. I have already indicated my determination to attend.

I have already decided to spend the morning with you, and then to dash away to take the Oxford Tube, the coach link to the Gloucester Green terminus in Oxford, in time for the six o'clock start. "Speeches," reads the invitation ominously, "begin at six thirty." But when I arrive at the hospital at ten o'clock you are wheezing down on the bed, essentially quiet but with intermittent episodes of disturbed movement during which you seem more than usually distressed. I sit quietly by your side watching the hours slip by, anxiously considering my options. With me I have the invitation card for the launch event with an extension number to ring in case of any change of plan. With each passing hour I defer my departure. The coach will take one and a half hours, and I will need a further hour comfortably to reach the coach stop at Victoria. As lunch time approaches I rise to my feet, bid you farewell with a kiss to the forehead, and make for the stairs. Once out in the hospital grounds I had intended to walk along the London Road towards the station. Instead I take a walking tour of the forecourt, and double back again to the ward. Once more I am staring down at you, attracted by a force field of love and compassion that I am powerless to resist. I have postponed my decision for a further hour. As the hour hand of my wristwatch reaches three, I rise to my feet again, and once more wish your farewell. I have deserved this break, I need it, and time is running short. Once more I am out in the forecourt, and about to debouch into the long and featureless main road. Instead, I stop by the boundary hedge, take out my mobile phone and contact the extension given and express my apologies. The well-bred voice of Kate Farquhar-Thomson from the other end expresses her regrets, but does not quite seem to know who I am. Now, for the third time I am staring down at you with a mixture of pride, love, resentment and relief. I stay there motionless for three or four minutes, and then whisper in the stillness of this room empty apart from the two of us "I will never let you down."

A vigil is a process of ethical waiting. It is a condition simply of being with: nonsensical in practical terms – except to those who wait, but very far from being meaningless. It is a way of saying we care, but its significance stretches way beyond that, since it is an act of witness to the moral importance of the you whom we wait upon. Even though you are unconscious, drugged, sedated, gently or not so gently snoring, hair matted though combed, your mouth open revealing teeth in poor repair as you lie between the crisp white sheets provided, clad in the patterned pale blue of an institutional nightgown, your legs shapeless in their anti-embolism stockings.

Vigilamus quia absurdum est.
Expectamus quia absurdum est.

Friday, November 15th

I 'phone Mary Hammond, a colleague from Southampton University who has written the chapter in volume two of the History on the Press's London Office. I ask her how the reception went. She sighs and says "What do you think? A lot of old men making self-congratulatory speeches." I am gratified to hear this, albeit predicable, news. Perhaps I have not missed so much after all. There will be plenty of occasions for chattering once the reviews are in, if - that is - so tedious and minority a publication actually attracts any reviews. Not for the first time I have preferred your silence to the wittering of the sages, and not for the first time, it seems, I was right. The application for continuing heath care, I gather, has now been sent off.

Monday, November 18th

What station do we play you on your new digital radio? At home it was always BBC Radio Four with its hourly news bulletins, its chatty magazine programmes, the anachronistically named Woman's Hour, the daily episodes of the Archers in their imagined, non-existent rural Midlands haven. Would the familiarity bring you back to yourself? We try it for a few hours, before the irrelevance of speech to an aphasic such as you currently are comes to seem too cruel. So we desist, and try my daily pabulum of Radio Three with its educated diet of classical music for the informed, until we recall the stark fact that in reality you hated it, perhaps because I so loved it. So we have settled for an evening of Classic FM with its cherry bowl of musical trifles, fruit picked from the stem and palliatively presented for those with weak cultural stomachs. In truth, you hated this too, but mainly because of the adverts, and because the station brazenly announced itself every few seconds. But the tunes are good and strong: perhaps the brain will be stirred by them at a level beyond, or below, the formation of words.

Every evening at eight they have something called a "whole works concert", as if it was unusual – or even something of an achievement - to play a whole work through from beginning to end. Tonight it is Haydn's Second 'Cello Concerto, a revelation to me because I only thought he ever wrote one, and I can vividly recall the fuss attending the discovery of that in 1968, and Mstislav

Rostropovich premiering it a few months later. The recording today is by the London Symphony Orchestra, in whose chorus I used to sing, under the baton on John Barbirolli. The soloist is the youthful, feted and fated, Jacqueline du Pré.

Barbirolli brings back memories of deserting you for the Bridgewater Hall ceremony last month. But Du Pré takes me much further back, to an evening in the Barbican concert hall in around 1984. I was sitting in the stalls in my dinner jacket because we of the London Symphony Chorus were to sing a Mahler symphony in the second half. Before the interval there was to be a performance of the Elgar cello concerto, performed as a come-back by the leader of the LSO's cello section who several months before had suffered a disabling stroke. That night he was to be the soloist, his effortless execution of this well- known but demanding work designed to demonstrate his full recovery, and his fitness once again to assume the leader's chair. But a few bars into the opening Movement he attempted the first of his virtuoso runs, and disastrously miscalculated his position on the finger board. He winced and swooped awkwardly back to the right note. At that moment I happened to look behind me, and notice that against the back wall of the stalls a large wheel chair parked, its chrome glistening under the arc lights. Perched on the seat was a miniature animal, hunched and attentive. At first I took it for a monkey, before I looked once more and dimly recognised on its distorted features the likeness of the once imperious Du Pré, come now to express her solidarity with another of the afflicted, and cruelly greeted with one more symptom of debilitation and distress. In the interval, I queued at the backstage bar and overheard one of the other basses declare, as he stood waiting and staring into existential nothingness, "I can never listen to the Elgar again without thinking of human pain."

Thursday, November 21st

For the last three Sundays we have been invited to Sunday dinner at the Purley flat of your friend and former colleague Dilys Bullivant. This week instead she proposes we eat mid-week at the excellent restaurant staffed by the catering students of Croydon College. She meets us at the hospital at six, and we catch the bus into central Croydon. As we make our way towards our table, my eye is drawn to a middle-aged white supervisor who is addressing a uniformed black waiter, clearly one of the younger students, in deaf and dumb language. There is a sheer attentiveness, a palpable concern and a gentleness of courtesy in the way she does this that I find intensely moving. The vulnerability of the waiter, his pride in his role, the studied respect accorded to him by the supervisor, all speak of a culture of mutual support and a sort of sustained humility that put the pretensions of fashionable London, the London of the media and the smart and exclusive clubs, to shame. Chastened by this sight, I take my seat with the others and order Guinea Fowl and Spiced Cabbage. As we chat about everything apart from you, I am suddenly and irrationally seized by gratitude for the mere fact of your survival, the thought that as we sit inanely gossiping, you are slumbering gently back in the stillness of ward. I am illogically glad that you are alive. The food takes about an hour to come – punctuality seems to be a low priority hereabouts – and about twenty minutes before it arrives we are joined by a male friend of Dilys's, a book illustrator and designer who has a second home, at which they frequently stay, on Mull. Shortly after the dessert arrives, the talk veers dangerously towards politics. Stuck for something to say, I ask him who in his opinion has been the greatest Prime Minister of his lifetime. He instantly counters by asking "Who's been yours?" I don't have to think long before mentioning that old labour warrior Harold Wilson, and add that it is a matter of some personal pride to me that my office is in something called the Wilson Building, and that Sir Harold not merely founded but conceived of the institution for which I work, sketching the first idea for a "University of the Air" on the back of a brown paper envelope in the interval between Easter Sunday matins and lunch in the town on the Scilly islands where he took his holidays. I should have known what was coming. Dylis's friend listened to me with supercilious and studied scepticism before declaring that in his opinion the only Premier since the war worthy of complete, unqualified approval was Margaret Thatcher, and listing her many achievements: the re-building of the British economy, the smashing of the trades unions, the Falklands war, etc., etc. Unable to take this reactionary nonsense for more than a couple of minutes, I butt in with a diatribe against the assault mounted on the mining industries of South Yorkshire, Derbyshire and South Wales, my bile rising as I discourse on the fatal insult offered not simply to particular industries and local economies, but to whole communities and ways of life. He will have none of it. "They had to go," he confidently asserts, "they had to give way before something more sustainable." When I call to his attention that what has actually supplanted the mining society in which you grew up has been a pervasive condition of near-total unemployment, a culture of welfare dependency and general despair, he retorts that anyone of spirit and initiative caught in that particular quagmire would leave, or else seek alternative modes of employment. The mere fact that anybody has stayed on to draw their benefits rather than clearing out and making their fortunes elsewhere is proof positive that Thatcher's victims received their just deserts as members of a sub-class of the spineless. Suddenly I lose patience and start shouting, as diners on adjacent tables look on. I am not simply defending the culture of the valleys: I am defending you and your people, those on the receiving end of history, the wretched of the earth, the powerless and unglamorous: the deaf and dumb black waiter- student, the ill-paid nurses back at the hospital, all those who receive little but of which much is expected. I end near to tears as we receive our modest bill. Answer me, you can now answer nobody: have I defended you well?

Friday, November 22nd

Today the ward sister informed us that you have been awarded Continuing Health Care by the local NHS panel. That we have achieved this result it a great tribute to the nursing staff on this ward who have spent the last week filling in a complicated application form with very many sections specifying the exact severity of every aspect of your impairment. The award covers every aspect of your treatment and care, your residence in an approved nursing home, your food, your medicines. We will be asked to select a home from a list that the local health authority will provide. The list covers this and two adjoining boroughs. We have three days in which to make our choice. Once we have done so, and a room becomes available, you will be transferred there by ambulance, and responsibility for your treatment will be handed over to a GP in the vicinity of the home. We will be able to visit as much as we like. After six months your case will be reviewed by a visiting team of doctors. Thereafter, it will be reviewed annually. As long as the panel is convinced of your total dependency, the funding will be continued at the present level. Should your condition markedly improve, the funding will be systematically decreased by degrees. Should you ever reach the point at which you are responding to rehabilitation, should you for example prove to be capable of following and obeying verbal instructions, some of the responsibility for your funding will be gradually handed over to the Social Services, who will eventually meet half of the bill. When this occurs, the element in the award that comes under the remit of the council will be means tested, placing us as your carers in a precarious position. As Debbie Swann had already explained, this is unlikely to happen for some time, if it happens at all. We have nothing to worry about in the short term.

In the afternoon we have meeting with Jasmine, the discharge nurse. She hands us a list of homes in each of the two boroughs that lie within easy reach of our house. Most are unknown to us, though we notice that two are within walking distance. One name stands out. The Lakeside home is at the bottom of the hill leading down from our home on the lip of the North Downs. For the last twenty Christmas Eves, I have sung carols there. On every occasion I have been struck by the attentiveness and visible compassion shown by the staff, both towards the residents and towards us. It is scruffy and under-funded. The wallpaper, as I remember it, could do with replacing. On the other hand, there is an abundance of concern that must be fairly rare within this much traduced sector. In the evening, we phone them up and make an appointment to visit.

Saturday, November 23rd

We have given ourselves a choice of nursing homes. The first is just across the neighbourhood park next to a recreational ground close to our home. Before visiting it, we check on its website, which looks fairly promising. It is, we are informed, "one of eleven care homes operated by the dynamic Abbey Total Care Group." Despite, or because of this, they are "a family run business operating in the provision of high quality personal care." The staff, we are further informed, are "friendly and experienced". As carers and relatives "we are welcome to visit at any hour of the day", though presumably not of the night.

The blurb is helpfully phrased, but somehow it gives off a chill. Hard to explain why. I am used to the promotional talk of institutions in the sphere of Higher Education, and perhaps I detect in the enthusiastic vocabulary too many tell-tale signs. "Dynamic" is one of them. Does anybody who is genuinely dynamic, moved to purposeful and energetic action, describe themselves as such? "Business" is another, "high quality" a third. Granted that any organisation that wishes to survive must prove itself solvent, and even put aside a running surplus so as to improve and expand, I do not particularly wish to commit you to a set-up which advertises the profit motive as one of its guiding principles. In higher education "excellence" is too frequently a cover-up for mediocrity; the more run-of-the-mill a college or university, the keener it is to claim this banal badge. "High quality" is a turn of phrase giving rise to much the same suspicion. I would not be surprised on our arrival to find the place closed.

At mid-morning Benjo, his girlfriend Hannah and I dawdle down the side of Sainsbury's to a passage overlooked by barred windows and graffiti where a Farmers' Market in progress. We inspect the plaice and tuna on the fishmonger's stall and decide not to buy any before traipsing through the park, its tarmac path covered by a patina of wet leaves – yellow, brown and hectic red – like the pattern on a William Morris wallpaper. Somebody has constructed climbing frames for the children out of architecturally arranged limbs of wood and car tyres. A middle-aged father is swaying backwards and forwards on a swing, his bundle of a baby on his lap. A pigeon limps backwards and forwards on its one working leg, holding the other in the air like a plea for help. Through a gate and across the road we emerge onto the rectangle of turf known locally as "The Wreck". At one corner stands the home in two converted and gabled Mock Tudor residences overlooking a row of well-kept hedges and a brace of tennis courts. Tall chimneys like those on Richmond Palace crown its two stories, the upper of which is stuccoed with cream-painted pebble dash, the lower of plain red brick. Dog toothing above the double-glazing. Burglar alarms and security flood lights decorating the façade. Three notices read "Vehicles Parked at Owners' Risk." Ravens caw in the bare trees. Altogether, the home has the blank and efficacious stare of a middle manager towards the end of his shift.

Up a flight of three steps we stand between potted plants and ring the doorbell, which burbles like an ailing bird. After five minutes a detached voice speaks through the intercom, inviting us to press and enter. In the Axminster carpeted hallway we are met by the owner, who shakes me by the hand and takes us to a large and well equipped communal area on the ground floor. In the distance male orderlies in green gowns are hoovering the carpets; further on, residents in pyjamas and nighties sit in armchairs around a cavernous common room. I am struck by an atmosphere that appears to resemble the apotheosis of polish. The owner describes the structure of the Care Group. From what we can gather, all eleven homes represent the family concern: this may be the original one, but it has produced several siblings, all of which seems to conform to the same practicable model. They are especially proud of their food, as evidence of which he produces a daily menu with choices and delicacies of every kind. He asks us how we are going to meet the bills. When I mention Continuing Care, his interest perks up. You will be cared for gratis, he assures us, until such a time when your social will equal your medical needs, at which point we will be asked for a smaller or greater contribution, depending on the local council under whom your care will then fall. Our own council, he warns us, is known not to be especially generous: if you own a house, you may well lose it.

I return in a state of deep depression, realising that I have had exactly the same reaction to this well organised and resourced institution that I have to most five-star hotels, which is why I often prefer to say in B and Bs. To me, the whole radiated an air of almost offensive luxury. I just hope that all care homes are not like this.

In the afternoon we visit the Lakeside Nursing home at the bottom of the hill. In the hallway we are met by the smell of cooking. The wallpaper is ill chosen and the paintwork dull and frayed. The duty nurse chats to us for about twenty minutes and shows us round. She remembers our choir. Residents wander to and fro in an atmosphere of protected freedom. The whole place gives off the unmistakeable air of slightly dowdy love, like a pair of well-worn slippers. I immediately decide to send you there.

Monday, November 25th

At long last the rude mechanicals from the Estates department have arrived to mend the faulty lights in your room: the fuse, the bulb. Two genuine dogsbodies complete with an atavistic demarcation dispute. They check the angle-poise in the corner next to your bed, the dud panel in the ceiling but, they sagely inform me, they may not replace what is wanting. He who mends succeeds they who merely check, but even he may not get the lights to work. Tomorrow we will welcome Him, or possibly Her, who ensures all is operational. The following day perchance the Come, O come Emmanuel who actually switches them on. And next week we must leave…

I have told the hospital that we would like you to be admitted to Lakeside as soon as possible. They phone through and find that a room is available on the first floor. We will, however, have to wait a few days while it is redecorated. A member of the staff will call in at the hospital to talk through the future with us tomorrow.

Tuesday, November 26th

This morning we enjoyed a meeting with Harriet, the "Quality Assurance Manager" from Lakeside, a trained nurse who's worked on the medical wards in the Royal Free. Originally, she's from the West of Edinburgh, as her vowels proclaim. German father, mother of Italian extraction. As a result, she tells us, she finds nationality, let alone nationalism, a bit of a farrago, is much exercised by next year's referendum on Scottish independence, and fears that she may wake up on the morning of September 19, 2014, finding she requires a work permit in order to carry on with her rewarding job. She's re-assuring about the home, though she stresses that many of the residents are suffering from Alzheimers: "You realise we are a dementia home." People wander around the corridors, and have to be discouraged from entering strange bedrooms. Just as long as you continue in your present incapacitated condition, she confirms, your care will be fully funded. You will be re-assessed after three months, thereafter at intervals of six. It is not much of a prospect, but at least the huge financial burden we all feared is no more than a distant threat. In view of the nature of the home, would we not, she asks us, like to visit the home once more so as to re-consider our initial impression? I have little doubt about my decision, but tell her that we will call by very briefly tomorrow before confirming arrangements, both with her and with the hospital.

Wednesday, November 27th

Back to the Lakeside, which as before is both tatty and loving. Before setting out, I check on their website. It features some of the buzz words I so distrusted before, but adds the following statement of intent: "All residents are seen as individuals with their own rights, likes and dislikes, dreams and ambitions. We aim to help each individual resident to achieve or sustain whatever it is that puts a smile on their face. This could be from something as simple as helping to fold the napkins for supper to taking them out to their favourite shop for the day."

In addition, they offer something called Namasthe care, so when I arrive I ask what the word means, and of what this particular form of therapy consists. The word, it seems, is a Sanskrit one, and there is something about it that I recognise. When it is explained, my mind goes back to the last day of October when I first recited that Buddhist chant given to me by my friend Elizabeth over your recumbent form: "Nam-myoho-renge-kyo". "Nam", I recall, is a contraction of "Namasthe", and like it, means, roughly speaking "I honour and respect you." It also implies the familiar oriental greeting with joined, supplicatory hands and slightly bowed head, a gesture of acknowledgement, of mutual awe and respect. The term is an ancient one, as is the philosophy underlying it, but its application to dementia care is quite new. Clinically, it seems to correspond both to a set of practices and an attitude. The practices vary with the patient, and range from foot massage to aromatherapy, depending on temperament and need. The attitude is dictated by a determination to venerate the individuality of men and women who sometimes no longer know who they are. It is a way of communicating intimacy and awareness when everything in the medical circumstances of the recipient would appear to militate against it. A way of reinforcing the personality at the extreme edge of dissolution, of applying care, less as part of a pragmatic programme (though that too is present), than as an overwhelming categorical ethical imperative. The greater the impediment, the more severe the impairment, the more the meaning grows and glows, both as obligation and, oddly, as personal fulfilment, even as pleasure. This is no out-of-the-way observation since plenty of people in apparently menial occupations – the lady who once served us on the waterfront at Gavrion on Andros, the taxi driver who during our present ordeal has picked our son and me up daily from our home to bring us here - grasp the essential reality of this. It is at one with the delicacy of an ethically alert life: work as prayer, what the Benedictines used to term the Opus Dei. It is what the Metaphysical poet George Herbert meant to convey in "The Elixir", his poem about the sanctity of work: "He (and I will now add "She") who cleans a room, but for thy sake, Makes that and the action fine."

Now I realise why I chose this home. There is an affinity in this mind-set with an abiding philosophy the clearest twentieth-century exposition of which occurs in Martin Buber's small masterpiece *Ich und Du,* I and Thou. An English translation does him scant justice:

> In the relationships through which we live, the authentic You is innate in the You we actively meet. Confronted as a social being in all its uniqueness, each of us can be addressed by this

> ultimate and basic word, a "Thou" earthed in the essential and *a priori* nature of every encounter.

In other words, basic to all human relationships worthy of the name is a recognition of the utter, irreducible unrepeatable character of each and every person. We neglect this at our peril; we honour it even when every outer sign of it has been obliterated. It is the most fundamental essence that there is, and it is foundation of every cogent moral system. I and Thou; Thou and I. This is the Thou, my darling, whom in you I continue to address.

Thursday November 28th

When we arrived back at the hospital this morning, we were told that a consultant called Dr Loke wished to speak to us. He took us to the large side-room in which our earlier conference with Debbie Swann and her team took place. Loke is of Asian extraction, in his mid-thirties perhaps, polite, knowledgeable, and an expert on chests. He told us that yesterday they X-rayed you and found a nodule on one of your lungs. A tiny nodule, a miniscule nodule, almost negligible, no more than a cubic millimetre in size. Under normal circumstances, had you been a different kind of patient, a patient in a less extreme position, they would have investigated further, perhaps taken a biopsy to the lab, maybe – had the specimen proved malignant - operated to remove the lump. As it is, they are faced with a decision based on a calculation of probabilities. They have to calculate the likelihood of somebody in your condition outliving the period over which, should the lung be cancerous, the disease might be expected to develop. On the whole, they consider the likelihood to be small. They have therefore decided to do nothing. When you are transferred to the care home, they will leave instructions to this effect.

I was struck by the mildness of Loke's manner, and the lucidity of his exposition, so I decided to take him into my confidence, air some of my difficulties, and some of our dilemmas. I took him back to the week in late October when it seemed to us that you were being starved to death. We are still not sure of the medical background to this crisis, and the nature and logic of the decisions then taken on your behalf. Nor are we sure just how much effect our minimal intervention had on the outcome.

He had consulted the notes, and gave us the clearest explanation of all these questions that we have had to date. At the moment when your naso gastric feeding tube became blocked, it was felt that to replace it through a difficult intervention in the endoscopy department would have brought forward your decease. Your death in any case was then felt to be imminent as the expected result of the removal of your tracheostomy. In fact, it was confidently expected within a very few days. If they did not replace the tube, you would thus die anyway, but it would not be from the effects of starvation or dehydration. So they waited, you struggled on, and a slightly more optimistic neurological assessment encouraged them to reinstate feeding through a different, more stable and comfortable, route.

Encouraged by the clarity of this summary, I was emboldened to raise some of the ethical and legal dilemmas in which we, and the doctors too, have been placed. At what point might it be legitimate and justifiable, to allow you to die, or to take steps to ensure that result?

He was emphatic in his reply. Whatever may be the case in Belgium, in Switzerland or in a minority of American states, euthanasia as such is always illegal in this country. Watering and feeding comprise normal care. There is, therefore, an obligation to provide it, whether in hospitals or care homes, unless it came to be felt that to supply or to restore it would of itself shorten life. In that case there is a consensus to the effect that it should be withheld. It was on that basis, and with that justification, that the decision on your case was taken last month. Then I asked him about the assent form that I had signed prior to insertion of your PEG in early December. He answered that signing it had not technically amounted to an act of assent. What I was in effect affirming was my awareness of the risks involved in the procedure, presumably to safeguard the interests of the hospital in the unlikely event of the intervention going wrong.

There is nothing in the world to beat clarity. It is all that most relatives ask. Well, it is all that I ask.

When we entered the Oasis Restaurant this afternoon, the whole place had been themed along the lines of The Wizard of Oz. The original Judy Garland film was showing on the screen above the lunchers. Dr Butt was in his usual position at the head of one table, surrounded by admirers and sycophants, and several members of staff had dolled themselves up as characters from the film. Morag McIvor was in the queue just behind us. She asked us how you were doing; I asked her how she fitted into the scenario of the film. She told me she was "the Wicked Witch of the West".

13 MALINOWSKI'S BAND

Masquerades are a folly of the season, but not one of which you were especially fond of - that is - required to perform in them. Spontaneity is a quality you have always valued, but obligation frequently drew your ire, or at least your sullen resistance. A spur of the moment girl, you were taken more by the mood of the moment than by the spirit of an occasion. Was it ever thus?

I was pondering this question this afternoon when an email arrived from Swansea. It was from Professor Margaret Kenna, the Social Anthropologist you failed to visit on Anafi in 1973, and it carried two pictorial attachments. When I opened them, I was confronted with a couple of images of you half a century ago, in or around the year when, according to the poet Philip Larkin, "sexual intercourse began". The first image was taken in early summer and showed a fresh-faced woman in her early twenties lounging on the veranda of a public building in a metal chair with plastic strings. You are looking directly into the camera with your Cheshire cat grin, wearing a floral blouse with a silken neck scarf beneath a dark twin-piece woollen suit, the skirt hem of which rests about an inch above your knees. Your left hand is lightly placed on your head, in a gesture both coy and inviting. Young men on seats in the background strike intellectual poses, as if each fancies himself a Harold Laski in the making. Some of them may seem to be smoking pipes, and all are arguing with a dashing vigour of address. The buildings in the background are in the style of nineteen forties Art Deco. From these hints, I gather the veranda must be that of your Alma Mater, the London School of

Economics. Of one thing there is little doubt: you look, at twenty-one, carefree and unaffectedly happy.

The second picture is taken a little further back on the same veranda, and in it you are dressed identically. I reckon it must have been taken later the same afternoon, and in it you squat on a bench with four fellow students, all of whom apart from yourself are studying Anthropology. You are the only lawyer present. Careless of the pressures of work, you are convulsed in mirth and holding a tray out straight in front of you. To your left, a lanky student called Nick smiles toward you with complicit enjoyment while mock-playing on the cross struts of a plastic crate, as if it's a washboard. To your right, a bespectacled sociologist called Chris strums on the strings of the metal chair which you have apparently just vacated. Margaret is in the middle, smiling wanly into the camera. To the far right, beatific and precociously maternal, stands your best friend, Jan.

You are all imitating a skiffle band of the period, or more accurately of the previous decade. You are not yourself an anthropologist, but the atmosphere of this plucky, seditious band of young students had become essential to your health and wellbeing. And, perhaps as a result of their joint influence, you yourself could write anthropologically.

Back in South Wales that Easter you sent them all a postcard. The front shows a back-and-white photograph of The Square, Porth, touched up with lurid, technicolour paint: a bright red bus, a shop front daubed the same colour and, behind, an artificially emerald slag heap. On the message side you have scrawled in blue biro "The colour on the card doesn't do justice to the place". Then you've added in an unmistakeable tone of mild sarcasm:

> Dear All, Having a super time here in Porth. The weather hasn't been too good but the place is so beautiful it doesn't really matter – there's so much to do here – like pictures, telly, reading law books in Welsh, eating delicious Welsh food like chips + leaks + looking at the historical coal mines + chapels. The natives are very homely + there's no language difficulty. Wish you were here. Love, Cath. P.S. The Truth – ROLL ON NEXT WEEK.

Thus you wrote, mock-anthropologically, a participant observer of your own place and people.

But, as for that spirited band of young musicians, the object of their satire originated half a century previously far, far away from either Wales or London.

Kiriwina is the northernmost district on the island of Boyowa, one of the smallest of the Trobriand group to the northeast of Papua New Guinea. It is so tiny, many charts do not show it, and even Google Maps draw a blank. To find it you have to turn to a text published in that seminal year of the modernist sensibility 1922: the year of Virginia Woolf's novel *Jacob's Room,* of James Joyce's *Ulysses,* of the first abridgement of Sir James Frazer's influential classic *The Golden Bough,* and of T. S. Eliot's gloomy poem *The Waste Land.* 1922 also, however, saw the appearance of a sober ethnographic monograph called *Argonauts of the Western Pacific,* on page 51 of which is a map of this obscure island. In 1917 it had been visited by its author, a Polish gentleman then thirty-three years of age, a gentleman serious, bespectacled and balding. Bronislaw Malinowski had come to Papua in search of a subject on which to write. Before the war he had been attracted to the newish subject of Social Anthropology, and had studied patterns of economic exchange among the Australian aborigines at your very own LSE. He had travelled to Australia in the company of the Oxford ethnographer, Robert Marett. When the following year the First World War broke out, he found himself trapped. As an Austrian citizen, he could not travel back to England without being interned as an enemy alien. He had chosen to stay in Australia, and to accept a bursary from the government to conduct a close study of the social and economic lives of the Trobrianders.

Malinowski saw himself as a pioneer, a new broom in the social sciences. His book begins with a stout defence of ethnography's right to be considered a science on a par with chemistry and physics. He was fed up with his academic forebears like the aforementioned J. G. Frazer. "The time when we could tolerate accounts presenting the natives as a distorted, childish character of a human being," he confidently asserts, "are gone. This picture is false, and like many other falsehoods it has been killed by science." As if to prove his point, his book contained a witnessed account of the people of the islands, among whom he had spent four years. There were photographs to prove it. In one of them, taken in 1918, he is sitting on a two-bar wooden fence flanked by near naked male islanders, two to each side. All of the men are holding one-string gourd guitars which they balance on their knees. Malinowski, dressed in standard

European's tropical kit of white linen and spats, is looking posed and self-conscious, with his face slightly averted from the camera. He too is attempting to play a one-string gourd guitar. The islanders, who are gazing at us rather than at him, are looking bored.

Malinowski went on to become the founder of the LSE's department of anthropology, then among the most illustrious in the world. It was because of this scholar, and the tradition of field work he passed on, that by the mid nineteen sixties so many bright young people had been attracted to London to read his subject at this particular School. Several of them numbered among your closest friends. It was Malinowski's methods and views, by and large, that they absorbed there.

In 1962, Malinowski's private diaries, written in the antipodes, were published, showing him to have been neurotic, heath-obsessed, mother-fixated and controlling. Nonetheless, in 1963 a room in the LSE was named after him, a study room on the first floor of the building, placed at the disposal of students of his subject. This room had a bookcase, on an upper shelf of which lay a reproduction of that photograph of Malinowski with that band of Trobriand Island musicians. Reproduced in several of his biographies, nowadays the picture seems quaint, mainly owing to a shift in – and confusion between - historical perspectives. The attitude and the content of the image partake of a kind of oldness presenting itself a kind of newness. The instruments being played were among the oldest and simplest on the planet. We cannot hear what style of music they were performing, but it is a fair guess it was something which, in terms of musical history, far preceded, say, a Haydn string quartet. It was a very ancient kind of music indeed. What in

1922 seemed new about the performance silently presented in that photograph was the proto-pop line-up of the instruments. By 1964, when you and your fellow student satirists were hamming up your mock performance on the roof of the LSE, this was no longer the case. You were children of the Second World War. It was the music of the war and the years immediately following it that you had ringing in your ears, rather than the gourd instruments of the Trobrianders, a Haydn quartet. You had grown up listening to shellac recordings of jazz, skiffle, and the crooning of Bing Crosby. Even now, Margaret can perform a fair imitation of Motown. Seen in such a light, Malinowski had been another kind of pioneer, not merely of social science, but of rock music as well. When you were all searching around for a caption for this iconic image, you adapted the refrain from one of Crosby's greatest hits, issued in the year of the Armistice. The song was named "MacNamara's Band".

So, what were you all singing on that afternoon in 1964? Your song, you told me, ran:

> Oh, me name is Malinowski, I'm the leader of the band
> Although we're few in numbers, we're the finest in the land
> We play at wakes and weddings and at every fancy ball
> And when we play the funerals, we play the March from Saul…

ANTHROPOLOGY AND SATIRE: *Above,* Bronislaw Malinowski and a group of local musicians in the Trobriand Islands in 1917; *Below,* Catherine and a group of fellow LSE students satirizing the above, on the roof of the London School of Economics in 1964.

Malinowski, of course, had been real enough unlike the MacNamara and his men, or so I had always thought, until you put me right. In fact MacNamara's men had been brothers from Limerick, two of whom had settled in the United States in the early years of the twentieth century, and formed a quintet, then a trio, hiring themselves out for ceilidhs, weddings and funerals. Crosby's hit tune, first aired in a movie in the last year of the war, had just the kind of bouncy jollity to which you personally always responded, even if you preferred the Beach Boys. Your performance was a spirited jape. But jokes lay couched within jokes, since what could have been further from Bing's chirpy melody than the stately dirge by Handel alluded to in the last line of the refrain?

It is this unheard, jaunty tune with its adapted first line that you and your fellow merrymakers are playing to me across fifty years, composing a group of your own in tribute to - or in mockery of – well of what? In this cross-cultural saga, just about everybody I suppose was pretending. Malinowski was pretending to be a Trobriand islander, and signalling failing. His gig as portrayed in the photo of 1918 appears to be an active demonstration of the great ethnographer's guiding philosophy of "participant observation", yet his detached and slightly aloof expression, his expatriate manner of dressing, his pallor and balding pate set against the Afro hairdos of his fellow musicians, mark him out as an outsider. Meanwhile, it is we (as, back then, it was the Trobrianders, in some respects more sophisticated and knowing than he) who are observing him. Crosby was pretending to be an Irish America from the wild Irish West. They in their turn were pretending they had not migrated.

And you and your jolly companions, Catherine Cariad, who or what are you all purporting to be? Are you imagining yourselves as Malinowski with his aboriginals, as Bing with his backing group, or as Bing imitating Malinowski, or Malinowski masquerading as Bing? (That, at least, is unlikely). And, last of all, here am I, as you lie there unconscious, kidding myself and you I've made sense of these successive guises and disguises…

Malinowski had no doubt whom he was portraying back in the years following the Great War. He was depicting people whom in 1922 it was still possible to refer to as "natives", among whom he appears as the only non-native subject. Yet surely the irony would have struck him: everybody is a native of somewhere. Malinowski himself was a native of Kraków, I'm a native of Kingston-upon-Thames, and you are a native of Porth.

So let us consider together this prospect of yourself as a subject of anthropological enquiry. This headmaster's daughter from the valleys who had come to the big, bad capital to consort amongst the newest of the new: the anthropologists, the leftward-inclining young men and women of the university's smartest school, the would-be Harold Laskis and parodic buskers of academe. 1964 may have been the year after sexual intercourse purportedly began. It was also the year in which Betty Friedan published *The Feminine Mystique,* and when Second Wave Feminism came coursing towards the shore. You curled your hair around your ears, as they are curled now, took to lipstick in fashionably pastel shades, pencilled mascara around your eyes, and started to buy your clothes from Biba. The provincial duck turned into a surprising sixties swan. You read Friedan religiously, and devoured *The Catcher on the Rye.* Lawyer though you were, you caught the Anthropology bug and imbibed the works of Margaret Mead, a yellowing paperback edition of whose *Coming of Age in Samoa,* with its panacea of primordial permissiveness as imaginary as Malinowski's recital, is even now, when I return to our home from the hospital, staring at me from the bookcase. Back then you reminded your anthropological friends of Betty Bryant, the girl from rural East Anglia in Arnold Wesker's 1959 drama *Roots,* who comes to London and finds herself a boyfriend called Ronnie, who is Socialist and Jewish like so many of your male LSE friends. Betty too, a native of rural Norfolk, is a subject of anthropological enquiry, and like you she is a person in transition. In the last Act, Ronnie deserts her, but her closing monologue, part of which you once had by heart, was a paeon to her own, hard won articulacy.

> Listen to me someone. (*As if a vision were revealed to her).* God in heaven, Ronnie! It does work, it's happening to me, I can feel it's happening, I'm beginning, on my own two feet – I'm beginning…

It took members of that generation to claim, not simply to have re-invented, something as ancient and as fundamental as speech. In your case, my darling, what was being reborn in those daring days, was your own inborn and inherited *hwyl,* the eloquence of the chapels honed to other, subversive ends. You quit the safety and discipline of Canterbury Hall, the university's residence for first year girls in Cartwright Gardens with its nightly curfew, and moved to share a flat in Shepherd's Bush with three anthropological girls. That July you first visited New York, where you recorded "a sense of well-being and travel and of events", a forward propulsion and an optimism have never quite left you. In November you met your black boyfriend Dave Bouavier, and took the birth control pill for the first time. It took members of our generation to claim, not merely to have re-discovered, but almost to have discovered, something as old and as basic in sex, in the spores of Margaret Mead with her wet dream of promiscuity in South Sea Islands.

You had shed Wales, or at least so you told yourself, yet every few weeks you took the train back to Porth to go to the Empire cinema with Gill. You were bold and daring, poised at a precarious moment of experimental freedom. For all that, you needed to be cherished and loved, like so many other members of your and my liberated, old and new tribe. In 1927 Malinowski had written:

> We have been comparing two civilisations, the European and the Melanesian, and we have seen that there exist deep differences, some of the forces by which society moulds man's biological nature being essentially dissimilar. Though in each sphere a certain latitude is given to sexual freedom, and a certain amount of interference with and regulation of the sex instinct, yet in each the incidence of taboo and the play of sexual liberty within its prescribed limits is very different.

You travelled between Porth and London, tasting your freedom, as all the while the letters came: courteous and nail-biting letters from bashful, sheepish admirers. In January of that year, a fellow student exhorts "I feel like something out of Beckett today…Has anyone ever written you a love letter? I would love to know how the average undergraduate copes with that sort of Dilemma. I usually find them (love letters) terribly embarrassing and have long since (6 months) given up writing them, or think I have, or…". From Westbourne Street, Hove in April, a student pleads to you in arch, self-conscious prose "I suppose I had better prod your memory a little so that you know who's writing to you. We met at a pub in Essex called The Pig and the Whistle and I took you out dancing about three times after that…Perhaps if you are not doing any studying still, you will find time to drop me a line…" From Eddington in Birmingham, an overture arrives in June, reading "If you have a spare moment between lectures I would love to hear from you…Next weekend I would like to go out again if you are agreeable…" From Working Street, Cardiff an articled clerk writes in May "I was hoping to see you during your Easter vac. but however I did not. I did catch a glimpse of you in a car driving through Penygraig on Good Friday, but that was all. I was 'too shy' to call round and see you, although the thought did occur…" You did not meet your shy Welsh admirer; instead you wrote your sophisticated anthropologist chums in London that slyly ironical postcard: "so much to do here – like pictures, telly, reading law books in Welsh, eating delicious Welsh food like chips + leaks + looking at the historical coal mines + chapels. The natives are very homely + there's no language difficulty." You never did learn at all properly your mother's "native" Welsh.

You kept all those old-fashioned, chivalrously phrased pleas for your favours tied up with a length of legal red tape in the bottom of our bureau. They are letters from the lovelorn and the hopeless, chivalrous even in their pimply lust. This was the year of the great sexual shift. Yet the great rock hit of that supposedly libidinous season had as its refrain a paroxysm of coyness: "I Wanna Hold Your Hand".

14 DECEMBER: THREE CLIFFS BAY

Sunday, December 1st

Advent Sunday. *I wanna hold your hand.*

As you lie there I have been discussing our predicament with Susannah Martin, a speech therapist and clergyman's widow we have known for some years. Susannah has an incisive manner occasionally verging on the brusque, and she prides herself on knowing her own mind. She is, however, a deeply thinking person, and religious to her bones. She does not know you well, but I suspect she likes you. Certainly she surprised me somewhat by the tenderness of her concern. She asked me whether you had made a Living Will. I told her that I was not sure what that means, so she told me that "living will" is a shorthand phrase for an Advanced Decision (alternatively an Advanced Statement) laying out what you would wish for yourself if and when you come to lack capacity, as you do now. All sorts of specifications can be made if you fill out and sign the relevant form, provided that is that you possess capacity at the time you do so. You can refuse certain kinds of food, or certain kinds of care. Should you be admitted to hospital, you can also opt in advance not to be subjected to certain forms of medical treatment, though whether that extends to refusing basic care and life-lengthening drugs I am not so sure. Had you signed such a statement six months ago, you would have made my position a lot easier. As it is I have had to proceed largely by hunch and guesswork, aided by my memory and general sense of your preferences complicated by my own moral instincts which have not always been in step with yours. I am still tormented by the suspicion that I have done the wrong thing.

Susannah is currently nursing a daughter severely injured in a road accident. She is now determined to make a Living Will on her own behalf "should I ever end up in a position such as Catherine's".

Monday, December 2nd

7.30 p.m. A minor victory: you sneezed.

Tuesday, December 3rd

This morning you will be transferred by ambulance to the Nursing Home. I have a prior engagement in Cambridge, and have decided to leave our son to oversee your short journey, and to settle you into your new home.

I take a late morning train from King's Cross to Cambridge in the company of the Donne scholar Francesca Bugliani, a pious Catholic and a fan of the new pope. On our arrival, Trinity's Great Court is as empty as ever, and almost oppressively quiet. Entering at the Great Gate, we cross to the Ante-chapel to view that human monster Isaac Newton in his frock-coat, fingering his prism. He looks magisterial, travelling through his strange seas of thought alone, and just a little bored. William Blake took him to epitomise scientific reductionism and a denial of mystical possibilities, yet this cantankerous Master of the College and later of the Royal Mint, laboured for years over a commentary on the biblical book of Numbers.

Then to the Wren Library where, I have heard, the Trinity Carol roll has been placed in an aisle for public perusal. We pull back the red baize cover, and peer beneath the glass to find a strip of parchment about two metres long, with medieval music crookedly set out in in staves. Here are the familiar Christmas songs, in unfamiliar guise: "Hail mary full of grace", "nowel, nowel, nowel", "Now make we merth al and sum", "There is no rose of swych vertu," the remote ancestors of Nine Lessons and Carols, one musical corner stone of modern seasonal rejoicing. And here it is, the first inscription of the Agincourt Song, named after its refrain "Deo Gratias Anglia", as in the Laurence Olivier film of Henry V. So, early as it is, the roll must date from after 1415, the date of the battle.

To lunch in the hall, where I find myself sitting next to my old friend Jean Khalfa, Director of Studies in French at the college and an editor of the radical Parisian magazine *Les Temps Modernes*, founded by Sartre in 1945. He has been working with the postcolonial scholar Robert Young on an edition of the correspondence of Frantz Fanon, the French-trained psychiatrist and revolutionary who, basing his arguments on his own clinical work in Algerian hospitals in the nineteen fifties, devised a theory of the cleansing effects of violence on the mental wellbeing of the Wretched of the Earth. I ask him whether Fanon knew Camus. Remotely, it seems. So I bring up Camus' distaste for the violent tactics of the FLN, and his well-known statement in reply to a question posed by a student after the Nobel dinner, that he would not endorse policies that might endanger the life of his own mother. This has always struck me as a deliberate, and unfashionably held, act of choice. But Khalfa is not sure that his views and Fanon's were so far apart. Camus understood the other side, he asserts: he understood the needs and motivations of those who plant bombs in pursuit of a cause, even if publicly he found it necessary to dissociate himself from the consequences. This is not quite how I read Camus, who has always struck me as being deeply humane. An intellectual espousal of ruthlessness in support of liberating objectives was one aspect of the cultural mentality of the nineteen-sixties, but it was one that horrified, and still horrifies me.

Over coffee I fall into conversation with one of the chaplains, with whom I bring up the subject of Camus again, but this time in connection with Pascal and moral choice. He reminds me that, after Pascal's death in August 1662, a piece of parchment was found sewn into his clothing. It read 'Greatness of the human soul... Joy, joy, joy, tears of Joy.' Then it echoed Christ's dying words from *Matthew*: "My God, My God, why hast thou forsaken me?' which the evangelist then gives in the original: 'Eli, Eli, Lama Sabachtani'. These must be one of the few instances in the Gospels of Christ's own words, since they are in Aramaic rather than in the Psalmist's Hebrew. As for Pascal, nowadays he's a unit of pressure and a programming language. Re-visiting Cambridge, you do learn a thing or two: mediaeval music, maths, political theory, Aramaic and the science of computing, all in one morning.

Back to South London, grabbing a poinsettia plant from a florist on my way through Victoria Station. Down the length of Auckland Road, dark already at four o'clock, though mercifully paced by street lamps. You are slumbering quietly in Room 20, which the management have decorated in time for your arrival. As I enter this strange space, I take hold of your limp, white hand. Look, I've brought a new notebook I'm writing in to show you. I got it at Paperchase in King's Cross: hand-stitched in India with a green and white cover, embossed with flowers, 3-D false pearls, a tea-pot, and a clock face. Our son thinks it a "girly" choice, but I tell him it's so unusual and tasteless it will be hard for it to get lost. "Look at what Dad's bought," he implores, and you dutifully open your eyes, then close them again. The room's a bit stark as yet: laminated floor, pine plywood furniture, pastel walls. I brighten it up marginally with the poinsettia from the station and the chrysanthemums from the hospital shop. Tomorrow there's a party at two, and Father John will play the piano. For years I have sung carols in this loving home. Little did I dream I'd ever see you in here.

Wednesday, December 4th

This morning, I take my bearings. The Lakeside Nursing Home is cobbled together from two adjacent Victorian houses, with an awkward join between them that involves a sharp 90 degree bend in an upper corridor where I am already getting lost on the way to and from your room. On the landing, relicts of more affluent days, are some stained glass windows with fetching amber and claret panes. Nowadays, however, the carpet is fraying and vomit green, and the lower walls are covered in peeling maroon wallpaper. Above it all there drifts the faint stench of cooking, though I must say all of the staff are warm and very friendly. They bring us sandwiches at regular intervals, and pots of good, strong tea.

We spend much of the day here, but must leave your room once every two or three hours whilst you are expertly tended to and turned. While this is happening, we sit in a club room across the landing, where each afternoon Dokia, a blowsy Greek Cypriot in her late fifties, assists the milder dementia cases by getting them to assemble words from the letters contained in a specimen sentence crayoned at the top of a white board. I am writing this in the club room now, surrounded by pastel shaded walls and occasionally glancing up at the back garden beyond the generous window pane. Around me are comfortable arm chairs in a questionable shade of pink, and the table cloth bears a monochrome likeness of the Houses of Parliament, with London buses tricked out in red. The ceiling has tulip-shaped uplighters and the floor is of a light coloured laminate material imitating oak. There are potted rubber plants in three of the corners, and a guitar leans against the wall behind the Toshiba flat screen. A glass fronted cabinet is topped by a pig-tailed girl doll on a miniature rocking chair. On the walls are framed collages of dried leaves, two certificates of membership of NAPA (The National Association for Providers of Activities for Older People), a poster of the floodlit Roman Colosseum and three cork notice boards with postcards from former residents or visitors sending greetings from Bournemouth and Tenerife. A low book case near the door carries an odd range of titles: a W.H. Smith Road Atlas, Luciano Berti's *Florence,* cookery books, Jilly Cooper's *Jump!* and Margaret Atwood's *Life Before Man.* A Nigerian nurse called Bola puts her smiling, scarified face round the doorway. They are ready for us now.

On the Glasgow Coma Scale you are now number 7, we learn. 3 represents deep coma or death; maximum awareness counts as 15. Are you half way up, or half way down? In reality, every score below 9 is taken as severe. But, courage girl, you used to be 5. For eye movement you score a whole 3, since you open yours spontaneously. But when this afternoon we played you your favourite programme on Radio 4, "The Archers", followed by your second favourite "Money Box Live", you stared straight ahead, with no sign of recognition or enjoyment.

I walk downstairs to join the home's annual Christmas party, to which relatives, friends and carers of inmates are invited, and fall into conversation with Norma, an upper-class woman whose husband died in the home a few years ago, and who ever since has charitably acted as compere for these events. She is interested in and sympathetic to our predicament and savvy about the law, though what she has to tell me mostly extends what I already know. Did you, she asked, when you had capacity, cede me enduring Power of Attorney so that I could make on your behalf decisions about money, treatment care, should you ever come to this sort of a pass? No, I answer truthfully; neither of us ever considered it. In any case, you always ran a mile from matters of that kind, would not discuss your only brother's death early last year once it had unexpectedly occurred. Provision for an unwelcome destiny was simply never in your nature. She advises me to arrange a Deputyship through the Court of Protection. Such a step with be most convenient for us both in the long run. For the moment you are in drastic need of total care, and the Borough is footing the bill. How will it be when and if you improve, and medical argument for comprehensive public funding can no longer be sustained? The weekly fees at this home currently stand at a little over £500 per week: to meet them out of our private pocket would eat up much of my income, and most of our hard earned savings as well. Would you have countenanced this, even for a minute? Would you not rather, as a niece of yours now writes to us from America, rage that the lucid and sardonic self you once were should have to spend everything you have in order to extend the life of the diminished self that you have since become?

Thursday, December 5th

Babita, the lead clinical nurse, tells us about her fifteen-year-old son who wants to read Medicine at Cambridge. She is a Hindu, but she observes the principal feasts of most of the world's major faiths: Diwali, Eid and Christmas. Her first husband was a Hindu, her second is a Shia from Iran. "I brought my son up as a Hindu. But now he is telling me that Science and Religion don't mix. I tell him that I am an Indian, a Rajput, my people were originally from Rajastan. I was born under a certain star, I am Saturnine, a hard working woman. And I worship Hanuman, the monkey god, I have him in my shrine at home. I have all of the gods there: I have Shiva and the Lord Krishna, and Durgah too. And I have the Virgin Mary and Mahomet and the Buddha, and Ganesh and Allah, I worship them all." Then conspiratorially she lowers her voice and adds, almost *senza voce*, "We are not living in Heaven now, innit? We are living in Hell, where Lord Huniman presides. I like to look after the old and the frail, not everyone has that gift. If you exercise it, the Hindus say, you go to Heaven. But I will never get there. I am wicked woman with two husbands, and I divorce, innit?" Babita is forty-three, with henna hair that used to be the colour of jet. "I change my hair colour," she tells us, "when I change my husbands." Babita has a red uniform, and laughing bedroom eyes.

Late afternoon, and our son is speaking distinctly within three inches of your face: "Hello, Mum, it is Benjo, your son. We are both here. Are you inside there somewhere? We know that you are, and we are going to stay here until you come out. We're not going anywhere."

Then Babita comes in and is cloistered with you for half an hour, during which I hang around in the club room next door. When I am shown back into your room, you have been propped up on your pillows, your hair has been brushed, lipstick has been applied to your lips, eye-liner to your eyes, rouge and makeup to your lips. Again you are a beauty, but not quite the sort of beauty you always used to be. The hair is too straight, the lipstick and mascara too thick. The attention is very well meant, so I am both moved and touched by it, though to be honest, when I entered the room at first, I was reminded of the mortician's art. This is Babita's idea of you, and Classic FM softly playing in the background – "Smooth Classics After Seven" – adds its mite to the subterfuge with music that in your conscious life you would either have avoided or else turned off. I sense that the effect is intended for me as much as for you and, for this respite and thoughtfulness, I am almost tearfully grateful. Such small mercies.

Friday, December 6th

Alone with you, once more alone. Is this condition worse, more gruelling, than your straightforward physical death would have been?

On the radio, tributes pour in to Nelson Mandela who died at home in Pretoria yesterday. For years I have waited for this event, expecting to be stirred by it into an agony of solidarity and compassionate awe. Instead, today I feel dead to everything: to my own pain, but also to that of others. Mandela's achievement was to confront and to face down an almighty presence in the shape of an unrelenting political regime. To me now it seems more challenging to confront an absence, that of one's life partner when her body and maimed brain lie visibly before one in bed. How I miss your banter, your irreverence and your common sense: how I miss your repetitions, your bad puns, your insights, your blind spots, your nagging, your support, your resistance, your procrastination, your sarcasm, your insights and your fears. How I miss our slight tiffs, and our occasional standoffs. The ripple of Radio 4 sounding upstairs from where I worked in my basement study, each of us withdrawing for an hour or so as to claim our respective "space", before meeting once more in companionable, ordinary fellowship.

Saturday, December 7th

Your friends John and Liz called round for a couple of hours, during which they divert me with talk of gamey meats, venison and swans. Can anyone apart from royals, they inquire, dine on the latter? Ah yes, I reply, remembering a neighbouring college to my own, the Fellows of Saint John's college in Cambridge, enjoy that privilege. In a moment of compensatory frivolity I quote them the limerick:

A certain young lad of Saint John's
Attempted to bugger the swans.
Said the faithful old porter:
"Here: take my daughter.
Them birds is reserved for the dons."

Then, whilst you are being turned, we are out in the corridor once more, and when we are well beyond earshot, I ask Liz whether she notices any change in you. Not really, she answers. Maybe your open your eyes a bit more regularly now, "though whether she is actually seeing anything, it is hard to tell." After your friends have left, our son moves the tip of one of his fingers across your wide open eyes to see if he can detect any tracking response. "Well, did you?" I ask. He answers with a curt but disappointed "No." For the first time the terrible thought occurs to me that you may in effect be blind.

Sunday, December 8th

As we enter the room this morning, you are wearing your new Size 14 cotton nightgown from John Lewis. Out loud I compliment you on your appearance wrapped in its mauve, flower-patterned folds. Nothing. Your eyes blindly swerve as I utter my endearments.

Liza, a tall nurse from Macedonia, pianistically trained and with ambitions to becoming a music therapist, enters and, after tending to you, she serves us tea. Until recently, she tells us, she was living in a flat opposite Pizza Hut on Westow Hill at the top of the slope on which the nursing home stands, with two female cousins who shared a bed. When the landlord found out about this convenient and convivial arrangement, he chucked all of them out with one weeks' notice. Now she lives with her Greek boyfriend in South Croydon. It is quieter down there. "He used to make wine in Greece, but it is more difficult here. Now he works in a bar in Croydon, but he is looking for something better."

This evening, researching once more the anthropological you, I've been rummaging in the drawers of your bureau for more of your diaries. March 1966: you wrote "Coup in Ghana." Aged 23, you were temporarily living back with your parents in Porth. In Hove, yet to meet you, I was poring over my set books for Prelims: G. E. Moore's *Principia Ethica* and Jacob Burkhardt's *The Civilisation of the Renaissance in Italy*. You were bickering with your beloved father because you were frustrated at not being able to find a job. In Moore's philosophy book I read: "In order to shew that any action is a duty, it is necessary to know both what are the other conditions, which will, conjointly with it, determine its effects; to know exactly what will be the effects of these conditions; and to know all the events which will be in any way affected by our action throughout an infinite future. We must have all this causal knowledge, and further we must know accurately the degree of value both of the action itself and of all these effects; and must be able to determine how, in conjunction with the other things in the Universe, they will affect its value as an organic whole. And not only this: we must also possess all this knowledge with regard to the effects of every possible alternative; and must then be able to see by comparison that the total value due to the existence of the action in question will be greater. But it is obvious that our causal knowledge alone is far too incomplete for us ever to assure ourselves of this result, that an action is our duty: we can never be sure that any action will produce the greatest value possible."

I had no experience as yet against which to measure these thoughts on the law of unintended consequences. In Wales you wrote: "Snow. I must do things. Read D.H. Lawrence short stories in bed. In a state of limbo. I must come home for shorter periods." In Hove I read from Burkhardt's history book: "How far would the influence of a man like Biondo of Forli have reached if he had written his great monuments of learning in the dialect of Romagna? They would have assuredly sunk into neglect, if only through the contempt of the Florentines, while written in Latin they exercised the most profound influence over the whole European world of learning. And even the Florentines in the fifteenth century wrote Latin, not only because their minds were imbued with humanism but in order to be the more widely read." Back in Porth you applied to the London Borough of Hounslow, and got a job. A youth employment officer, but it was a job.

I am not sure that I can carry on like this.

Monday, December 9th

I have invited my resourceful and compassionate friend Dr Rachel Darnley-Smith to see you. Thirty-four years ago when I first met her, she was a nineteen-year-old music student at Lancaster University, taking a year out from her studies and lodging in Muswell Hill. Now she runs a music therapy Masters programme at the University of Roehampton, having taken her doctorate at Durham last year. Ten years ago, together with her civil partner Helen she co-wrote a standard textbook on the practice and profession of music therapy. Five years ago, Helen died of cancer. Rachel knows about love, loss and bereavement. She knows a lot about music too, and the varieties of healing that it can provide. If she cannot heal you and console me, then nobody can.

She arrives a little late and meets us up at the house. We share a modest pub lunch, then walk along with her to the care home. Patiently she sits with us for about two hours, moved and perhaps a little embarrassed by our situation. After a while, she suggests we sing some rounds. In good voice the three of us perform "London's Burning" and "Row, row, row your boat" across your recumbent form. Then Dokia, the middle-aged Greek Cypriot woman who runs the recreational club along the corridor, calls round for a chat. She uses a lot of word-play with her geriatric patients, so I tell her about the round that can be sung, with variations of phrase length, to the tune of "Frère Jacques" and the accompanying sentence "Life is but a melancholy flower." The puns on "butter", "melon" and "cauliflower" are a little beyond her at first, but she listens carefully as we sing it through twice and explain that "but a" has become "butter", that "Life is but a melan…" has become "Life is but a melon" and, finally, that "…choly flower" has become "Cauliflower". At length, the penny drops. I copy out the words, and she promises to try them on her group. Perhaps she will, perhaps she won't. You would have considered the puns too obvious for words, perhaps even verging on puerile. Probably, as we run through it for the umpteenth time, you would have let out a deep, ridiculing, yet complicit sigh.

Tuesday, December 10th

On Friday I am due to sign a "Non-resuscitation form" at our doctor's; next Monday, during an interview with the home's administrator Harriet, another form outlining the nature and extent of the care that you are offered here. Once again your future seems to be in my hands, even if I possess so few rights under the present law. Do I – do we – want you to live for an appreciable period in this liminal condition, or would we prefer you mercifully to be allowed to die? This has been the over-arching question all along, yet day by day, week by week, it rears its head again from different directions and in different forms. And each time it catches me in a new, unpredictable mood. Today I would prefer to let you go; tomorrow I might feel quite otherwise. Even now, with you snoring softly beside me on the bed, gratitude at your mere survival seeps gradually back. Without you, even in this semi-conscious state, I would feel half the man whom I have taken myself to be for more than thirty years. Without you, in a very pressing sense, I simply would not feel myself to be me.

They have dolled you up in a nightdress of pink, a colour you seldom if ever wore. They have straightened your hair, and laid you out in an unfamiliar position on a strange, technologically versatile, bed. Daily I struggle to maintain the you-ness of you in the face of the reasonable and compassionate provision of those to whom I have of necessity entrusted the difficult task of your care. This is a work of love if you like, but I am not sure that you do like. Would not the authentic you the memory of whom is already slightly fading, have protested with "Why didn't you kill me before?" Well, I tried.

This evening we read you Chapter Seven of *Mansfield Park.* How excellently Austen evokes both unwilling envy, and half justified self-reproach. Fanny's jealousy on observing her cousin Edmund assist the attractive and manipulative Mary Crawford in her riding, is very well done. But not half as well as Edmund's bitter feelings of self-recrimination on realising how he has neglected her for four whole days together, so infatuated has he grown with his trim and sturdy young pupil. Edmund, of course, has done nothing very much amiss, nothing that anybody but the officious, hypocritical (and hyper-critical) Mrs Norris would accuse him of. Yet he has permitted his social and physical excitement get the better of more delicate and lasting obligations, betraying him in the process into sins of omission and of neglect. His self-reproach is all the more galling to himself because, in the eyes of others, its occasion had been so very slight. How well do I recognise this process of constant, if venial, marginalising of you in the presence – real or imagined – of some other, superficially more desirable, other. Too late, too late.

Thursday, December 12th

What is a wise and considerate law? One that defends the weak against the strong, the disadvantaged against the advantaged, the ailing against the healthy, the unfortunate against the fortunate, me against you.

In your situation you are supposed not to know your own mind, and I am supposed to know mine. I have a capacity for decision, you at present have none. Thus the wise and considerate law – in this case the amended Mental Incapacity Act of 2005 as incorporated into the Mental Health Act of 2007 – protects your rights against anyone who might be tempted to abuse them – including my tormented self. Accordingly I may not take decisions on your behalf, seeing as I am not you. Hence any "you" that I might care to hypothesise – could arguably be held to be, and probably is, a projection of my active if inchoate wishes on your helpless passivity. In vain do I argue that, when lucid, you took such an action in relation to others; in vain do I protest that, judging from your antecedent attitudes and statements, you would have wished matters to proceed in such and such a way. That "would have" is a conditional perfect tense too hypothetical for practical use. In any case, so the law maintains, it is suspect since ripe for abuse.

Had you, while rational, made that living will, declared in writing that, if deprived of reason or awareness of the external world, you would wish others to take steps to end your life, your inclinations would have been protected and your instructions obeyed. Again, however, the conditional perfect is a grammatical and logical mode too blunt for effective use. You made no such declaration. Imagining you having made one, we cannot now, even with our intimate knowledge of your temperament, construct what you would have said.

Provisions to ensure your wishes were respected well may have been taken, had your decline into the twilight been a gradual and progressive one. Under those circumstances foresight would have suggested provision for future decisions to be taken on your behalf whilst you were still on the upper slopes. This, it appears, is the scenario that governs the present law. Your collapse into semi-consciousness was too rapid for any of us to feel a need for such prudence. For the same reason, you never invested in me a Power of Attorney that might now enable me to administer your affairs or make choices concerning your treatment or care. Should I wish, acting in your own best interests as I perceive them, and guided by my sense of your philosophy, to take steps to end your existence, I could and can do nothing.

This morning I 'phoned an anxious relative and explained the law as it stands as an attempt to safeguard such as you against unscrupulous partners. As for caring partners, she inquired, is nothing offered to assist them in their vigilant office of love? There is, it appears, presently no answer to this question.

Friday, December 13th

Benjo cradling you in his arms, Benjo with his tender capacity for love imbibed largely from you. I have, I reproach myself, given too little overall, and do not perhaps deserve quite so much in return.

This morning to the local doctor's surgery where we see Dr Rinaldo. Short, polite, intelligent and informed, though as Benjo quickly observes, he does not always complete his sentences. We discuss our options concerning resuscitation, concerning which he remarks soberly that it would be most unlikely to work anyway, so we might as well get him to sign the relevant form to that effect. He has, he stresses, a duty of care, and sees it as an obligation to treat each and every one of your medical conditions as it arises. He will not, however, at this stage bother to investigate further or to treat the small nodule recently discovered on your lung, since this would entail troublesome, and for your possibly disturbing, visits to the Royal Marsden in Chelsea.

This afternoon, some hours after we left, there was a further call from the surgery to say that the nursing home is concerned about your physical condition. Dr Rinaldo will attend just as soon as he can. We walk briskly to join him, but arrive a few minutes too late. Are told that he suspects an infection of the windpipe and has prescribed Clarithromycin, the antibiotic with which you were successfully treated by one of his colleagues last summer. As we enter your room, you are taking in the contents of a nebuliser from a mask. By now you seem to have rallied, though Babita tells me that you are constantly and impulsively pushing out your left hand, which has led to the wrist stiffening. *I wanna hold your hand.* She has contacted the nearest hospice, St Christopher's on the Penge side of Crystal Palace Park, in case either of us require counselling. At the moment I feel I could benefit from some. As she leaves, Babita suddenly asks me "Are you alright?" I ask "How would you feel in my place?" Babita looks me in the face and replies "Don't make me cry."

We settle down to read you from *Mansfield Park* again. In Chapter 11, Edmund is seated at the piano, caught like a moth within Mary Crawford's attractive glare when what he really wants to do – what his better nature invites him to do – is to accompany Fanny out onto the lawn to view the constellation Cassiopeia on a perfect late summer evening. I notice once more his faults of omission, so parallel to my own. Meanwhile Fanny herself is caught between the social pull of the Glee singers into which she is reluctant to be drawn, and the prospect of the lawn and the overarching sky as glimpsed from the windows. Once more the furniture, the spatial disposition of feeling.

Saturday, December 14th

Janet the Namasthe nurse massages your back, your arms, your face (which you seem particularly to enjoy) and then applies aromatherapy, a skill that she has studied in Florida. She is a light-skinned Jamaican with a rich and friendly bur; every three hours she arrives from the office downstairs to turn you. She asks whether, as a matter of course, you wore makeup. I say yes, though the nursing team have not as a rule been applying the Blush Tint No. 10 (clove), the 16H Pinceau Eye Liner from Bonjour of Paris, and the No. 7 brows pencil with the subtlety that you once employed. You were never much made up: more enhanced.

The self-accusation continues. Will this ordeal never end? I did not deserve you.

I have been advised to seek consolation and advice from the "Cruise Bereavement Service", which sounds like some organisation to which you might apply should your shipboard holiday unaccountably be cancelled. Why, in any case, should I require grief counselling when you are not at present dead, but in this state of life-in-death, death-in-life? A bit tactless, I thought.

I loved you more than any other human being in this cold, unforgiving world: the purest, the most beautiful thing.

Sunday, December 15th

We have come to dress your tree, a Norwegian Spruce four feet high with an artificial robin perched on top, courtesy of the local Garden Centre. Such has been a social ritual for twenty-seven years, during which, ten days before Christmas, our son and I would withdraw to the basement living room to perform a ritual of adornment before inviting you downstairs to inspect our handwork. During his first two or three years, you and I had shared this homely yet exotic ritual in an attempt to surprise him. We still have a photo of him aged two and a half, gaping upwards in sheer wonderment at the multi-coloured miniature bulbs, the tinsel, the baubles dangling from the branches. When he was old enough to take on your role, we sought in turn to surprise you, inviting you down to inspect the result of an hour of careful artistry. It became your prerogative to gasp in pretend astonishment. Now we have erected a small tree in the corner of your bedroom at Lakeside. When we have finished we angle the top section of your hospital bed so that our minor masterpiece is within eyeshot. "Look, mum," calls our son, "the tree. We have finished our tree." You are facing in the right direction now. Your eyes remain tightly shut as you slumber on and, when they eventually open, they loll blindly back and forth, not a flicker of recognition or understanding in them. This, I knew, would be the most difficult moment: the instant when we knew for certain that the familiar wife and mother we knew has fled, probably never to return.

"Look!" our son repeats with a mixture of affection and desperation, "the tree!"

He plays you "Cool" and "The Dance at the Gym" from West Side Story on his Galaxy S3 phone. He has forgotten to bring the speakers so holds the device next to your right ear. He is a veteran of OUDS musicals and has blue-tacked two college posters advertising the undergraduate show "Musicals and All That Jazz" that we saw together, holding hands in parental pride, in the Magdalen College Auditorium during seventh week of the Lent Term in March 2007. This is some of your favourite music too, lively and spiked with danger, that I learned from both of you to love. As the glitzy sounds leak across the room, I am transported back to North Devon, a summer camp near Woolacombe, in the August of 1961. The film of the Bernstein/Sondheim Broadway spectacular was newly on general release. A self-conscious group of grammar schoolboys, we took a bus along the coast to Lynton and Lynmouth, twin towns across a confluence of rivers, to watch it at a cinema. I had been kept from such secular thrills by the confines of my choir school during the cloistered, cathedral-girt childhood I have so often sought to describe to you. From the jumpy music I inhale a petroleum-perfumed scent of peril, liberation and feud, Shakespeare slicked and modernised, Puerto Rican Sharks against waspish Jets. You meanwhile, five years older and already a Law student at the LSE, had set sail for France, embarking at Dunkirk on the first of the month, leaving from Calais on the fifteenth, tasting foreign delights that for me were still some way in the future, but of which I was already afraid.

That afternoon, as we left the darkened cinema and came out into the blaze of a later summer afternoon, we decided to walk part of the distance back to the camp site along the beach. A huddle of bathers had gathered at the edge of the Bristol Channel, from which there emerged a stretcher between bearers. On it, a diver in a wet suit, a diver with pallid face. From his abdomen like an immense arrow protruded the glistening length of a harpoon, his clenched hands steadying it around the open wound as they dragged him up the sloping shore towards help. Peril, pain, heartache, things I knew very little of. As they eased the diver's body up the beach, he moaned with every step.

Tuesday, December 17th

The Parry Rooms in the Royal College of Music in South Kensington. I am here to deliver a talk to a group of colleagues from the college and my own institution. This January we launched a joint project to chart the changes in the way in which people have listened to music across the centuries from the late Renaissance to the present day as recorded in their private diaries and letters, as well as in published accounts. The project, and the electronic database connected with it, have now been running for slightly under a year. We have covered most musical genres, many times, places and different categories of listener. Time we conferred and pooled our findings.

I arrive at nine, slightly ahead of the others and, as they appear, I scrutinise their faces for signs of concern. Few by now can have failed to hear about your condition and our predicament. Just how dire it is, however, few of them know. Will they ask if you are better? Will they inquire when you will be joining me at home, perhaps for Christmas? On greeting me, few mention what must be on several of their minds. Pleasantries are exchanged; the subject is avoided. But in every conversation comes the moment when each feels the need to ask. I explain as best I can a situation which few if any can have experienced at first hand. They attend to the awful facts in silence, and an awed pall descends. Then I watch as each in turn endeavours to recreate an equivalent tragedy in their heads, a scenario in which they are intimately involved. I watch each and every one of them as they fail. There is a studied and welcome avoidance of standard expressions of sympathy. They will not damn you with a cliché, nor insult me with trite commiserations. By and large, these men and women are too intelligent and sensitive for blunders of that sort.

After lunch I take the stand and talk about a subject that I have been researching all year, in Florence and Venice, always in your company: "English Listeners in Italy" from the seventeenth century to the late twentieth, illustrated by brief extracts from the musical works concerned. It will afford me an opportunity to compare English taste with Italian across the period in question. To start with, I want to take them back to one of the earliest sources we have for my theme: *Coryate's Crudities.* Using my own words and Thomas Coryate's, I endeavour to evoke an afternoon in Venice four hundred and five years ago. I begin:

> The Feast of Saint Roche: Saturday, August 16, 1608. In the upper hall of the Scuola Grande di San

> Rocco in Venice, beneath a ceiling of biblical scenes gorgeously painted by Tintoretto, a concert is being held in honour of the fraternity's saint. The programme consists of motets by Giovanni Gabrielli accompanied by a consort of sackbuts, cornets and violas de gamba, and of solo songs by Bartholomeo Barbarino, a forty-year old former organist of Pesaro Cathedral and an accomplished falsettist, performed by the composer himself with chitarrone continuo. Barbarino thinks his own voice "raucous", but an English visitor disagrees. Thomas Coryate is a clergyman's son from Odcombe in Somerset, an Oxford graduate and sometime jester in the court of Prince Henry. He has walked to Venice from Northern France and now he sits in the audience beneath those Tintoretto frescoes. As Barbarino starts to sing, he is charmed. The soloist, he later reports, had a "peerless and (as I may in a manner say) a supernatural voice for clearness…I always thought he was an Eunuch which if he had been, it had taken away some part of my admiration, because they do most commonly sing passing well, but he was not, therefore it was the more admirable. It was nothing forced, strained or affected, but came from him with the greatest facility that ever I heard."

All of this is well and good, especially as I have brought along a recording of Barberino's song. What I have held back, however, is any reference to my emotional investment in this scene. This January, just as the project was getting underway, you and I caught the plane from Gatwick to

Venice. I had skipped a university meeting to go, a dereliction of duty scarcely mitigated by the fact that the meeting was eventually cancelled owing to a heavy fall of snow. We knew that we were taking a risk in going to the Adriatic in mid-January. Our fears were confirmed. When we woke that morning and turned on the wireless, the weather reports were more than usually gloomy; snow storms were predicted all over the UK. By the time we were up and dressed, flakes were drifting diagonally across the window panes of our upstairs bedroom. When our driver made an appearance, the pavement outside our house was coated several inches thick.

The plane stayed on the tarmac for three hours as the wings were de-iced. When we reached Venice it was after dark, and we almost missed supper in La Calcina, our hotel in Dorsoduro where Ruskin once stayed. Afterwards we lay in bed listening to the background silence of the city. No cars, just the lapping of water in the Giudecca canal, and the very occasional human cry. Flocks of birds swept past the windows. The rattling of wine bottles in a crate, the exiguous bleating of a mobile 'phone, the rustling of a laundry basket. You were poorly and stayed in our room on Sunday morning while I rushed across the Accademia Bridge to catch the last half hour of Solemn Mass at Saint Mark's. I wanted to check if the acoustics were as Charles Burney described them during his visit of August 1770. Burney was researching a *General History of Music.* "This church", he reported, "is not very happily formed for music, as it has five domes or cupolas, by which the sound is broken and reverberated before it reaches the ear."

When I got back to our hotel room, your nose was deep in Jan Morris. "We have", you confidently announced, "positively to visit the Scoula di Santo Rocco. It is full of wonderful Tintorettos." That afternoon we set off. It was the Feast of Saint Sebastian, so on the way we decided to take in the saint's church. As we trailed along the canal, past the house of the composer Luigi Nono, knots of policemen were conferring. Our minds full of the film of Daphne du Maurier's *Don't Look Now*, we posited some unearthly crime: an atrocity, a body dumped in the canal. When we arrived at the West door of the church, it was locked. We were told to return in twenty minutes, and at eleven the doors swung open to disgorge more police. Sebastian, we then gathered, is the patron saint of the Venice constabulary. They had gathered to celebrate his Mass.

Inside, Sebastian was draped in every permutation of pain. Behind the main altar he stood manacled to a pillar, one arrow through his knee, another through his chest, while to his side a posse of archers prepared new refinements of torment. In a side chapel Paul Veronese had depicted him dragged to his place of execution by a crowd of russet-gowned officials, then clubbed brutally to death, as his eyes explored the heavens.

Two hours later, we were in the upper floor of the Scuola. I stood in the large upper hall gazing up at the ceiling on which scenes from the Old Testament are illustrated in gaudy choreography. To see them in more detail I was looking downwards at the inclined mirror provided for visitors who prefer not to crane their necks, when suddenly I realised that you were no longer by my side. After a panicky moment or two, I found you in a side room. Tintoretto's 'Crucifixion' occupies the Sala dell'Albergo off the main hall: quite a large room that seems nonetheless too small to contain it. You were staring up at the painting to where, amid the swirling horses' heads, the sweat and bustle of Calvary, Christ hangs centre, arms outstretched in blessing, effulgence like a gossamer fan spreading downwards from his embrace. The embrace enfolds the Roman soldiers as they struggle to raise the twin crucifixes on which will hang the two thieves. At the foot of her son's cross, brown-habited, stands his mother. In the background, storm clouds gathered.

That evening, after a confused hour or two wandering around the back streets without any firm sense of direction, I proposed we dine al fresco at a tourist restaurant I had spotted just downstream from the Rialto bridge. We were holding hands in the candle light, by the glow of which I noticed tears in your eyes. "Why", you asked me, "is so much of the art in Venice religious?"

It was a fair enough question, though we had already walked appreciatively round the Doge's Palace in which the temporal realm is illustrated in all its splendour, popes hanging alongside earthly leaders – were not the popes both? – and where, in the Grand Council chamber, seventy-six portraits of the doges line the walls just beneath the coping, and the central panel of the ceiling is given over to Veronese's *Deification of Venice.* Even here, in the epicentre of the city's maritime and political glory, pride of place is ceded to Tintoretto's *Paradise*, which, the guide books had informed us, is the largest oil painting in the world. At the apex of the southern wall, it stretches across and dwarfs the dais on which the high and mighty of the republic once sat and conferred. Saints and angels aspire upwards to where God and his mother stand in compassionate triumph, lording and ladying it over the known universe, recalling the minds of the potentates beneath them to the limits of civic power.

"Well," I replied over the candle-lit table top as plausibly as I could, "we have mostly been looking in churches."

"But why is there so much pain?"

"It is the central Christian myth. Besides, Venice was a plague city. Many of the churches were built to ward off the menace, or else to give thanks for release. Saint Rocco was an anti- plague saint. He was imagined to effect cures. That is why the Scoula was erected in the first place, and why on the ceiling he is shown being received into Heaven. You must understand."

That night you were angry with me. Or was your rage directed against the ubiquitous nature of suffering as illustrated by all of that art?

Now, after the symposium, I journey back to South London to see your body stretched out in pain on a bed. A pain that maybe you cannot perceive. But I can.

Wednesday, December 18th

Winchester Cathedral, 6.30 pm. I am seated in the nave of this great church where as a boy chorister I sang, clad in purple cassock, stiff white ruff and surplice. The annual carol service is about to begin. The wooden rood screen with its surmounted cross rises in the distance towards the chancel.

Jane Austen lies about thirty feet to my left, beneath a large grave stone that does not mention her novels, but speaks instead of the gracefulness of her mind. Besides me sits one equally graceful: a Kleinian psychoanalyst, whose husband is also a former chorister. We fall into conversation, and I mention you, compelled not only by the desire to unburden myself to which I gave way yesterday at the Royal College, but also in response to a receptiveness that I sense in her. She asks me about my years here, and I tell her about a poem I once wrote with a refrain that went "Save me from the cruelty and the dying music." The cruelty is well known to her, because her husband, now a canon of the established church, was exposed to it in the war years some time before I arrived. Then she says, taking me briefly by the hand, "I don't know how you both survived."

I talk to her about Choir Time, the first two weeks of the Christmas holidays when our services were required for celebrations like these. We were not permitted to go home. On Christmas Eve the dean held a Turkey Feast at the fourteenth-century Deanery, which we were invited to attend. The first year I did this was 1957, and I was just ten. In advance the senior choristers took us aside and told us that the climax of the feast the Dean would call us up to the dais one by one, and ceremoniously cut our throats. That afternoon we were told to go down to the town and purchase the razor blades with our small pocket money. In the evening, after the Christmas pudding, silence fell on the hall, and the Dean invited us up one by one by name. He asked us for the blade. We handed it to him. He took it out of its sheath, and then handed it back with a smile. He was a very good New Testament scholar.

Every Christmas you would ask me "But why do you go back?"

Now the choir are standing round the tall Christmas tree by the West door singing John Tavener's "The Lamb". Tavener died on November 12th this year after a long illness. His funeral service, a ticket only event, was held here. His son is about to enter the choir. "Save me from the cruelty and the dying music."

Thursday, December 19th

A card from a university friend evokes you as you were in Chelsea in the 'sixties:

> "Hi, Cathy, remember me? From the good old days of Finborough Road, miniskirts and eyeliner and a train to the south of Italy. Our friend Janet provided us with a huge bag of rolls. Then to the south of France, in a chalet near Saint Tropez, and a weekend in Paris in the snow."

Yet you remember none of this, cannot even to all appearances recall me your husband as I sit beside your bed in a subtle pool of light shed by the dwarf Christmas tree you cannot see amid the gloom of a fading December afternoon. A mutual friend whom you once described to me as being "too serious for her own good" – yesterday called our predicament "Not a nightmare, but Hell on earth". To be sure it feels like an act of condemnation, so that it is hard to resist the notion of some agency – human incompetence including my own, or else divine fury – in the face of these events. I feel more guilty than angry.

Behind the Christmas tree hangs a reproduction of Camille Pissaro's painting "Fox Hill in the Snow" made by the exiled French artist in 1870-71 and depicting a sloping hill just up the road from here in the same time of year as this. The painting always hung on a wall in our drawing room, and in 1985 it suggested to me a poem describing a man plodding up hill to meet his lover:

FOX HILL IN THE SNOW

after Camille Pissarro

On an ice stilled winter evening
a man is striding uphill through
purple tracks of snow.

Above him an acacia stands.
He climbs this snaking slope
in a top hat, placing his spats
through all the mudded slush of time.

A light falls soft against the glass.
Across the sodden landscape I tread
now the twilight leans, flaking like
bread against the polished window panes.

The acacia yawns like a splayed beetle or
sea anemone caught in a cross-drift.
He feels the path oozing before him,
his prints half brushed with the clouds'
leavings, a deepening stain of mauve.

Two women pass, wrapped in their
secrecy like queens. Their shadows blend;
his shadow bows. Voiceless,
his greeting smoulders through the frozen air.
He labours upward to the crest,
lingers there and scrapes his shoes.

The lamp falls soft against the glass.
Resting, he breathes and stares.
On an ice still winter evening
he stares at a man striding uphill
through purpled tracks of snow.

The walker was me and the lover, of course, was you. The poem won a small prize, so you 'phoned up your friends and announced "Robert *bach* has been commended." But at the presentation ceremony in Earl's Court Square, Norman St John Stevas quite forgot to read out my name, much to your disappointment. So we married instead, and learned what true contentedness was with a growing boy in an absurd and lovely house with its knotted beams and cacophony of books, its upright piano sweetly sour, its narrow bathroom with twin wash basins in which you rinsed our clothes because, though we could well afford a washing machine, we could never in twenty-seven years agree where it should be installed. Then one day a priest called round and your nonconformist agnostic hackles arose, so that one basin overflowed and on Advent Sunday the ceiling of the dining room collapsed as you stood amid a ruin of plaster and wailed "I tell you, no good ever came of this religion!" It was, and it remains, a perfect setting for our marriage, a place as eccentric and quixotic as us.

What shall we do, you and I? We cannot speak to one another, and you no longer know my name. We cannot properly look at one another, and you do not recognise my face. You are a thing, the bare bones of a creature, slumbering and secreting in an institutional bed. I have a moral obligation, but to whom? To a you that is no longer you, cherished by a me who am gradually ceasing to be the self you knew and loved. Only with difficulty can I now reconstruct the people we were before this egregious accident occurred. The presents pile up under the tree. The messages and cards accumulate, yet cool in urgency. No longer is there an emergency, but a repeated recasting of nothingness, silence and regret. Plus the thudding of traffic outside the double-glazed, metal framed window I am slowly learning to hate.

The nurses turn you and, when we re-enter the room, you are lying propped up on a pillow and groaning with your nose in the air. Your hair is uncharacteristically swept back, your skin is pale and serene. I say to Babita, "She's a beautiful woman, isn't she?' She replies, "Yes, she has strong features, the love of your life.'

Outside there is a sudden shimmer of rain, and Babita sweeps back the curtains. "Look!" she cries "Hailstones!" A flash of lightning is followed by thunder. Half humorously I remark "It's God. He's angry with me." Babita looks at me in astonishment and says "You've done nothing wrong."

Friday, December 20th

At two this afternoon Heather from the salon at 47 Westow Street turned up to cut your hair for Christmas. I was alone by your bedside when she called, bringing this journal up to date in a comfy arm chair. As Babita brought her into the room, she looked down and her eyes filled with tears. About five years ago her husband, a prosperous Pakistani business man in his fifties, died quite unexpectedly. After he had complained of a dull pain in his torso they opened him up and found his body riddled with cancer. Now I hugged her as she said "I'm sorry, but I have lost so many people: my father, my husband." We withdrew into the corridor while they prepared you. She was crying continually and said softly as I embraced her again "I don't know how you cope." I don't know either, though I am glad of the fleshly consolations of the squeeze.

The Namasthe nurse came in to attend to you. Before she left the room, she looked into my anxiety-ridden face and said "Don't worry. You mustn't worry." I said "It's hard not to." Then she told me that, twenty years ago, her older child, a fourteen-year-old boy, was killed during an armed robbery on his uncle's house in New York. She lost her father and, the day before he died, he said "Life is a holiday. When you have enjoyed your holiday, you go home." "If you are worried, her spirit will be troubled. Live on all of the good memories." She is a Catholic from Kingston, Jamaica, and in South London she attends Saint Chad's Church. Throughout all of these three last, gruelling months, I have not met a single irreligious nurse.

Saturday, December 21st

The winter equinox. I am doing the Guardian Lovers' Special Review Crossword. The name for which I am searching must be a pun, since 8 across is Hubert Humbert's 29 down. 29 down is lover, so Lolita; and 26 across is Count Vronsky's 29 down, ergo Anna, and 20 across is Professor Higgins' 29 down question mark, hence Eliza. In this cryptogram all people are grouped in couples, and everybody has a partner except me. Suddenly I am kneeling beside the bed in tears asking you why you have left me alone, I who am so poorly prepared for such a condition, I who have always dreaded loneliness more than any other state on earth. Then, before anybody comes, I dry my eyes clumsily with the corner of a sheet. Surely it must be the epitome of solitariness to be plunged into mental isolation by a seasonal crossword.

Sunday, December 22nd

Two programmes on BBC Radio 4 this afternoon on science and its relationship to the humanities. They are the final episode of "The Monkey Cage", and the punningly entitled "Science Taken for Wonders". I asked our son whether there is any such field as Science, as distinct from the individual sciences. He answered "Yes, there is: science is quantification. Science is measurement." So, I ask myself, what is the proper scientific attitude towards you: that your consciousness has been measured, pronounced negligible and, for the present at any rate, is therefore not there? Now your eyes open as our son trails a piece of silver foil across what I take to be your field of vision. I suspect that you may, at last, be tracking it, so I ask him whether he agrees.

He is very definite with his 'No'. "Mum", he explains, would never have seen the foil that close." Besides, I had held the foil at too wide an angle to subtend to your line of sight. (That I gather is what angles do: they subtend). "One has to experiment systematically; perform the procedure over and over again. Science, essentially, is bloody-mindedness.'

What, I am feebly thinking, is the connection between the son who insists on his professional scepticism, and the young man who crouches by your bedside, cradling you in his arms and repeating passionately "I love you, mum. I'm here; we're both here." Where are you, my ever cherished darling? Are you locked in? Is there any you left to lock? Can you be re-built from the inside out or from the outside in?

I have brought a colour photograph of you into the care home so that the staff can see what you really look like. So far they have, with the best possible intentions, brushed your abundant hair behind your ears and swept it back over your forehead to reveal all of your face. The photo I have brought was taken on an August afternoon in 2010 in the garden courtyard of the Hotel du Manoir in Tours. Roses are in bloom on a sill behind you as you sit in a garden chair exposing your shapely upper arms and bestowing on the camera a mild smile tinged with scepticism: quizzical though not strained, the faintest suggestion of the Cheshire cat grin written on your thin and curling lips. The following day we were to visit the English poet Stephen Romer along the river in Amboise. There we sat drinking his neighbour's white wine as he and I discoursed on poetry, surrealism and the differences between French and English verse. As we talked, his Italian mistress lolled in a hammock reading Balzac. You sat quietly taking all of this in, sensing I suspect a fundamental sadness or even loneliness behind the handsome poet's cosmopolitan assurance, his learned and carefully chosen words: an unease that ultimately revealed itself as homesickness. When the professional business was over and done, you steered the conversation gently to earth by chatting about The Archers. With marked enthusiasm Stephen told us he listened to the homely British soap opera on his short wave radio every afternoon.

This evening I told Father Andrew that I was consumed by remorse over you. He said "It's inevitable, part of the general wash of feeling; we always think that we could have done more, or better." I'm not sure that it was an entirely satisfactory response to my condition, but amongst Anglo-Catholics it is the sort of answer that serves. A stern evangelical, or a law-abiding papist, might have returned a different answer. He did not inquire "Remorse over what or whom?"

Tuesday, December 24th

A superfluity of commiseration, mostly well meant, almost always misplaced. Outside the corner pub I almost bump into an old acquaintance: a retired army officer married to a health worker, both of whom take themselves for Christians. Drunk to an absurd degree, lurching as he speaks, he proves a Job's comforter. He hiccups and looks philosophical. "Do you mind if I speak profoundly?" he inquires, affecting a serious air. There follows a litany of platitudes, truisms of sympathy so banal one expects the very pavement to shrink in shame. His "you are in a difficult situation" (Well, thanks,

I hadn't realised that). His "we are in the hands of fate" (the originality of which staggers). His "anything we can do", leading up – one confidently expects – to absolutely nothing at all.

His sober and embarrassed wife, a health worker at another local hospital, makes more sense with her "We cannot redeem every situation" ("We" being the NHS).

At noon I join the church choir for the slim lined Eucharist and carols we have staged every year for the last twenty in the nursing home. Benjo and his girlfriend will join us. The choir master has promised that we will sing you a carol round your bed. But when we all troop up to your room you are being nebulised, and Babita, in a fit of officious panic, is reluctant to let us in. We overcome her resistance through a concession: only six of us will enter the room, and the rest will join in from the corridor and stairs. Once the nebulising mask has been removed, you almost resemble yourself. Graciously to all appearance you incline the ear to a couple of verses each of "Ding, dong merrily on high" and "Oh come all ye faithful" and a reluctantly offered rendition of the secular fob-off "We wish you a merry Christmas." In response you utter a growl which I interpret for them as an expression of gratitude in a rare dialect of Welsh.

More clumsy comfortings pour in: "Thinking of you" (thirty-two times thus far); "Hope you get better soon" (twenty-six times). Christmas cards from friends one has not met for thirteen years proclaim "We were so sorry to hear…" (twenty-seven times). And, again and again, "I don't know how you cope".

During the nine lessons and carols from King's, Benjamin Britten's lovely and precocious antiphonal "Hymn to the Virgin" – "Of one that is so fair and bright; Ave Maris Stella" – vainly struggles against the dry sound of the nebuliser, rending its delicate textures. Nothing could be sadder than this.

Wednesday, December 25th

When we judge the time to be right, we fetch each of your presents in turn from under the tiny tree: the blue glass vase, the Chanel No. 5 Eau de Toilette, the newly framed photograph of Benjo's graduation from Balliol – how proud you were that day – Lucy Inglis's book on Georgian London, three silk kimonos ordered via the internet from China, each in a different shade of turquoise. As we open each in turn, we rustle the wrapping next to your ear and say "Listen, mum, this is for you". Once the wrappings have been removed, we hold each present in turn against your cheek, hoping against hope that you can feel the smoothness of the vase, the texture of the book cover. Against the exposed portion of your bare right arm we pass and re-pass each smooth kimono, pretending that you can sense the softness of the silk. We open the box of Chanel No 5, and dispense one spray of scent close to your nostrils, letting the rich aroma diffuse into the room. There is absolutely no response.

At midday the staff at the home provide us with a tasty turkey dinner in the club room, complete with wine. We are just tucking into our puddings when Jason, whose family owns the place, puts his head round the door and asks if we are alright. "Yes," I say. "We are as well as can be expected. We have just been discussing Pascal."

Thursday, December 26th

Last night I dreamed you were in prison in a small town in the Southern United States. It was the sort of jail that used to feature in cowboy films, with bars stretching right down to the bare floor. You were in a cell, and I was on the outside. You were standing and to my amazement as I moved to and fro in an attempt to attract your attention, you moved in sympathetic unison, mimicking my movements. I cried out in my sleep "It's true: she's moving!" upon which I woke up alone in our marriage bed with a feeling of utter dejection.

Continuing to read you *Mansfield Park* out loud, I realise that we two are inhibited from outright grieving in much the same way as the young people in the novel mounting amateur production of "Lovers Vows" in the absence of Sir Thomas Bertram are encumbered in their acting. We have, in Austen's words, "all of the disadvantages of education and decorum to get through." In other words, we are too English.

Discussing the implications of your state with our son, I casually ask "Do you think that it's easier to be an unapologetic intellectual in USA than in England?" He retorts "I should say that it's easier to be an unapologetic anything outside England. In England you need to apologise for everything."

Friday, December 27th

This afternoon, whilst keeping watch and ward by your bedside, we received an unexpected visit from Dr Ali, a physicist colleague of our son who teaches at Imperial College. Ali is a Shia Muslim of part-Iranian and part-English extraction. He is both a specialist in the testing of theories of Modified Gravity and a devout, law-abiding follower of Islam. I thought that he would have quite a bit to say about our situation from the double perspective of a first-class scientist and a devotee of a religion widely condemned in this country for its perceived bigotry. "Religion," he remarked, "is like a loaded shotgun; hand it to the wrong person and he will commit a murder." For all that, in his considered view, the vision of an all-knowing creator God who sees and sustains all things is both noble and majestic. The Holy *Qu'ran* is not responsible for outrages committed in its name: it does not countenance pointless violence, and its attitude towards women is generous. The holy text has nothing whatsoever to say about burkahs or women not driving cars, or even riding camels. But there is a need to be tolerant in both directions: for the Turkish parliament to banish the wearing of head scarves on the grounds of Turkey being a secular country is as repugnant as the French government to place the same restriction on its employees, or for the Saudi government to insist on women covering their faces. What is important is for people to continue talking, creating the sort of inter-faith dialogue that flourishes in this country. Even this is imperilled this week by the wave of retributive inter-community violence unleashed by the conviction of two

Nigerian converts to Islam for the coldblooded murder of the British serviceman, Lee Rigby.

And what of you, I ask him. The decisions we ultimately take on your behalf, he suggested, can only depend on the balance struck between a commendable reverence for life, and the quality of existence within reach. A very low quality of life may not be worth preserving. The British law says much the same, although the decision nowadays is effectively lodged with the doctors. On this matter, too, the Abrahamic faiths are for the most part at one. Islam, he stressed, is a strongly pragmatic faith.

Last month Megan McIvor asked us "Is either of you two gentlemen religious?" It is useful to have an answer to her question from a commonsensical adherent of another of the world's great faiths. The attitude set out by Ali possesses the ring of rationality. It is in step with most world religions. I have not yet had the chance of consulting a Jain, who would presumably take the principle of the sanctity of life further than we have.

Saturday, December 28th

This morning, as we were scuttling downhill rather late for our daily visit to you, a panicky phone message arrives from the nursing home. You have bad chill with phlegm to the chest, and their suction machine has broken down. There is no chance of replacing it over the weekend, so their advice is that you are sent back into hospital pro tem. Since this is a Bank holiday period and equipment cannot be ordered until Tuesday, you would be there for several days. Though we have made it clear that we do not wish you to return to the wards, we reluctantly agree to this arrangement as a temporary measure. When we arrive, preparations are already well under way. The ambulance team have been called, and you are being made ready. Benjo is wearing his dark green hoody from a production of *How To Succeed in Business Without Really Trying* in which he acted at Lincoln College, Oxford in February, 2007. He sooths your brow as I discuss the situation with the nurses. There is a blast on the bell downstairs, and two middle aged women in khaki uniforms ascend the stairs. We leave the room while you are winched out of the bed onto the ambulance trolley, and, as we accompany you down on the rickety lift, we are asked to which hospital we would like you to be sent. Taken aback, I mention King's in Denmark Hill, to be told that the ambulance people have just come from there. "There's a hefty wait at A. and E; they're very busy this morning". Recalling that Croydon University hospital will have your notes, I indicate that we would have no objection if you are taken there; we will come along for the ride, and hold your hand. Babita gives me a brief kiss before we quit the home. Now we are in the abdomen of the vehicle, you on stretcher in your new light blue kimono with the geisha girls under a flowering white cherry tree, and the plumes of the nebuliser streaming out into the body of the beast. Benjo holds your hand, and one of the ambulance women croons "It's alright, Catherine darling," as I sit back and take notes. A and E is not crowded this afternoon. One of the ambulance crew explains your case history insofar as she understands it to the admissions clerk, who inaccurately enters the details into the system on her desktop computer. Our name comes out as "FRASE". A woman in the bed opposite is dragging on the NHS equivalent of a hookah, with a dial on top to measure her lung capacity. Despite this, she seems almost spry. Attracted by his hoody, she falls into conversation with Benjo about *How To Succeed.* The room is Spartan and divided by blue plastic curtains, the atmosphere almost relaxed as you purr into the chattering silence. The hundredth nurse we have seen since October arrives and introduces herself: "Hello, Catherine, I'm Priscilla." With the help of a health assistant, she peels off your kimono and performs some "quick obs" with a portable blue machine. Then she dresses you again in a regulation blue cotton "Sunlight" gown. A House Officer called Doctor Hoque arrives and quizzes us about the reasons for your admission. He wants to take a blood test, and to administer antibiotics through a cannula inserted into your vein. We are both quite firm in resisting these steps; the second at least seems unnecessary and, besides, they represent just the sort of intrusive intervention we are now attempting to avoid. To our surprise he is very amenable, insisting on our rights: "Just let us know what you want us to do. We cannot go against your wishes." This is the first time that we have heard these words.

We have placed a tiny speaker in your right ear. It is connected to Benjo's Samsung Galaxy, through which we play you a recording of the pianist Paul Lewis playing Schubert impromptus. The lady opposite is now flanked by two male police officers who are talking to one another, and pointedly ignoring her. "People around here accuse me of being too lenient," complains one to the other. "But I know my job. I mean I was in Victoria the other day…" Another eager female junior doctor passes between the beds: pale, thin, concerned. My flesh rises. Depression creeps back.

Once a bay becomes free in a neighbouring ward, you are wheeled into it. Above the bed hangs the sixty degree angle of an operating light, its two tilted eyes gawping like those of an outsized fly on the end of their stalks. I gaze across at you, and note that your ears appear to have burgeoned as the rest of you has shrunk. A male junior doctor arrives, confronting us with a new version of an old quandary. He has been counselled by his colleague and wants to discuss our needs. He asks me who is next of kin." "Me", I say, "but I do not have power of attorney."

It occurs to me that you need to know quite a bit about the law in order to make a distinction like that, which leaves most people, most distressed relatives, nowhere. For once, the proviso seems not to matter. In any case, we have now agreed for an X-ray to re-assure ourselves that the nodule on your lung has not grown, but have baulked at the intravenous drugs and the bloods. We have, he now informs us, choosing his words carefully, decided on a "ceiling of treatment." The phrase is new to us but, just so long as such a limitation has been fully discussed and agreed between family and doctors, it is it appears a perfectly legitimate course of action, or non-action, to observe. To that extent at least, a measure of discretion remains to us.

Sunday, December 29th

They have transferred you to a General Ward and in the process of turfing you from one bed to another have lost your pale blue kimono, which Benjo had placed in a plastic carrier bag underneath the bed in A and E. Disconsolately he goes off in search of it. No luck.

In the evening we take a taxi back home with our usual firm. The driver this time around is a bearded fifty-five-year-old from Kashmir. He asks what is wrong with you and, when we explain, retorts "The imam from our local mosque here is in a coma for six months. When he recovers, he has forgot everything. EVERYTHING. Except the Holy Qu'ran." He drops us off at the house and, after we have paid him, remarks "She will be alright, N'sha Allah."

Monday, December 30th

You have been moved to yet another ward. When we find out where you are, your kimono is in a bag by the side of your bed. Opposite you sprawls a West Indian girl in plaits moaning to a consultant from behind a blue plastic curtain "You are not the one who is going through this pain. You sit there and you do your tests. I am not a lab rat. That is what you are making me feel that I am." They agree to discharge her and, half an hour later she is on the phone pleading "Can you do me a favour? Can you come and pick me up? I need to get out of this hospital. I am going home. Could you reinstate my carers, please?"

After lunch we receive a visit from Belinda Baumgartner from the Intensive Care Unit. She recalls your time there and recounts the daily meetings with the medical team taking care of you. She even recollects us reading you from *Emma*. "Look how far we have come," she remarks, either in encouragement or genuine amazement. "When she was discharged from ITU, we were led to believe your wife was on the way out. Now look at us on the threshold of 2014." But, lying supine in bed these last few weeks, your muscles have started to waste away, especially along your upper arm.

You could do with some Occupational Therapy and Physiotherapy, she thinks. It is the responsibility of the health services to provide these in the community: "She deserves the very best, and you should demand it. Pester them every week." Before she departs, she observes "I bet you could write a book about the National Health Service, couldn't you?" Benjo says softly, "He already is."

Tuesday, December 31st

Back in the nursing home, with your brand new suction machine. Here, for the next three nights, the nurse on duty through the still watches is Edmund, an Igbo from the Alhambra State of Nigeria. When we arrive you are poorly, so he brings sheets and a table fan from downstairs to cool you down. We want to see the New Year in and so tonight we will stay with you, as he talks to us about his past. Edmund lost both of his parents in his country's acrimonious Civil War: "I've got no family, nobody at all now." Brought up in South London, he attended Archbishop Tenison's Grammar School near the Oval, where he was in the same class as a brother of my friend and Cambridge contemporary, the writer Gabriel Gbadamosi. The two brothers were products of a Yoruba father and an Irish mother, and seem to have inherited the charm of both. "Yes, I remember him," Edmund responded when I mentioned the name: "A mixed race boy. He was forever nicking my pencils and sticking them in his bushy hair." After failing to get into medical school, Edmund took a Masters degree in Immunology in London, and for several years worked in the research department of Guy's Hospital on HIV. A second application to medical school foundered for lack of funding. So he re-trained as a policeman, and now works the other two days a week as a Special Constable in Brixton. "But I didn't want to do that full time, so I took this extra training as a nurse." He looks after you with especial, tender care since "I believe in God, and he sees everything." There is something sad about him, and something at the same time jolly: something philosophical and resigned. With us he is the performer of his own mottled history, but he is also a solitary who lives by himself in a flat off Beulah Hill. Nobody else in the home seems to be aware of this array of facts, though they work alongside him for half the week. Night time is his cell, his penance and his grotto.

Wednesday, January 1st, 2014

Cheryl, the Assistant Manager here, is from Kingston, Jamaica and, before being appointed here, worked as a Senior Staff Nurse at King's for thirty- seven years. She is small, efficient and cheerful, though dismissive of current trends in nursing. "Nowadays, as soon as they qualify, they go into management. It's all about paperwork nowadays." She works here for four days a week, arriving shortly after five in the morning, staying until eight at night, or even ten, whatever the job requires: "For my job satisfaction," she says. I have never seen her looking downcast, or even tired. Her accent is like honey from bees fed on flowers of the Eucalyptus. She bustles out of the room, a living embodiment of the Namasthe philosophy, talking of the red mark on your bum you acquired during your recent short stay in hospital. "A number one redness," she assures us. "Nothing to be worried about."

Saturday, January 4th

Three months since your cardiac arrest, and still you lie there yielding little if any sign of consciousness, slumbering away with your usual night sounds, occasionally opening your eyes as Benjo crouches over you murmuring "I love you, you know" in the stillness of a Saturday afternoon with cars slipping past on the wet roadway beyond the double glazing and the grey, empty suburban pavement.

This morning had Miranda Villiers on the 'phone. An Oxford Greats graduate who studied Philosophy under Elizabeth Anscombe, onetime secretary to the Tory MP for Brighton and Lewes, a keen musician and communicant Catholic, she is among the most perceptive and intelligent of all our friends, but still there is the need to explain as she asks "was it a *massive* stroke?" When you first entered this nursing home, this is precisely the case history that the majority of the staff assumed. It is very far from the truth, but the words "hypoxic" and "tracheostomy", almost unknown to me until a very few months ago, come slowly and unwillingly off my tongue (though, as slender compensation for the devastation they convey, I am touchingly proud to know them). I fill in the background. "I am so sorry" she says, and this for a woman who with her husband John has accompanied sick and disabled pilgrims to Lourdes annually for the last fifteen years. They have recently published together a history of that voyage of dedication, and of the shrine.

Your friend Sylvia writes to you. A retired town planner, twenty years ago she married the artist Roger Ackling, who has made a speciality of burning parallel patterns on pieces of driftwood by concentrating sunbeams through a magnifying glass. They settled in the converted stables of an Arts and Crafts stately home a few miles to the south of Sheringham in Norfolk, from where he could gather his materials – flotsam and jetsam – on the beach. Three years ago, he was diagnosed with Motor Neurone disease and, unlike Big Ben, he has stayed the course. He is now very weak, and unable to speak or to feed himself. His wife writes: "I think about you a lot and you are – in a halo of emphatic, concentric strokes – WONDERFUL. I am so sorry that I am such a rotten friend that I am not coming to see you and be with you. The truth is that it is difficult for me even to go out to Holt, as Roger can't be left on his own for too long. So no chance of hopping up to London while Roger needs me. But we spend generally peaceful days looking out at the lush green and the pale grey Gwen-John-ish flints outside, and remembering how nice the summer and the outdoor life is. Cathy, I know that you will be well loved, but I hope that you're not too uncomfortable, bored, frustrated, or however it feels to be you now."

Sunday January 5th

You talked to me in the old days of dreams, the continual dreams about those no longer there. You meant your brother Peter of course, and almost every morning since the February of 2012 you emerged saddened and a little frightened after a reverie of him. Now I awake after a night time vision of greeting you, alive and cheerful, at the door.

Tuesday, January 7th

We are called at 9.30 a.m. by Cheryl: you are very bad and the doctor has been summoned. Then a call from the surgery: a GP will be there by midday. At 11 another more urgent call from the home: your breathing has grown more laboured, and we should really be on our way. At the entrance we meet Harriet the manager with a serious face. In your room a black nurse is holding your hand. Babita takes us aside: should they, she inquires, send you into hospital yet again, or are we happy for them to continue treating you here? When we express our preference for you staying where you are, Babita turns her deep brown eyes on us and tells us you are on your way now, but will only depart if we give you leave: we should let go of you, for your sake and our own. After consultation with the staff we agree that 0.125 millilitres of morphine should be administered by injection pending the arrival of Dr Deegan, who is now expected at about half one. So we read to you from one of our son's Christmas presents, the latest compilation of sardonic autobiographical essays by David Sedaris: *Let's Explore Diabetes with Owls,* the story called "Memory Laps".

Babita returns on her regular round. She gives you your medicine then, placing her hand on your forehead, begins intoning very softly a blessing from one of the Vedas:

> Lord Krishna, see her on her way,
> Lord Ganesh, clear her path,
> Lord Huniman, remove all impediments,
> Shanti. Shanti. Shanti.
> Peace, peace, peace.

I find this recital so comforting and meaningful I ask her to repeat it again, and then again, and finally ask her to send me the text when she has time. It has certainly refreshed me as thoroughly as the much more familiar ministrations of the Christian priests.

When Dr Deegan turns up, she is a buxom and friendly married woman in her mid-forties. Bright eyes behind heavy-framed glasses, thick fingers and rings on her capable hands. Unfamiliar with your ups and downs, she takes this lapse for a final seizure, and recommends that if necessary the dosage of morphine should be increased. There is a sort of compassionate, loving fatalism about her. She has, one senses, seen many such cases before, and assumes without being told that we are reconciled to the worst. After six or seven minutes, asking the home to contact her again if your condition deteriorates any further, she takes her leave.

A while later, the staff bring us a late snack lunch. As I sit there, cheese sandwich in hand, Benjo informs me that I have fallen into a "brown study". I inquire as to the derivation of that telling phrase which I have always understood to mean "striking an attitude appropriate to a portrait painted in brown, or sepia". To my surprise I find that there are instances of it going back as far as 1532. David Copperfield at one stage falls into a "brown study" while walking along the beach. "Brown" apparently used to mean "sad". But, whatever the precise etymology, it is perfect for that state of mind or body in which abstraction verges on melancholy. It can be profoundly attractive, or attractively profound, in others, but it helps if you have a basic sex appeal first. In unattractive people, it is apt to appear merely as gloom. I cannot say that I feel picturesque or attractive, just ineffably sad.

Wednesday, January 8th

Yesterday you were at death's door; today you are breathing naturally and looking calm. The reason is that they have at least put you on the correct antibiotic. Your ebbing life has been framed by approximations and mistakes. During your brief recent sojourn in hospital, having been correctly informed that you have never been allergic to Penicillin derivatives, the doctors prescribed a course of Amoxycillin. After only half of the ten-day course of treatment, they released you without the Discharge Report that should have informed the home how to continue with your care. When your chest infection occurred, the GP was reluctant to prescribe Clarithromycin for a third time, and put you on a full course of Doxycycline, perfect for chest complaints, but an upping of the antibiotic stakes. After seven days, the discharge report having turned up, and the staff having been disabused of their mistaken impression that you would react against Penicillin-derived drugs, you have been placed on Amozycillin, since then you have thrived.

Friday, January 10th

Would you have taken your life had you been aware of the imminence of your present condition some time in advance? Would you have given us permission to end it in the event of your present level of incapacity?

Robert bach, I suspect you know the answer to that question.

It would be an easier one to answer if there was any common consensus on matters of absolute moral principle. Instead, we have a congeries of differing legal dispensations. I have been thinking tonight about the operatic conductor Teddy Downes. My brother Malcolm, founder of the Buxton Festival, worked at Glyndebourne as an Assistant Stage Manager in the early nineteen sixties; before his own death, he recalled Downes' wife Joan, then his fiancée, peddling happily in the early morning through the East Sussex lanes after assignations with him. But in 2009 Joan was diagnosed with inoperable pancreatic cancer, while Ted was deaf and increasingly blind. In the summer of that year they and their son Caractacus travelled to the Dignitas Clinic in Bern, where with medical assistance they put an end to their lives.

In accordance with article 115 of the Swiss penal code, euthanasia has been legal there since 1942, provided it is not facilitated by another "for selfish motives". It appears from a programme on the radio this evening that it has also been legal in Belgium for more than eleven years, from 28th May, 2002. Belgian law provides for the assisted suicide of people who are terminally ill or in unavoidable and incessant pain, provided that the decision is taken by the patient her- or himself, and that it is voluntary and well considered. At the moment five people every day avail themselves of this provision. In 2012 there were 1,432 such cases; last year there were 1,816, a rise of 27%. 53% of them involved people in your age group, between 70 and 90 years of age. Currently the Senate is debating extending that right to children. The churches by and large are opposed, both to the present law and to it extension. None of this would have helped you, or us.

Saturday, January 11th

I am following your friend Sylvia's train of thought. What can it be like to be you now? Perhaps everybody knows to some degree what a comatose or semi-comatose condition might be like: everybody, that is, who has ever fainted. I recall a particular moment in January 2009. I was enduring a blood test in Dulwich Hospital after a night without food. I recall queuing for my turn, then sitting next to a desk manned by the medical orderly who was about to take my blood with a syringe. I looked away and then there were things looking down at me, things that were human faces, though at first I did not recognise them as such. Sounds that were human voices, though again I did not recognise them as such, were echoing between me and these unrecognised apparitions. At length, the sound patterns settled into the disyllable that composes my first name, though I had no sense of its meaning, nor that this locution might possibly possess any connection with myself. Indeed, to begin with and for several seconds, I did not register the fact that I had a self worthy of naming, nor had I an inkling of thus being invoked or addressed. The disyllable hovered in the air, the things that were really faces distorted and, I can only now suppose, grimaced.

For a long fraction of a minute I thus lay suspended betwixt being and non-being, both out of and in the world, cognisant to some degree, yet not sure what or whom I was cognisant of. Until, that is, blood flowed back into the relevant portions of my cerebellum, and I was once more me, the entities peering down at me were once more faces, the space around me a room in a hospital to which I had recently been called, the disyllable the name of one slowly restored to himself as consciousness nudged in like the tentative motions of an advancing tide.

Is that how it is for you as I hang across your bed and, with peremptory affection, pronounce the three syllables that compose your name? Does recognition fitfully flood back?

How Austen's cynicism tunes in with your own. The circumstances of Maria Bertram's marriage in *Mansfield Park*, her motives for finally accepting Rushworth: a mixture of spite, hurt pride and a great desire to feel herself important and free – fit absolutely with your understanding of human nature, supposing as you so frequently did that venial considerations govern so many apparently high-minded actions. Which did not prevent you from being on occasions the most sentimental of beings. Arguably indeed, it was your temperamental tendency towards sentimentality, and the gap between such an attitude and what you observed around you, that predisposed you towards cynicism and satire. Are satirists spoiled idealists?

At 7.10 this evening, after being turned, you were in great distress. So we placed speakers on either side of you and played you the lingering Andante from Mozart's Piano Concerto No.21 (Mainz Chamber Orchestra, Walter Klein pianist and Gunter Kerr conductor). As you listened, your breathing gradually slowed down to the tempo of the music, momentarily quickening as the movement drew to a close, then subsiding into a deep, slumbering repose.

Sunday, January 12th

A colder day. Your sister Margaret, her husband David, and their son Steve are expected at 2. They have not seen you for three months. I am very concerned as to how they will react. They arrive slightly late and mistake the floor, taking the lift up to the landing above, having been told to go to "the second floor" by a nurse evidently raised in America. We meet them in the club room and escort them into the bedroom where you are lying on your side, snoring gently. A sort of appalled hush ensues, as Margaret negotiates her wheelchair around the end of the bed. We move the large armchair on which I usually sit to make room for her. She sits directly opposite your pillow, her large, tragic eyes conveying apprehension mixed with alarm, as she scans your face for traces of alertness or of life. Are you worse or better than she expects? Beyond the two sisters on a low table stands a framed black-and-white photo taken against the back fence of your parents' home in in Porth sixty-eight years ago. Aged around three, you are sitting cross-legged in the middle of the picture wearing pig-tails and your party dress, and flanked by your siblings: large, smiling, protective sixteen-year-old Margaret to your right, quizzical Peter, already urbanely detached in his twelve-year-old's short-trousered flannel suit, to your left. You have been told to look straight at the camera and not at one another, but the dynamic of a generation is already present, the overt emotionalism of the elder sister giving way to the precocious, droll sophistication of the brother. Your abashed and self-conscious face is turned ever so slightly towards him, as is already aware that this is the direction that you will take: towards doubt rather than faith, reason rather than passion. You were the one who chose not to take your degree in Wales. You will go gladly to the LSE and mix with pipe-smoking twenty year olds pretending to be Harold Laski. And yet it was Margaret who, a couple of years later than the photograph, won a competition with an essay on the Co-operative movement, went on a funded trip to Czechoslovakia and returned full of glad tidings about the world inhabited by the Soviet Union who had only just ceased to be our allies in the great ideological struggle against Hitler. The Iron curtain had only just descended. Despite the misgivings of Churchill, whom everybody in the Valleys hated anyway, the future seemed bright, and soon you saw yourself as part of it. As you lie there, we play you Kiri Te Kanawa as the Countess singing "Dove Sono?", snatches from *West Side Story* and the Monkees. At home Margaret has a video snippet of you wriggling your hips across the floor of her Essex home in time to the latter. Now you lie passive and unstirring throughout.

Wednesday, January 15th

I have arranged to lunch with my former colleague and fellow contributor to the *History of Oxford University Press*, the book historian Mary Hammond. We will meet in Pizza Express on the Euston Road, opposite the main entrance to the British Library. I have co-edited a couple of books with Mary, who is one of my most valued friends. Married to a film historian, she now teaches at Southampton University. She has recently completed a monograph on the publication history of Dickens' *Great Expectations,* and, celebrating a task well done, she is up in London for the day. You were always very fond of her.

Two years ago, Mary lost her mother, who had made matters easier in the last few months by leaving a Living Will. Now she asks me about our future, on the supposition that you are going to survive.

"The problem is," I say, "I can't really decide what Catherine wants, or would want."

"What do you think, under equivalent circumstances, that you would want for yourself?"

"To decide that, I'd need to know whether I'd be in a position to choose one alternative rather than another. We can't be certain she has sense of the reality of choice. Not can I possibly guess, were I plunged into the sort of limbo she supposedly inhabits, whether I'd have any understanding of the meaning of choice, either."

"But you may be able to get some sense of what the person you now are believes the person that you would have then become might want..."

"Provided that hypothetical person retains any sense of the person I presently am. But we cannot be sure that I would retain that sense. Nor can any of us be sure that she retains an equivalent sense of her old, maximally aware, self. All such arguments depend vitally on a conviction of continually. I have the impression that the law as it currently stands, rejects that very supposition, precisely because it is so easily abused..."

Thursday, January 16th

A well-deserved reproof from South Wales. Complaining that you are "very ill", I solicit the assistance of my friend Wynn Thomas, Professor in Swansea University of the Literatures of Wales, in translating your grandfather's anthem. He dispatches an expert rendition within a very few hours, expresses his sincerest sympathy, then tells me that he and his wife have been sitting beneath death's ample, extended wing since she received radical surgery for ovarian cancer four years ago "We celebrate every day anew, and are astonished that we have survived together this far." So much sadness. Last year Wynn served as External Examiner for the viva of Karen Caesar, a doctoral candidate of ours who had written a thesis on Peggy Eileen Whistler, the Uxbridge-born twentieth century novelist filled with a sense of a double inheritance, English and Welsh, who under the pen name Margiad Evans wrote a series of fictional and autobiographical works depicting these psychological and geographic borderlands. Whistler, who suffered from epilepsy from the age of forty, died in 1958, at the age of forty-nine. The viva was a great success, as was the thesis, yet six months later Karen died in Addenbrookes Hospital, Cambridge from cancer of the pancreas. Not for nothing do the great religions agree that the essential reality against which we must all pit ourselves in one way or another, is our shared mortality.

Even under these circumstances, I have flashes that amount to premonitions of your homecoming. In one of them, the Swansea train speeding across Wiltshire and Somerset, settling briefly outside Bristol, then drawing majestically across the mouth of the Usk at Newport via the noble, painted cast iron work of the bridge, within sight of the darkened masonry of the keep. Advancing more slowly after Cardiff, it trundles across the luxuriant Vale of Glamorgan with the wispy rumour of your very own Cwm Rhondda to the North until, as if in solemn penance, it toils past the Satanic steel works of Port Talbot, until the blissful Bay of Abertawe opens before us. Except that in my fantasy it carries on round all the bays of the Gower peninsular: Langland, Caswell, Three Cliffs, Oxwich, where it mysteriously stops.

Now I am there in imagination, we have decided to sing you your favourite chapel hymns. So different are they from my High Anglican fare, they seem almost exotic. You had turned against the preaching in gaunt Bethlehem chapel on Mount Pleasant on the slopes above your childhood home. But in these last few years, every morning on rising, you burst raucously into song with Horatio Palmer's "Yield not to temptation, for yielding is sin." And then your favourite verse:

> Shun evil companions, bad language disdain,
> God's name hold in reverence, nor take it in vain;
> Be thoughtful and earnest, kind-hearted and true;
> Look ever to Jesus. He'll carry you through.

In your diary you had noted your best friend Gillian Edmunds of 101, Cemetery Road, Porth had got herself a new coat in Morgan's in Cardiff. The preacher announces a fresh number as together we turn to the new page in the hymn book, and we follow:

> When upon life's billows you are tempest- tossed,

When you are discouraged, thinking all is lost,
Count your many blessings, name them one by one,
And it will surprise you what the Lord hath done."

Friday, January 17th

Depressed all morning. Very little achieved. Put up a picture, bought a pot, re-organised one of your drawers, made lunch.

Tried to mark examination scripts with you lying there puffing, as you always said of nocturnal me, "like a grampus". What, I wonder belatedly, is a grampus? According to the *Oxford English Dictionary,* it is "a cetacean of the dolphin family." Or it is "another term for Risco's Dolphin". Or else "another term for a killer whale". We have joined the Leviathans.

Tuesday, January 21st

Your LSE friend Jan has come to call on you from Norfolk. She asks about the causes of your condition, and I mention that in the hospital you were suspected of suffering from a version of COPD, the smoker's complaint. I ask whether you smoked heavily as a student, before I knew you. She recalls the 20 Consulate menthol cigarettes in the cellophane-wrapped blue and gold packets you stowed away in your handbag. In the early years of our relationship, before you quit smoking, you used to hide these Consulate packets away in a drawer. Then you would sneak off to the garden for a quick fix, extinguishing the stubs in the flower pot to the left of the back door.

You were always cautious in your way. In your twenties you and Jan shared a second floor flat with four other girls at 4, Finborough Road, on the borders of Fulham and Earl's Court. "Chelsea", you called it. Your room was at the back, overlooking roofs. As a young adult, you preferred it to Mount Pleasant. It meant that you had come of age. But when the others proposed painting the bathroom blue, you recalled Mr Pooter in *Diary of a Nobody,* and the bath at his house in Holloway that he painted red and then bathed in, only to emerge as splendid shade of puce.

Wednesday, January 22nd

6.10. The phone rings six times and then falls silent. I rush downstairs and dial 1471, which calls up the last number. It is the care home, which I call back straightaway. Edmund the night nurse answers. He informs me in a sober, South London-inflected voice "It's the Lakeside Care Home. I'm sorry to have to inform you that your wife passed away this morning, sir, at about 5.30. I am so sorry."

I tell him we will be down there about eight. Benjo and I go into a bear hug, his face tense with grief. After a few intense, silent minutes I say "She wouldn't have wanted to live like this. We did everything that we could." A bit later I say "You never know what to do under these circumstances, do you?" He replies "Well, put on some trousers. That's something."

As I pull on my pants I say "Oh, these early morning phone calls!" "Well," our son replies, "At least we're free from their tyranny now." At eight I phone your sister. When I announce your death, the phone goes dead. I try later, and am told that it was an electrical fault. "But it was what we were expecting anyway."

Before we leave the house, I pocket my Aunt Madge's copy of *The Book of Common Prayer*, and scribble onto a portable notepad the phone number of Canon Andrew. As we arrive at the door to the Lakeside, we bump into Edmund who is leaving at the end of his shift. He looks apologetic, brings us inside, and then asks us to come upstairs. In the corridor outside your room he explains that he had come to turn you at five, after which you had seemed peaceful. When he looked in on you half an hour later, there was no sign of movement or of a pulse. I ask if the doctor has been, and if so, which one. Yes, he says, the duty doctor called but did not stay long. "It is what we were expecting," he had said.

We walk into the hushed room. You are on your back in your floral, turquoise dressing gown, your mouth open much as it always was in deep sleep, your skin paler than of late. Your eyes are closed as I touch your brow, which is cold, then give your body a hug. Now even I cannot persuade myself that this is you.

At a loss as to how to proceed, I fish the prayer book out of my pocket. It is duodecimo size, black with a plain gold crucifix, printed by Henry Frowde in Oxford and bears a bookmark for my crazy aunt. I turn to the order for evening prayer, sure that I will find the Lord's Prayer there, then remember that the evensong version is shortened, shorn of its "power" and its "glory", so I turn back to the order for Matins and read the whole thing aloud. After it, Benjo says "Amen."

I pocket the slender volume, then ask our son what he thinks the cause of your death might have been. "Perhaps she got fed up of all these visits," he suggests. "Yes," I say ruefully, "Perhaps it was that."

We sit on either side of you, looking vacant. Then I ask Benjo if he minds if I call the priest.

He shrugs and says "No, not at all." So I leave a message for Andrew, who calls back after ten minutes to say that he is on his way with the vicar. "He's the boss."

The religious caterpillars enter, clad in their habitual robes. Father John asks "Have you contemplated this moment?"

After the priests have left, I suggest that we carry on reading Jane Austen. Our son asks me to read, and in my confusion I repeat a section that we have already read. It is the chapter in which Fanny walks over to the Rectory and meets Mary Crawford on the doorstep. She pulls her inside, as Edmund has pulled us, and offers her a chain to wear with the cross that William has given to her for the forthcoming Mansfield Ball. When Fanny realises that the chain has been a gift from Mary's bother, the rapacious and manipulative Henry, she demurs. Mary persuades her to accept. Austen's description of a young girl not knowing what to do for the best, anxious to acquit herself honourably, yet equally anxious not to give offence, a young girl in awe-struck love of her elder brother, as you were in love with yours, constitutes in its ambivalent, humour and affection, the perfected form of Last Rites. This was your third, and final, death.

Thursday, January 23rd

So, we have lost our wager. Were we right or were we wrong? You will not answer me, because even the putative self with which faith or imagination endowed your passive form for the last four months has now taken its leave of us.

I have one additional thing to say, the first of many final things, even if from now on you cannot or do not respond. I have, at the very least, to thank you for turning me into an authentic person with substantial dilemmas, rather than someone who continues to linger, as so many intellectuals feel that they are condemned to linger, on the outer margins of life. The choices that you have forced on me since the beginning of October are the most fraught, and ultimately irresolvable, that I have ever faced. Now I am as true to life as Dr Rieux, the physician in Camus' parable of the dying on which I lectured back then, a proper existential protagonist, as actual, as weak and as strong, as a character in a novel. You have rendered me fictional, and in the process have made me real.

Friday, January 24th

Last night Benjo and I talked into the early hours about an appropriate way to commemorate you. Do you recall your dread of graveyards? How in 2009 I was preparing my biography of the poet and surrealist David Gascoyne? One evening we were returning by foot from an expedition to the southern Paris suburbs to photograph the Bahaus-style residence where in 1933 he had visited the painter Julian Trevelyan? How we made a wide detour so as to avoid crossing the Cimitière Montparnasse on our way back to our hotel on the Rue de l'Ecole de Médecine? Or your reluctance to ascend the gentle slope leading to Beachy Head in Sussex, since the way was lined with benches bearing a forlorn dedication to a deceased former resident of the Costa Geriatrica of Eastbourne? You shook your fist at the statue of the ninth Duke of Devonshire in his Cambridge Chancellor's robes outside the Grand Hotel. Not even the fact that Debussy had completed the orchestration of *La Mer* in that grandiose building could make up in your eyes for the aristocratic connections attested to by that statue. Or a return trip in 2012 to Zennor in Cornwall where I once set a play about D. H .Lawrence, when you refused to complete the coastal path from St Ives because a dedicated bench lay every few yards? How do you commemorate someone who resents and fears the fact and furniture of commemoration? What did you tell me?: "Just stuff me in a black plastic bag and leave me outside the front door."

I told you, Robert bach, stick me in a black plastic bag and leave me outside the door.

Catherine cariad, they would not take you away. Anyway, a black plastic bag does not remotely do you justice.

Why crave justice? I'm the lawyer around here.

Because I need to do justice to you, even if you might have resented what I do in your name. Mourning is for the mourners, not for the mourned. Well, this is how the discussion began. Then our son said that there exists more than one conception of justice. The truest way to do you justice is to respect your wishes, even if they go against our own inclinations. How do we balance our needs with what we remember of your personal convictions? You disliked ritual of all kinds, disliked and abhorred it. Yet how are we to remember you, how make your departure real if there are no elements of ritual and symbolism in the "performance" (a term our son questions). I want a picture, a coffin, something that symbolises you, bodies you forth, externalises you, even if you yourself would have baulked at these things.

I do baulk at them. You know that I do. Put me down, Robert bach, put me down. Leave me outside the door.

Catherine cariad, once more we are fighting the English Civil War.

Well, I am Roundhead, you know that.

And I, Catherine cariad, am a Cavalier. Once more we are entrenched in this on-going tussle between the icon makers and the iconoclasts, those who would tear down the rood screens and those who would put them up. The Puritans were against all forms of theatre, you distrusted religious cant. In Venice once we bickered for an hour whilst dining by candlelight within sight of the Rialto bridge because you said the religious art of the city offended you and weighed you down.

It did weigh me down.

Yes, I think, she's like Dorothea Brooke in *Middlemarch* dismayed by the statues in the Vatican. Two provincial girls dismayed by what lay beyond their cultural reach. They should both have broadened your minds. You're Beatie

Bryant again, Beatie before Ronnie opened her eyes and ears.

You mean before some man opened their eyes and ears. My organs of perception were always in perfect working order.

But your mind was closed.

Robert bach, this is growing wearisome. Stick me in a bag. What does Benjo say?

He is rather subtle, actually, subtler than both of us. It is his contention that the very rejection of symbolism and ritual itself embodies an aesthetic.

Well, doesn't it?

All those gaunt Welsh chapels. The spare aesthetics of truth is not something I appreciate or really understand. I need illusion. I desire and require the "willing suspension of disbelief".

And I always wanted disbelief. It is what kept me alive.

I can't act in that cold rational spirit, and you should not require me to do so. I do what's absurd because it's in my nature and, anyway, it brings your life and death out into the open: *Ago quia absurdum est.* I am not alone in this. Some of us feel cheated unless we are provided with an illusion. We need to be transported. I am shedding Pascal's tears.

No, you are not alone. It is what Funeral Directors trade on. And your tears are killing me anew. I cannot breathe, and I am dying anew. You are drowning me in your sodding needs.

That is what our son says. You are right, and only your needs matter. He thinks my needs are self-serving. I should stop strangling you with melodramatic grief, and set you free to be yourself. But have I no right to a freedom all of my own? If my beliefs are killing you, your disbeliefs are doing the same to me. Every Ash Wednesday when I returned from the ashing I had to wipe the evidence off my forehead so you would not see. I had to live a lie in order to accommodate your conception of the truth.

Our son asks: Isn't there a Greek play that begins like this? There is, and it is called *Antigone,* except that, from certain points of view her dilemma was more straightforward. At least she was performing the burial rites for a brother who would have wished for a decent burial. She would never have stuck Polyneices in a bag, and he would very much have resented it if she had. At least I am not leaving you to rot. I am Antigone attempting to do the decent thing by an unappreciative Polyneices, however inconvenient and embarrassing that might prove to be. And you are Creon trying to prevent me honouring you as I see fit.

Robert bach. Stick me in a bag. Re-cycle me.

Catherine cariad, if I did that I would feel that I was betraying you.

Robert, I am just a body in a fridge. Externally that is what I now am, even if the embalmers will do their best to help you believe otherwise. I am only real insofar as you choose, individually and collectively, to remember me.

That is what the pictures, the symbols, the flowers and so on are designed to let us do.

If they do that, they are a distraction and a lie. I am still what I was when I confronted you in Venice, and my convictions and aversions have not changed. Besides (and she flashes her Cheshire cat grin), *it is getting very late and I want to get to bed.*

Our son says he feels very close to you, even though you have gone. I congratulate him on his "Negative Capability", eliminating himself in order feel close to you. But then, I go on to argue, ritual itself represents a different kind of capability. It is a way of transcending the self in the contemplation of others, of "otherness". Today you are the "other" whom we are endeavouring to honour, even in the face of your own resistance.

I am a freedom fighter. I am Welsh. I do not want your ritual or your needs. I want to be myself.

I am trying to set you free.

No, you are murdering me again on the open sword of your superstition. Let me be, Robert bach, let me be. We were everything to one another while I lived. Isn't that enough for you? What was that poem you wrote me once?

I was downstairs, and you were downstairs. The wind was howling in the chimney stack and growling outside in the wood. I wrote:

FOR CATHERINE

Your voice more than God's
Has convinced me of this,
Like the sound of a gong as it strikes true:
Many waters cannot quench love;
Neither can the floods drown it.

I heard it in the caresses of the breeze
As it pawed the corners of our ancient
House, heard it in my left ear,
Which softly sung it A.

And what did the ear-drum mutter?
We do not love what we desire and
Cannot have, we do not love
The delirium we crave:
These are intolerable things,
Agents of self-oppression.

What we love is what we have:
The baby's cry in the garden,
The sheet cast aside after kissing,
The joke once mint-new, now a phatic
Ceremony of calm, the ticking of the
Wall clock, the chipped, named mug,
The mongrel piano downstairs,
Slowly going flat.
Love is possession. Outside the door,
Delusions stomp, furious and begging, like

Blind, lame dogs.

Well, Robert bach, isn't that enough?

Wednesday, January 29th

I have agreed to travel back up to Cambridge to attend another reading by my friend Sebastian Barker, named after the saint whose arrow-shot image we saw over and over again in Venice. It is four months since the reading in Canterbury; in the interval his cancer has continued its inexorable advance, and there is little hope. He and some his friends will read extracts from his latest volume of poems, *The Land of Gold* in Trinity Chapel at five o'clock, still at this time of the year a dark enough hour to welcome candle light. I enter the familiar building, the pews to the north of the choir are filled with faces on which is written a kind of speculative awe. Mortality is in the air, and concern tempered by love is evident on the features of several members of his quite large family, including three children by two former wives.

Since Sebastian is now quite feeble, the task of reading is to be shared out between him, his third wife, the poet Hilary Davies, and the Cambridge based poets Richard Berengarten and Clive Wilmer. Clive goes first, after a brief introduction by one of the current chaplains. He remarks that Sebastian's recent writing has been marked by a new tightness, variety and grace, as if the whole of his life's work has been winnowed down to a perfect form and a ready reticence. He reads some of the poems and then hands over to Hilary, followed by Richard. Finally, it is Sebastian's own turn to read. He once told me how much of an ordeal he found the act of publicly reading his poems. This evening, however, his nerves and apprehension seem to have deserted him, to be replaced by the authority of his illness. From his wheelchair above the chancel steps he reigns supreme, as with a kind of loving dexterity, riding the weakness of his breath, he intones 'A Ballad of True Regret':

Never to look on the clouds again,
Never the flowers, nor seas.
Never to look on the sparkling rain,
Nor Easter in the trees.

Never to tread on the forest floor
Mottled with pools of light.
Never to open the kitchen door
To walk in the starry night.

Where will I be, when you are here
So full of life, so full of cheer,
And I am in no place we know
Where I and all the living go.

This, my darling, is the place you now inhabit, a place I can only dimly imagine, devoid of sensation and thought, a palace of regret, if only it were enabled by memory. Though since, four months before your body eventually expired, your memory had already succumbed to your breathlessness, how can I kid myself that you are equipped with a memory now?

In a previous professional existence Sebastian worked on an Oxford thesis on the physiology of breathing. The ironies of his present situation are not lost on him. After the reading we all retired to Côte restaurant, almost opposite the main gates of St John's, at 21-24 Bridge Street. If you could remember anything, you might recall that, slightly over twenty years ago, it was a branch of Garfunkel's where we regularly entertained our four-year-old son. The table at which we dine tonight is lined with several poets, Jungian analysts and me. The Jungian analysts included the wife of the Scottish writer Robert Nye and the current spouse of Richard Berengarten, one of the poets who assisted in the reading tonight. Emboldened by drink, at one stage I launch into this posse of pseudo-sages, denouncing theirs as a pretend science. Sebastian pretended not to hear. Later he sat closer, and mused through his hoarseness on the perversity of a one-time expert in the science of breathing being felled by his own lungs.

15 EPILOGUE: OXWICH BAY

Saturday February 1st

This evening Hilary phoned to say that Sebastian died of a heart attack yesterday morning. The seizure was sudden, in their home in Wargrave Avenue in Tottenham. By the time the paramedics arrived, he was past saving, despite their best attempts to revive him. Perhaps, under the circumstances, he was the less diminished one, passing straight from an, albeit painful, consciousness into the barren wastes of "no place we know/ Where I and all the living go", with no intermediate waiting room of mindlessness. Hilary's tone as she tells me about his going is sombre, but I sense she feels that I have had an even harder time. She, unlike me, will have no memory of a Sebastian who is no longer Sebastian, of an empty body in which her beloved once dwelt.

Wednesday, February 5th

The Funeral Directors we have chosen for you have two chapels of rest: Cedar and Willow. You are in Cedar, the right hand one. The youngish undertaker greets us after unlocking the door and then says "Wait just a moment while I uncover her". He disappears, fiddles with lights and then stands in the corridor, asking in a serious voice "Are you ready? We have prepared her as you wished. The clothes you sent are on her. I've just sprayed her with Anais. The boots were OK, but I couldn't manage the watch. It wouldn't go on her wrist, so I have just popped it in a plastic bag".

We enter this narrow and apologetic space, under subdued lights. To the left stands a lightwood coffin, draped across which is a green, gold edged velvet pall, partly covering the trestle legs. Inside it is a waxwork that might once have been you. Propped in the corner, stands a lid with a brass plate that reads "Catherine Fraser. Died 22nd January 2014. Aged 71 years." So we would have to calculate your date of birth retrospectively, as if you lived backwards, with death the definitive event.

You are in your blue and sand wash cardigan, and they've put on your matching turquoise earrings and necklace. Your face has sunken, and rouge has been crudely applied to your cheeks. You look stately, older, crosser, like a grumpy headmistress trying to remain calm. You are also a lot stouter, and when I lightly touch it, your skin feels artificial and cold. Your sweet upturned nose is just the same, but the corners of your mouth are turned down, as they never were in life, your lips have thickened, and your clothes look all wrong on you. Against your woolly you clutch a posy of lilies already fading. I remark on how stout you seem, and Benjo says "When you're dead, you don't get a lot of exercise". You'd have enjoyed that joke. Why do I see you breathing? I look again and, yes, you are breathing again. More easily now, my love.

It is the coffin-ness of the coffin that it so unappealing. Is there any way of decoffinating this pious box?: "I'll have the decof' please."

Green carpet, textured beige wallpaper. Skirting boards scrupulously clean. A studied absence of dust. On opposite walls hang two framed prints in sober brown, one labelled

"Freesia", the other "Digitalis". On the ceiling a circular smoke alarm dimly flickering, like an absent-minded lighthouse. In front of it, an illuminated green sign pointing to the Exit. In the far corner, an assortment of red and white flowers on a white painted metal stand. Artificial, of course. I feel them just to make sure.

There is a tap on the door and Will announces a call from the second doctor who is required to counter-sign the relevant form. I take over the mobile phone and hear an Asian voice ask whether I am satisfied with the causes of death listed by Doctor Number One. Since the first doctor alone attended following your decease, this procedure seems oddly pointless, but is, Will now informs me, an extra provision installed twenty years ago after the Harold Shipman scandal to ensure that the first doctor is no fortune hunter intent on securing your estate. Since I was not present at the death either, I tell him to go ahead and sign. After briefly expressing his sympathies, he hangs up.

We still have to decide whether we want this coffin in church for the ceremony. I ask Will whether it can be brought in the night before. Yes, he says, that will be quite possible, but will add two hundred and eighty one pounds to the cost. Then we flee homewards, away from this awful artificial tranquillity, clutching the plastic bag with the kimono in which you were taken away, and the box of Anais. When I unpack it in the bedroom, there is no sign of the watch.

Monday, February 10th

The watch has turned up, curled round the lid of the Anais bottle inside its box. I have had it ticking beside me all night, keeping last summer time. Too late to correct it now. We have come to take one last look at you, and as we do so, we read you the chapters from *Mansfield Park* about the ball. They seem just right, with their evocation of a young girl's coming out in the old sense, her trepidations, fears and delights – the very experiences that defined you fifty years ago – falling on your alabaster ears.

Such delicacy and quaintness of grammar, enough to make you smile, except that you don't. "Fanny's heart sunk"; why not sank? "The entrance of the Grants and Crawfords made a favourable epoch." Epoch presumably in the Greek sense, implying an inception, or an interruption. "A partner, a voluntary partner, secured against the ball began," meaning presumably "before the ball began." We have a lot of fun with this, and kid ourselves into believing you do too. Knockabout verbal humour of the sort you would adore.

What caused me to fall in love with this face, I ask aloud, casting one last regretful glance before we leave: the turned up nose, the grey-blue eyes, the russet locks, the lips curled up in a grin that even the artifices of the mortician cannot quite disguise? Or the single mole on your now bloated neck, just southwest of the smooth outline of your larynx? The map of a marriage and of my intimate desire. Bestowing one last kiss, I abruptly turn away.

Wednesday, February 12th

10 p.m. Nowadays faith has produced some incongruous bedfellows. Radio 3's nightly discussion programme, recently re-styled *Freethinking,* offered a rare opportunity to drop in on an agreement between two British intellectuals at opposite ends of the political spectrum. The former Marxist critic Terry Eagleton, cradle Catholic, former Marxist theorist and doyen of the academic-literary Left, was intense but amicable dialogue with the reactionary ultra-montane philosopher Roger Scruton, a latter-day Anglican, over the continuing need for a Being to whom Eagleton, with uncharacteristic deference, referred to throughout as "The Almighty". In the chair the one-time Methodist Philip Dodd goaded both of them in his characteristically chuckling style, as all three attempted to communicate via a transatlantic link with the atheist Peter Watson. Perhaps at the contrivance of the General Synod, Watson's Skype link with New York kept on breaking down, whilst Eagleton's from Virginia remained firm. Late in the conversation, Eagleton rhapsodised over the eighteen-year-old nuns with whom he once served as a seven-year-old altar boy in Manchester. One of them, now in her eighties, has just visited him and told him that back then in the nineteen-fifties they all had "a lot of fun". Very honest, this: I was once almost thrown out of a pub for laughing too loud over Eagleton's memoir of his Catholic childhood.

Thursday, February 13th

Your absence from our house shrieks from the walls. It is something almost as palpable as your presence was. As I worked and wrote downstairs, your presence above me was sometimes an implication, a suggestion or insinuation, conveyed through muffled and distant sounds, through minimal movement and customary association: a feather fall of breath, a stirring in another room, on another floor, a rhythm indistinctly sensed. Your absence, in stark contrast, is something directly heard and seen: it is an accusation, a menace and a threat.

Friday, February 21st

We have called it a celebration, not a funeral, and here you are on the front page of the Order of Service, above the words "Catherine Fraser, teacher, mother and wit", smiling faintly out at us all from the courtyard of the Hotel du Manoir in Tours, your richly textured skirt covering your knees, your shapely arms showing amidst a bouquet of flowers in the pots that stood around you that August morning. At the back of the brochure is the black and white likeness of your beaming face from the veranda of the LSE in 1964. Between them stretched an adulthood, only part of which I shared. You were forty when we met, already fully formed with your likes and dislikes, your atheistical opinions and your unquestioned and vehement politics. We have dragged you into church, and there you lie in your pinewood coffin on its trestles, beneath a card bearing a colour photo of you in the kitchen of our lodging house in New Haven, Con, during my academical visit of October, 2009. You look as if you are rebuking us. You are rebuking us. The *crachach,* you are telling us, have prevailed at last. I have few excuses, I have to admit.

To assuage you, we begin with Dylan Thomas, your devotion to whom was as close to devoutness as you ever got in seventy-one years. Then we launch into your second favourite chapel hymn:

> Yield not to temptation, for yielding is sin;
> Each vict'ry will help you some other to win;
> Fight manfully forward, dark passions subdue;
> Look ever to Jesus; he'll carry you through.

I read one of your favourite lyrics of A.E. Housman's – "Loveliest of trees" – and then your friend Jan from days together in a flat in Finborough Road, Fulham, tells of your resistance to a plan to paint its shared bathroom blue, before reading the passage in *The Diary of A Nobody* in which Mr Pooter emerges a vivid shade of puce after causing the bath to be done in red enamel. Benjo plays the Allegro ma non troppo from Beethoven's Sonata Facile in G, and then reads your favourite French poem, Théophile Gautier's "Soleil Couchant": impressions of sunset across the roofs of Paris as viewed from the Pont de la Tournelle. Upstairs in the bedroom at home there is a photo of you standing next to its parapet in a long blue dress whilst pointing up at the name of the bridge fixed to a nearby lamp post. I have asked your colleague Liz to talk a bit about our stay two years ago in Lake Garda as a preamble to an extract from *Twilight in Italy.* It is a passage about the Lemon Gardens along the shore of the lake, one of which we visited on a sultry afternoon; we were on the Lawrence trail again. The novelist Zoe Fairbairns is reluctant to deliver the passage from *Pride and Prejudice* in which Mr Bennett interviews his daughter after her rejection of the Revd. Mr Collins. So Father John reads it instead in a voice indistinguishable from that of the spurned suitor. After a lusty but incongruously lugubrious congregational airing of "Count Your Blessings",

I evoke our union, its comic incongruities, its haphazardness, its anachronisms:

> How could anybody resist a wife and lover who still referred to BBC Radio Four as "The Home Service"? Even your sophistication seemed naïve. Ours was marriage of talk about poets so persistent that casual visitors might have thought Dylan Thomas a house guest away for the weekend, a union of passionate toleration and humour between the daughter of a socialist headmaster, and the son of a Tory almost mayor, between a Baptist Sunday school girl and a cathedral chorister, a union of jokes and vivid daily discussions of subjects over which we hilariously disagreed. After which I would retreat to the basement to listen to Thomas Tallis whilst you leaned in your paisley dressing gown against the counter upstairs retaliating with pop songs and thrumming chapel hymns.

As if to emphasise the point, the assembled company then launches into the inevitable, but for once poignantly apt, hymn Cwn Rhondda.

There are two concert items. My dear old friend Dr Rachel Darnley-Smith, music therapist, 'cellist and Roehampton academic, executes a feeling performance of Saint-Saens's 'The Swan' from *The Carnival of Animals.* At the last moment I have also invited a Lawrence scholar, Bethan Jones, clarinettist, novelist, librettist and all-round fine woman, to play us and you the Adagio from the Mozart clarinet concerto. Bethan is from Pennard on the cliffs of the Gower, a passionate Welsh woman, and a deeply humane soul. As the long downward phrases of the movement unfurl I am carried back to the Palazzo Bettoni in Bogliaco one evening in September 2012, when she played the self- same movement to an audience of conference delegates under a ceiling of buoyantly ascending cherubs. You were there that day, and noted the cherubim in your diary.

In the crematorium we have set you loose: not as an ascending cherub, but as a banshee, *une fille folle*, a wild and wandering spirit. The undertakers' men are here in solemn black, so we march them in quickstep to the strains of Bernstein's overture to *Candide.* We have said Goodbye to good taste so here, already loaded onto the sound system, is Susan Maughan's "Bobby's Girl", number three in the charts for seventeen consecutive weeks in 1962, two years before that LSE photo. It is a hit of the times that catches your contradictions: the pre-feminist part of you that enjoyed Dusty Springfield, "Rusty Springboard" with her bee-hive hair-do and low camp, this jaunty song about a girl who sits at home moping because her boyfriend has someone else. If she can but get hold of him for to her sentimental self, "What a happy, thankful girl I'd be." Yes, sometimes you were that girl.

Saturday, February 22nd

At the far end of Oxwich Bay, twenty miles to the West of our home in Swansea, stands a church that must be the smallest and simplest in the whole beauteous Gower peninsular. Half hidden by Oxwich woods, it overlooks a rocky creek and is inaccessible except by a narrow path that runs immediately south of the large and showy Oxwich Hotel. People say that it goes back to the sixth century, though it was extended in the thirteen. The kernel of it may once have been an anchorite's cell, and a font in the churchyard may have been set up there by the Celtic Saint Illtyd, to whom the church is dedicated. One afternoon last August, shortly before you fell seriously ill, we strolled along the two-and-a-half-mile stretch of sands, then you removed your sandals and lingered on the margin of the sea, as I watched from the parapet of a distant bridge as, lost in reverie, you dipped your feet. After tea in hotel gardens, where we were pestered by early autumn wasps, we wandered along to the bare and tiny church, basic and unpretentious enough even for you. An exhibition by local artists was advertised. By the time we arrived, the building was locked, so we stood there beneath the crest of the hill, and I saw you dissolve into that distinctive mood of yours, a mood of instinctive communion with the spirit of a place. "Never mind," I dropped into the brine-washed silence. "We can always come back."

It is almost the Feast of St David, but this year I will not, as in our early days together, be posting you a bunch of leeks and when they arrive, expressing bewilderment as to who could have sent them, nor presenting you with daffodils over lunch, or stand listening as, staring dreamily out of the window at a prospect of Kent, you recite the first line of Housman's 'Loveliest of Trees', then expect me to remember the rest. Instead, we will be scattering your ashes on the edge of the sea in this cove of the Gower you had lately learned to love, near that ancient and simple Welsh church. Behind it, crocuses will be in flower, and this year for the first time I will probably envy them.

The thought had occurred to me that some at least of you might be buried in the Lilliputian church yard. So this afternoon the two of us sauntered down to the local vicarage in London, where we persuaded Father John, the Priest-in-Charge, to contact the vicar of St Illtyd's by telephone. After much civil humming and haa-ing, he put the receiver down. The Church of Wales - a branch of the worldwide Anglican communion disestablished in my grandfather's time - unlike its established sister church in England, does not, he regretfully informed us, concur with the interment of ashes on its property. We were at liberty to scatter you on the path leading from the hotel towards the church, though of course the breezes coursing off the Bristol Channel might then soon blow you away. "How was he?" I asked John, meaning the clerical colleague to whom he had just been speaking. "Rather unhelpful," he replied. "Welsh."

Friday, February 28th

At five p.m., Will 'phones. After an interval of a week he has retrieved the ashes from the crematorium, and will "walk them round" in about ten minutes. Half an hour later, there is a subdued knock on the door and, when I open it, he is on the step in his standard, sober clothes, a purple plastic bag dangling from his right arm. Good timing. St David's day is tomorrow, and in preparation for it, as he enters the front room, BBC Radio 3 is playing a Welsh folk song called "Wake of Pines" in an arrangement for harmonium and soprano duet. After five months you are home, but before I can unwrap you, Will calls my attention to an envelope I will find nestling close to your remains. It is, he assures me, a letter from the Crematorium "to certify that it is her." He informs me that the invoice for his services will arrive in ten days, then briefly bows and leaves with almost oriental courtesy.

I carry you upstairs and place you on the fraying green carpet of the bedroom, next to the wardrobe with your clothes. Carefully I remove the bag and uncover what is left of you in a plain dark brown screw-topped plastic flask, height 11 and a half inches, width 6 inches at its widest point, depth across the top 5 and a half inches. The width varies because, a lone concession to your femininity, the jar is waisted across its curved middle. At the front a label tells me that these are indeed the 'Cremated Remains of the Late Catherine Fraser; Cremation 116563, 21/2/2014.'

So, contrary to what I have previously been told, you were incinerated on the day of the committal. How heavy you still are, but how much of this kilo of weight consists of the cinders of the coffin, and how much of your dearly desired and beloved body? Rummaging in the bag again, I find the covering letter, which runs "I HEREBY CERIFY THAT The Registrar's Certificate for Disposal (after registry of death) of the late Catherine Fraser has been produced to the Medical Referee and has been filed by me in accordance with the Regulations made under Section 7 of the Cremation Act 1902 (2 Ed. VII c8) and Section 2 of the Cremation Act, 1952. The Notification Certificate of Disposal (Part C) has been (or will be) sent to the Registrar of Births and Deaths of the above district. ASTRUD MATANIEL, Registrar."

Is this truly what you would have wanted? My mind goes back three years to the January of 2011. I had just sent to the Oxford University Press the electronic files containing my biography of Gascoyne. To reward myself, and to rest up, I had booked us a few days in Jeake's House, towards the bottom of steeply sloping Mermaid Street in Rye. It had now converted into a stylish middle range hotel with antique furniture in every reception room and plush, curtained four-poster beds in every chamber.

It was on that very holiday break that I read you that passage from my second-hand copy of Pascal about man as a thinking reed. To fit into the seventeenth-century mood, I'd also brought along a dog-eared copy of the Everyman's Library edition of Sir Thomas Browne's *Religio Medici* bound in with his essay on cremation, *Hydrotaphia or Urn Buriall.* part of which I read out to you in the capacious and curtained double bed:

> Life is a pure flame, and we live by an Invisible Sun within us. A small fire sufficeth for life, great flames seem too little after death, while men vainly affected precious pyres, and to burn like *Sardanapulus,* but the wisdom of funeral Laws found the folly of prodigall blazes, and reduced undoing fires unto the rule of sober obsequies, wherein few could be so mean as not to provide wood, pitch, a mourner, an Urne.

Well, I am your mourner now, and an Urn is a splendid and acceptable thing. But brown plastic, a handy screw top?

Tuesday, March 11th

As a concession to my religious nostalgia we will scatter the first few handfuls of the incinerated you, not on the path, but on the craggy slope leading down from St Illtyd's towards the cove. You can always close your eyes to the ecclesiastical edifice above. At about two o'clock a party consisting of Benjo and his girlfriend Hannah, also Margaret Kenna who has driven across from Swansea with her husband, the classicist and intellectual historian Dr Chris Stray, and a clutch of relatives from Salford, gather to the right of the Oxwich Hotel to hear me declaim Thomas's "Death shall have no dominion" as defiantly as I can manage. They watch as I clamber on my weak left ankle down the shallow escarpment between dusty ivy and nettles. Opening the brown plastic cask, I encounter, not you, but the unexpected surface of a polythene bag, and have to call up to the others for an implement with which to pierce it. Eventually, I use my keys. Inside the ash is fine and white, and presumably as much coffin as it is Catherine. I invite Benjo to join me, and between us we strew about a third of the thin, tender powder onto the dingy foliage, avoiding the discarded plastic bottles and cans that are the residue of last summer's picnics.

No worry, my love, we will scatter the rest of you out in the bay, well beyond the reach of the crachach. There is a lazy and limpid stream that meanders off Oxwich Marsh down the broad and sandy beach towards the rippling tide where once you paddled on bare feet. We pause there awhile, as Margaret delivers her own adaptation of a poem by Brian Patten, and Benjo reads out a version of a Callimachus epitaph by William Cory, high church paederast and one-time Eton schoolmaster, in which we have substituted the Welsh endearment "Cariad" for "Carian" in the phrase "dear Carian guest". So it runs: "And now that thou art lying/ My dear Cariad guest/ A handful of grey ashes/Now at last at rest." We make our way in a thoughtful gaggle down to the margin of the sea where Benjo removes his shoes and wades into the lapping waves of the Bristol Channel. Slowly he empties the rest of the bag of ashes into the water, and stands there in his well-cut, sodden shorts gazing south. As you drift irretrievably out to sea, through my tears I softly recite a valediction I composed for you just yesterday:

LULLABY

Take her up, you shimmering waves,
Instinct with scintillating light,
And with your froth of laughter
Smooth the sorrows from her sight.

Take her where the jokes abound
And insurrection smiles like wine,
Where salt conjugates with sound
And satire coaxes every sign.

Take her up, deep-breathing sands,
In your granular embrace,
Wrap her in sardonic folds,
And kiss her subtly mocking face.

Take her where the words catch fire,
And puns fly unimpaired by sense,
Where mirth cascades through all the spheres,
And sobriety takes no offence.

Take her, mild and caustic sea,
Rock her gently in your tides,

And at every sly return
Waft her softly back to me.

Monday, March 17th

Back to London, for the first time without you. As the train draws out from Newport I turn unthinkingly in my seat to offer you a sandwich from the Buffet and realise that you are not there. Arriving at Paddington I think to take a taxi, but cannot bear the thought of travelling on the back seat alone. Instead, I catch the Bakerloo line southbound as far as Oxford Circus, then change onto the Victoria line to continue my journey onwards to our empty-seeming South London home. The evening stretches before me so, partly to fill it, partly for company, and partly for a much needed re-encounter with the female form, at seven I attend a life drawing class held weekly above a local pub. As a muzak tape of 1960s and 1970s favourites dribbles in the background, a slender and attenuated model disrobes and I look on with a mixture of artistic appreciation and thwarted lust. For periods of five, then ten minutes she assumes a series of postures of increasing complexity, her limbs crossed and posed so as to confront us with a congeries of perspectives and lines. My efforts are pitiful, but the kindly teacher Betty Frankenstein captures them on her phone, telling me that she will soon place them on the group's Facebook page. During the twenty-minute break I offer the model a drink, but she huffily declines, protesting that she will buy her own and, besides, "do you mind if I get dressed first?". When we resume there is to be a longer pose held for a full twenty minutes, but five minutes into the exercise, when the page of my sketch pad is still almost a blank, I recognise from the tape machine the opening strains of Johnny Cash's 1940 hit "You are my sunshine".

Within a few bars my chest is heaving, and tears are coursing down my cheeks. In vain do I attempt to shield my brimming eyes from my fellow amateurs. Mercifully, the session is drawing to a close, so as the others gather around I explain about your recent death, of which they knew nothing, and mention the fact that this is a song you always sang to our infant son when he was ill. It is, I tell them, as Betty gives me a welcome hug, associated with a particularly harrowing memory.

I do no tell them of what. But twenty-six years ago, when I was working as a Visiting Professor in Kuwait, we went to the local swimming pool one afternoon and afterwards stood at the top of a flight of concrete steps, chatting to friends. I was in charge of our son in his push chair, the brake of which I had neglected to apply. Carried away with the conversation, I took my hand off the handles to gesture a point, and at exactly that moment our four-month-old baby leant forward in the chair. I caught the movement out of the corner of my eye, and then looked on in horror as the vehicle lurched forwards and bounced down the steps, carrying our only child with it. When it reached the flags at the base, there was silence. After what seemed like an eternity, one of the attendants rushed forward, and at that moment the boy let out a wail, as the attendant lifted him in his arms and massaged his fingers to make sure his reflexes were undamaged. Afterwards, in a state of numb shock and relief, we retired to our staff flat and you placed our son across your shoulders, caressing his back and pacing up and down the lounge as you crooned out Johnny Cash's trite but moving lament.

Even before you died, I could not hear those lyrics without weeping. Now I clumsily take my leave from the disbanding art class, apologising for this ungainly emotional exhibition to Betty, who seems to think that it is all her fault and who wants to buy me a drink and offers to return my ten pound fee. I press it back into her hands as I retreat, once more apologising both to her and to the now clothed model, who seems to have relented in her attitude to this sad loner, watching me with a mixture of embarrassment and compassion as I slump towards the stairs.

Tuesday, March 18th

People remark I have lost you, but I must say I am used to it. Early on, you had warned me saying that evasiveness flowed through all the Ishmael women. Every Saturday afternoon, you informed me, your mother would disappear without trace. Among your many qualities you too excelled in such a well-timed elusiveness that I had grown quite habituated to losing you, several times a week. Usually, after one of the long walks we took slightly out of step, when you were standing right behind me. I had grown quite used this quotidian comedy, with me searching vainly about and you patiently resting in my blind spot, waiting for me to notice, waiting for me to care. I who so vainly ranged about, so busy looking that I could not see. Then your wry peal of laughter when I did see. And, when I made it up to you, your invariable cry of "There's sentimental!" Are you behind me, before me, beside me, even now? Are you sitting by window over your law books, unseen and unheard?

How can I live without your jokes and your gripes, or the calm you so often spread over the house, out into the street and wherever you went? You possessed, and for all that I know still possess, an alert, gently lapping tranquillity. One supernal afternoon I recall in the mountainous north of Corsica, just downstream from that skein-like cascade known as the Bridal Veil, when you perched on a boulder watching the year turn, shedding with your quiet intelligence all the sorrows of the previous few months. Your very stillness seemed to transcend time then, hinting at a pattern beyond itself:

RIVER CROSSING

For Catherine, Bocognano.

Not this chestnut glade alone,
the mountain brook sagging yearly toward winter,
not even the moss at the water's edge,
drab bees foraging amid old stones;

not even the arched Genoese bridge as it
gathers its load of ivy to the other bank;

not simply these, nor the red-haired girl
asleep on a boulder
dreaming of peace, seeing a
room in which Mother
moves her mouth over a morsel of sorrow.

The chagrin will return, dead leaves and the
stream's constriction;

the girl will go back to
where, on a fraying chair,
spent clothes lie curdled like regrets.

But, as snow plumes the mountain tops,
and at evening light fails again and
again, slowly in the remotest pass

the ice will begin once more
seeping towards summer.

My strangest beloved, my most beloved stranger, Farewell.

St Ives, Cornwall,1984

Brantwood, Lake Coniston, 2011.

9781916440012

#0014 - 291018 - C0 - 197/132/15 - PB - 9781916440012